THE NIXON-GLEASON ALIEN ENCOUNTER

PAUL BLAKE SMITH

Foundations Book Publishing
4209 Lakeland Drive, #398, Flowood, MS 39232
www.FoundationsBooks.net

The Nixon-Gleason Alien Encounter
Paul Blake Smith

ISBN: 978-1-64583-104-4

Published in the United States of America
Worldwide Electronic & Digital Rights
Worldwide English Language Print Rights

FOREWORD

by Douglas Caddy, attorney
Member of the Texas and District of Columbia Bars

"On two occasions, Gallup has asked questions about whether the government knows more about UFOs than it is telling us. The questions, asked 23 years apart, produced virtually identical responses. In 1996, 71% said the US government was withholding information, and in 2019, 68% gave that response. In a CBS News question asked in March of this year, 73% said the government knows more about UFOs than it is telling the general public, while only 20% said the government has told the public everything it knows about them. In the new Economist/YouGov survey, 65% gave this response. Interestingly, two-thirds in this poll approved of government agencies investigating UFOs."
—Forbes, June 3, 2021, "UFOs: Americans' Opinions On What's Out There."

Here in 2022, author Paul Blake Smith skillfully uses the close friendship between President Richard Nixon and actor Jackie Gleason, known as "The Great One," to bring to life a unique UFO story that indeed asks whether the government knows more than it is telling us. At its center is the question of whether, in the midst of the Watergate scandal President Richard Nixon in a quid pro quo arrangement, permitted Gleason exclusively to view the bodies of four dead aliens at Homestead Air Force Base in Florida on February 19, 1973, and in return, Nixon received from Gleason up to one million dollars from a special golf fund that could be used as "hush" money in the burgeoning scandal that eventually led to the president's resignation.

Smith marshals voluminous and convincing evidence that such an event occurred but ultimately leaves it to each reader as a member of the public opinion jury to return the verdict. I, too, am a member of that jury and easily reached my decision on how I would cast my vote after reading this book. However, in doing so, I might be accused of not being impartial. This is because I was the first person approached to take "hush" money and distribute it to the seven Watergate defendants. This occurred in the first month of the case over the July 4 holiday in 1972, eight months before the Nixon-Gleason alien encounter. As proof, here is the testimony of Herbert Kalmbach, President Nixon's personal attorney (who is a figure in this book), seated before the Senate Watergate Committee as he was being questioned by Samuel Dash, the Committee's Chief Counsel, on July 16, 1973, four months after the Nixon-Gleason event:

> Mr. Dash: Now, what was the first instruction you received to give the money?
>
> Mr. Kalmbach: Again, as I have tried to reconstruct this, Mr. Dash. The first instruction that I received, which I passed to [private detective Tony] Ulasewicz, was to have Mr. Ulasewicz give $25,000 to Mr. Caddy. I don't know much of Mr. Caddy. I understand he is an attorney here in Washington, D.C.. And as I recall it, this was approximately from July 1 through July 6 or 7. There were a number of calls. I would either talk to Mr. Dean or [Fred] LaRue [a presidential aide]. I would then call Mr. Ulasewicz, who, in turn,

would call Mr. Caddy. He would have some response from Mr. Caddy, and I would call back up to Mr. Dean or Mr. LaRue.

Mr. Dash: What was the response from Mr. Caddy?

Mr. Kalmbach: Well, the sum and gist of it was Mr. Caddy refused to accept the funds.

Mr. Dash: In that manner?

Mr. Kalmbach: That is correct. That was the end-all. There were several phone calls, but the final wrap-up on it was that he refused the funds.

Paul Blake Smith has produced a masterful work that not only focuses on the Nixon-Gleason event (and how it likely tied in with similar covert actions of President Dwight Eisenhower in the '50s) but also provides ample evidence of the Alien Presence on Planet Earth, which was told to me during the Watergate era by defendant E. Howard Hunt. Be aware while you are curled up in your favorite chair reading this fascinating book that simultaneously it is being read in the Intelligence Communities in countries around the world. As it should be. Enjoy.

Douglas Caddy
June 17, 2022
Watergate's 50th Anniversary

PROLOGUE

"Decades ago, visitors from other planets warned us about where we were headed and offered to help. But instead, we, or at least some of us, interpreted their visits as a threat, and decided to shoot first and ask questions after."[1]
—The late Paul Hellyer, former Canadian Defense Minister.

Richard M. Nixon's confidante and eventual biographer Frank Gannon[2] spent many hours interviewing the wily ex-president[3] in the late '70s and early '80s. Gannon recalled: "At one point during our labors in San Clemente,[4] I asked RN if he believed in UFOs and if there was anything to the whole Roswell/Area 51 business. He raised his eyebrows and rolled his eyes and I moved right on to the next subject."[5] To hardened critics, this reaction means that Nixon knew nothing of the subject and was skeptically dismissive of it. To anyone else, this silent treatment can be interpreted as the presidential retiree suspiciously clamming up when asked directly about a topic he should have been quite informed about. He commented freely on everything else, most verbally, but not this.

For decades, I have been quite intrigued—like just about

everyone else—with the riveting allegation of a covert late-night meeting between Richard Nixon, comic actor Jackie Gleason[6], and extraterrestrial beings (albeit dead ones). The legend of that meeting on Monday, February 19, 1973, has been aired over the past decades in mere book paragraphs and brief web pages with almost no legitimate research offered to support them. I wanted real digging, with real answers unearthed. Did the two mega-stars *really* travel to a Florida airbase one night to view genuine ETs and kept it hushed up afterward? Did they see *more* than that? What are the facts, and what are the falsehoods?

Much like two other UFO tales I took a shine to, I found no full-length nonfiction book about this topic. So, I decided to write my own. Thanks to encouragement from my always helpful agent, I pressed forward in fleshing it all out during the economic shutdown and pandemic mess of 2020-2021.

A few years before, I looked into the Nixon-Gleason allegation and wrote a few paragraphs about it for a chapter in my 2020 book, *President Eisenhower's Close Encounters* (foundationsbooks.net). I then reissued my 2016 book, *MO41, The Bombshell Before Roswell* (a-argus-books.com), with an all-new Bonus Chapter that expanded upon those recent Nixon-Gleason paragraphs. You'd think that would be enough, right?

Nope.

I still longed for deeper research that could be fleshed out in a complete nonfiction book, separating the wheat from the chaff. This proved to be necessary work since I discovered to my dismay, that some UFO researchers—some with less than savory reputations—have been inserting themselves into the story and making claims that, upon further review, are not valid or worthy of discussion to put it politely. I think with this tome I can correct the record, debunk some of the creative embellishments, add some new details, and set the record fairly straight, hopefully once and for all.

Much of *The Nixon-Gleason Alien Encounter* came together in the first half of 2021. It can be considered a kind of sequel to my Eisenhower-ET book in that Richard Nixon was, of course, President Dwight Eisenhower's loyal vice president in the '50s and evidently patterned his 1973 alien encounter almost exactly as the famous general-turned-president did (see Chapter Four). It was carefully prepared for in advance, not an impromptu affair at all. I have attempted to give herein as full an explanation of how it could have taken place as possible, nearly fifty years later, in accordance with indisputable facts and some amount of reasonable speculation. That requires setting the table first with data on Richard Nixon and his possible experience with extraterrestrial matters. As we're about to see, there is a caveat with each story. With the release of *President Eisenhower's Close Encounters* in 2020, the publishers inadvertently left out the critical final nine pages of a leaked January 1989 government document summarizing America's covert past with alien visitors.[7] Since these missing pages mention how other presidents after Eisenhower—like Nixon—continued a fairly simple secret agreement with ETs and described a bombshell revelation about a president-monitored ET program in the '70s, I have corrected this oversight and placed these missing pages at the end of *this* book to wrap things up properly.

Along the way, I have also pieced together pertinent information on some other celebrities, like Ronald Reagan, Bob Hope, Gordon Cooper, David Bowie, Nikola Tesla, and John Lennon. The ex-Beatle[8] became quite obsessed—much like Gleason—with the subject of extraterrestrial visitation and even had his own sighting in New York City. Nixon and Lennon were like fire and gasoline, perfectly suited to touch each other's raw nerves, but it turns out that they might have found a strong basis to form a friendship if they had just sat down to talk about UFOs and ETs. The same goes for Lennon and Gleason, perhaps even more so. They did not, of course, ever meet. Nevertheless, ill-fated Lennon's journey makes for a fascinating chapter in this book, and, in fact, the fate of *all* the celebs and locations involved herein seems to have been quite tragic or even cursed, which is noted in the concluding chapter.

I regret that I was not able to locate and interview Jackie Gleason's ex-wife, Beverly,[9] the original source of this story. She is now nearing ninety and may not recall that part of her life well. Even if she did, does she really have anything new to add? Over the years, she has related the shocking story three times and has never embellished it, watered it down, or retracted it. She has likely told all she knows. Thus, an interview now may not uncover much, if anything, fresh and helpful.

Since the publication of my Eisenhower-ET saga, one of its most noteworthy supporters passed away. Although I never met him, Canada's former Defense Minister Paul Theodore Hellyer[10] (1923-2021) deserves a quick bow of gratitude here. Paul spoke publicly numerous times of the Eisenhower contact and that the American government had been in touch "decades ago, [with] visitors from other planets," who calmly "warned us about where we were headed, and offered to help."[11] Hellyer was no deluded or misinformed fool. He served as a senior minister in Canada during Nixon's first months in office in America, and he continued as a Member of Parliament until just one month before Nixon's resignation. He once had access to intelligence files, government reports, and inside gossip alike, but he could not openly tell all that he knew in his retirement, perhaps fearing the loss of his pension and benefits.

I want to express my special thanks to anyone dedicated to getting out the truth and to those who review with an open mind all the facts to conclude fairly that mankind is not alone in the vast universe. I am thankful to those who are willing to calmly consider that we are being visited and monitored by other, more advanced races. More information is becoming available all the time, including military sources within a recent CBS *60 Minutes*[12] piece, recent proposed congressional UFO data-collecting legislation, and other nonfiction UFO/ET stories in the media as of late; it all intrigues and piques both this author and readers around the world to keep pressing and digging for the truth. Specifically, I wish to thank agent Patricia Baker; fellow author Douglas Caddy;[13] diligent researcher

Linda Moulton Howe; editor Autumn Weese, and the fine team assembled at Foundations Publishing in Mississippi; they have all been most kind and patient in helping get this book off the ground.

To properly launch this project, we need to establish some groundwork for the Nixon presidency by reviewing his *vice* presidency. The '50s were a time of domestic secrecy by our federal government. It is possible that secrecy was intended to keep the subject of UFOs and ETs from the increasingly curious populace to avoid triggering a panic. Was Nixon clued in to this veil of surreptitiousness? That topic is up next in the Introduction.

Overall, was any of this book's collection of data—or still other ET matters that have yet to be uncovered—ever shared by President Nixon with his devoted supporter Jackie Gleason? I believe Richard Nixon had plenty of knowledge he *could* have relayed to the world, but he apparently opted for silence for various reasons. I also believe that when the retired ex-president simply rolled his eyes during the Gannon interview. "Tricky Dick" was dutifully keeping up this government-mandated cover of quiet, showing he was still dedicated to the policy of silence, skepticism, and secrecy. A more honest approach, utilizing complete honesty, might have gotten him unwanted attention and possible recrimination.

Are we finally seeing through the tissue of lies today? Maybe. Perhaps this book will help focus our vision as we continue doing so. I thank you, the reader, for giving it your time and consideration today. I report, you decide...

Paul Blake Smith

July 2, 2022
World UFO Day

---

1. Chris Matyszczyk, "Canada's Ex-Defense Minister: U.S. Knows How Aliens Can Make Us Greener," *CNET*. February 27, 2011.
2. "Frank Gannon (White House Central Files: Staff Member and Office Files).", *Richard Nixon Presidential Library and Museum*. Yorba Linda, CA. s
3. Wikipedia contributors, "Richard Nixon," *Wikipedia* , https://en.wikipedia.org/wiki/Richard_Nixon
4. Wikipedia contributors. "San Clemente, California," *Wikipedia*.
5. David Emery, "Did President Nixon Hide Proof of Alien Life in a Time Capsule?" *Snopes.com*, March 24, 2018..
6. Wikipedia contributors, "Jackie Gleason," *Wikipedia*.
7. Ultra-top-secret-MTD, allegedly from Defense Intelligence Agency, January 1989
8. Wikipedia contributors, "John Lennon," *Wikipedia*.
9. "Beverly Gleason," *IMDB*./
10. Wikipedia contributors, "Paul Hellyer," *Wikipedia*.
11. Vicky Verma, "At least Four Alien Species Have Been Visiting Earth For Thousands Of Years From Andromeda," *howandwhys*.com, August 2021./
12. Aired May 16, 2021, reported by correspondent Bill Whitaker, CBS television network
13. Wikipedia contributors, "Douglas Caddy," *Wikipedia*.

PAUL BLAKE SMITH

INTRODUCTION

Nixon's UFO Foundations

"Nixon had all of the good stuff and wanted to share it with some of his friends."

Before we dig into the legendary American President Richard Milhous Nixon (1913-1994) and his knowledge of extraterrestrial visitation, we first need to review his eight years as America's vice president.

During President Dwight D. Eisenhower's first term (1953-1957), Vice President Richard Nixon—a former congressman from California—was not clued into most classified government secrets. First, that is simply the way seconds-in-command were treated by chief executives in those days. Second, Nixon was exceptionally young for a VP and considered somewhat immature by his peers. He privately complained at times that Eisenhower ordered him around like a private in the army.[1] Richard Nixon wasn't allowed that much power or influence because presidents don't like being overshadowed by their underlings. Eisenhower mostly conferred on super-sensitive issues and state secrets with older, more experienced statesmen, such as his Secretary of State, the Director of the Central Intelligence Agency (his brother), or old Army buddies of high rank with access to military intelligence files. But as "Ike" gave ex-Naval officer "Dick" more and more political and policy chores to handle, the younger man began to prove himself. As the first term passed, Mr. Nixon "grew into the job," as they say. By 1956, Eisenhower was rumored to be considering a *new* running mate for his re-election bid, but he settled on Nixon once again since he had ably proven himself to be obedient, competent, and generally helpful.

Thus, Richard Nixon earned the right to more inside secrets before President Eisenhower's second term (1957-1961) was completed. The vice president was now allowed into the private, closed world of *highly* classified projects. This was especially true after he let Eisenhower know he was determined to succeed him as America's president in the looming 1960 election. To these two conservative figures, continuity of government was essential, and thus even top secrets needed to be shared.

At some point in late 1958 or early 1959, it appears President Eisenhower let Richard Nixon in on *the* big secret: Earth had been visited by a variety of advanced extraterrestrials, and the U.S. government possessed crash-landed—and even *gifted*—alien craft as solid, indisputable proof. Moreover, Eisenhower personally met (at least two or three times) with a race of human-like aliens at secure, remote military airfields, as explained in this author's 2020 tome, *President Eisenhower's Close Encounters*. At that time, arrangements were made to get visiting ETs to agree to remain generally aloof and remote and not interfere with our society or trigger a panic. These particular humanoids seemed very much like us, at least physiologically. This is reflected in a leaked U.S. Army intelligence officer's training booklet from April 1954, which described one race as about five feet tall and nearly identical to humans.[2] They appeared to be, to this author, like "cousins" of homo sapiens, arriving for a "family reunion" from a similar planet.

Could such a nearly identical world with very human-like beings really exist in the cosmos, perhaps not too far from Earth? In November 2021, astrobiologist Simon Conway Morris from the University of Cambridge gave an interview with a respected science magazine[3] and claimed just that. In an article aptly dubbed "Astrobiologist: 'Surely we will meet humans from other worlds,'" he explained that he and his fellow researchers can "say with reasonable confidence" that a human-like process has occurred on other planets in the universe, utilizing "the theory of convergent evolution," which states that "random effects eventually average so that evolution converges, tending to produce similar organisms in any given environment." If so, such extraterrestrial life would have evolved "analogous to that of a human." He went on to state that other scientists have also reached this logical conclusion. Meanwhile, another story from a different science-based media source in November 2021 claimed that a "second Earth" had been located in the known universe, one with very similar properties as our own planet based upon scientific analysis of available data.[4] Obviously, more concrete information is needed on both topics, but it is now very exciting to reasonably theorize our planet and human race may well have a kind of "long lost twin brother"—perhaps even *several*.

Obviously, Nixon would have been floored, at first, by the tale of his boss's secret airbase alien contact. He was likely given a briefing report either just before or after huddling with the popular president on these remarkably sensitive issues. Thus ready, Vice President Nixon was by the late '50s allowed to sit in at high-level conferences to learn the latest details on UFOs and ETs. How do we know this? We can thank intrepid journalist Linda Moulton Howe[5] for uncovering the story of an eyewitness to these behind-the-scenes events.[6]

In April 1998, Howe first learned about an older, retired gentleman who had once served in the United States Army as a highly educated cryptographer. This member of the Army Signal Corps eventually worked for the Central Intelligence Agency.[7] As a result, the knowledgeable source possessed stirring UFO/ET information from the Eisenhower era. The ex-serviceman was living in Florida with "his health deteriorating" from diabetes. Realizing his time on Earth was limited, he was at last in the mood to share some tasty secrets. Linda Howe flew to the Sunshine State to meet him. She felt comfortable trusting his word. She came to refer to the former cryptologist by a pseudonym, "Kewper Stein."

Howe's secret source claimed in no uncertain terms that Eisenhower and, eventually, Nixon knew all about cosmic visitors to our world. At Mr. Stein's request, Ms. Howe did not post their fascinating audiotape conversations online until June 2014, after Kewper Stein had passed away. Before he left this world, Kewper Stein told Howe that he worked for the Central Intelligence Agency from 1957 to 1960. Since he knew so much about languages, symbolism, codes, and cryptology, the well-trained lieutenant was assigned to study some top-secret extraterrestrial autopsy films. The footage featured dead humanoids being dissected by Army surgeons, it seems. He was informed the celluloid was recorded in June 1947, in the desert near Socorro, New Mexico, apparently just after a spaceship crash-landed nearby. That was nearly a month *before* the now-legendary Roswell UFO affair.[8] There are many rumors and claims about this strangely unheralded event, but that's for other authors to explore.

According to Kewper Stein, Eisenhower eventually assigned Vice President Nixon to investigate the military's more serious, genuine cases of apparent alien fly-bys and landings, which were not released in their official *Project Blue Book*[9] report. The rest of that so-called "investigative program"—which ended during Nixon's first year as president—was window-dressing for the public, a deliberate white-wash that debunked the more easily-explained claims by American citizens during those seventeen years. *Blue Book* certainly did not reveal the most guarded and precious of all American secrets: that at least one living, breathing alien had been recovered from a wrecked metallic craft on American soil. But Kewper Stein knew this and further informed Linda Moulton Howe[10] that it and other such peaceable ETs were being housed in a top-secret military installation in the Nevada desert, a remote and inaccessible site surrounded by closed-off government property that stretched for dozens of miles in all directions. Today, we would call this "Area 51"[11] and nearby "S4" (some say for "Section 4" and others say for "Sigma 4").

Kewper Stein learned first-hand that President Eisenhower had grown increasingly exasperated at the lack of steady, reliable CIA reports on the alien-human communication going on in this Nevada base. The president expressed aloud his irritation at an Oval Office meeting that Kewper Stein attended. At that confab, the commander-in-chief personally selected Kewper to go on "several trips" to investigate the restricted Nevada site to find out just what was going on with the visiting ETs.

While touring the S4 site, "Lt. Stein" was allowed to read some secret CIA files on ETs and, at one point, even saw a live alien being! He could clearly make it out, "through a glass window" or one-way mirror, in another room, but he "never went in to see" or communicate with it—but his boss accompanying him on the trip did. Afterward, the boss told Kewper that the ET did not speak aloud because his communication "was only telepathic" within the next room. The gray, thin, entity would send answers to a CIA interpreter who worked with him daily "before he even spoke the question out loud."

Stein claimed that, in the spring of 1959, he returned to Washington D.C. and met with President Eisenhower, Vice President Nixon, and a CIA official at FBI headquarters. A few FBI officials took part in the meeting but not Director J. Edgar Hoover[12]. Stein gave these leaders a thorough briefing on his fact-finding mission. The evidence he shared included a variety of reports and photographic images of flying saucers and unknown aerial crafts taken by various sources worldwide. Eisenhower looked them over with substantial interest and made informed remarks. He seemed to know a good deal more than Nixon, who was seemingly "stunned" and somewhat "out of the loop" on the otherworldly topic. Who knows, maybe he hadn't been briefed until this very meeting!

One upshot of the 1959 get-together described by Stein is President Eisenhower's general dissatisfaction with the dossier. The president supposedly wanted still more insight on what was going on at S4 and MJ12, especially about possible alien abduction cases, interestingly. He also expressed disappointment that the conference reports did not include actual photographs of extraterrestrial beings, "like the ones you had before." Meanwhile, Richard Nixon absorbed all of this; did it fire him up even more to run for president soon?[13]

So, *if* this Kewper Stein data is true, we can see that even as vice president Richard Nixon knew explosive truths and kept his mouth shut. To everyone. Even to his ET-curious golfing buddy Jackie Gleason, mostly likely. There will be more on Gleason's ties to Nixon later.

After losing the 1960 election and the 1962 California governor's race, Nixon spent years stewing on the sidelines as a New York City lawyer, eager to get back into the political game. He saw his opening in 1968 and ran for president once more. Now a well-known name to Republicans, Nixon easily captured his party's nomination and, in the fall, ran a nearly flawless campaign. At one point, he stopped in southern Texas to inspect the Space Center in Houston, a tour guided by a supportive astronaut. Nixon wanted to show the world he was hip to outer space and scientific issues, and the public responded. In the fall, Nixon won a narrow national election decision. He spent the rest of that tumultuous year selecting cabinet members and staffers, setting up a "Southern White House" in the Miami area, and viewing ongoing NASA[14] space missions on television like all other fascinated Americans.

Taking office on January 20, 1969, the new president enthusiastically encouraged the American space program, particularly the Apollo[15] moon-landing mission. According to one UFO data site, "In 1969, Nixon ordered the US military to investigate a UFO that was seen by pilots and air traffic controllers in the vicinity of the White House. The object was described as 'a glowing red, football-shaped object.'"[16] No other source seems to support this alleged event, however.

PAUL BLAKE SMITH

Success arrived for NASA's Apollo program in July 1969 via the first human landing on the moon, and similar manned missions continued until late 1972. Apollo was initially conceived during the Eisenhower administration as a three-person spacecraft mission, superseding the one-person Mercury spacecraft program that put the first Americans in space (but not very far). After the first moon landing, sufficient flight hardware remained for nine more similar touchdowns with a plan for extended lunar geological and astrophysical exploration. Budget cuts, supposedly, forced the cancellation of three of these planned landings. Thus, by early 1973, there were no more planned trips to the moon.[17] Did this decision have anything to do with the secrets a safely reelected Nixon was up to with his showbiz golfing buddy at an Air Force base on February 19, 1973? We'll get to that later.

Either way, just as the lunar landings were ending, two more major space plans unfolded that were privately pushed and publicly endorsed by President Nixon.

First was "Skylab," the unique space station which successfully supported three-crewed missions with the goal of better understanding our ability to conduct scientific experiments in space. Second, on January 5, 1972, Nixon announced to the nation a new, reusable "Space Shuttle" to hopefully launch "in manned flight by 1978, and operational a short time later." Unfortunately for Nixon, the shuttle had several technical delays and didn't take off on such a mission into space until 1981.

Perhaps significantly, Nixon declared in that same speech on January 5, 1972: "We are learning the imperatives of universal brotherhood and global ecology, learning to think and act as guardians of one tiny blue and green island in the trackless oceans of the universe." Pretty flowery for Dick Nixon, but it is still a good perspective on space matters.[18]

By late 1972, just as these expensive space programs were progressing nicely and Nixon was basking in the warm glow of a landslide re-election while bringing the unpopular Vietnam War to a close, the Watergate scandal busted open like a can of biscuit dough. It expanded so widely and rapidly that it could not be crammed back into its damaged container, straining and staining Nixon's dreams of glory. Instead, he became perhaps the most hated and lampooned president in U.S. history, forever associated with underhanded dirty tricks, secret electronic eavesdropping, and private plots against his perceived enemies. Eventually, he would be remembered primarily for his resignation amid scandal and disgrace. In the years that followed, Nixon bravely battled health and legal woes while becoming a behind-the-scenes adviser to Governor Ronald Wilson Reagan[19] (1911-2004), who became the standard-bearer of the Republican Party. Reagan took office in January 1981, and some say soon spoke to those in the know on what was factual about the subject of extraterrestrial visitation.

According to an internet transcript that surfaced in 2005,[20] in early March 1981 new President Reagan met twice with a select team of advisers while relaxing at Camp David.[21] Allegedly, the classified meetings were set up specifically for Reagan to be briefed on the subject of UFOS and ETs away from prying eyes and ears. On Friday and Saturday, March 6-7, 1981, the information relayed to Reagan was supposedly recorded and later turned into a controversial transcript that features fascinating revelations.

In an online article by writer Steve Hammons from November 2007,[22] President Reagan was said to have already been somewhat familiar with the topic, having received a one-hour briefing from his CIA director in February 1981 (likely on February 23, as official digitized logs show). Reagan supposedly said of the alien presence: "Well, I knew a little about this subject before. Back in 1970. [President] Nixon had all of the good stuff and wanted to share it with some of his friends."

We'll stop here for a second and wonder if that included Nixon's golfing buddy Jackie Gleason. The entertainer, who was privately obsessed with the otherworldly topic, likely badgered the new president for any scrap of information. Reagan continued: "Nixon showed me some papers. Not sure about who authored them, but they...huh...well something about New Mexico and other places... Nixon was pretty...huh...well, you know...fascinated with it. He showed me something, some kind of object or device that came from one of their craft. Something that was taken from the New Mexico crash site."

This dovetails nicely with the information relayed within my 2020 book, *President Eisenhower's Close Encounters*, in which I aired the tale of a 1948 UFO crash in the New Mexico desert—in a rural canyon near the small town of Aztec[23]—that produced a secret U.S. military recovery and a removed communications device from the disabled alien ship. So, we can see a strong indication that the controversial briefing transcript might well be the genuine article. Reagan's alleged words in 1981, on what Nixon related eleven years earlier, seem spot-on.

On Friday, May 1, 1970, White House records show that President Nixon did speak by phone with California Governor Ronald Reagan for eight minutes, then Nixon attended to some government business and phone calls in his Oval Office. Later, he left for Camp David, Maryland. Nixon's first telephone communication on Saturday morning was with paranormal-loving Jackie Gleason, on the line from Switzerland at 9:10 a.m. EDT.[24]

After several more phone exchanges, the president and a friend impulsively hopped in a car and *drove*—themselves—all the way to Gettysburg, Pennsylvania. The unescorted duo wanted to visit Dwight Eisenhower's widow. Strange! It is unknown if Mamie Doud Eisenhower[25] (1896-1979) ever found out about Ike's alien contacts, and it is less clear if she chose to share her data with Nixon during that surprise visit. After a couple of hours of chitchat, the duo motored back to Camp David, where Nixon received and placed more calls, including long-distance calls to Jackie Gleason. *Another* call from Gleason was handled after the meal. Finally, records reveal President Nixon and future President Reagan hooked up on the phone yet again on May 7, 1970.

What was going on that required phone conversations with the two most UFO-curious Hollywood figures?

In July 1970, Nixon's official records show[26] Governor Reagan visited Nixon at the president's San Clemente beachfront estate, where they were able to speak in private, without a crowd of aides or pesky press (and, presumably, hidden microphones). Also, records reveal that Nixon sat with Reagan in the Oval Office in January 1971 and later again that November. There was actually much more contact between these two famous American leaders, but these are just examples that show how Nixon *could* conceivably have shared above-top-secret ET matters in private with trusted fellow conservative Reagan in that particular time frame.

Did Nixon *really* have a secret piece of a crashed UFO in his possession? Did he display it for his fellow southern Californian? We'll likely never know the complete, unvarnished answer. However, this book seeks to explore an even greater saga.

By the rocky end of his official White House tenure, President Richard M. Nixon had not uttered a single word in public about otherworldly beings visiting Earth. He obviously had enough trouble and controversy on his hands without stirring up more. He said nothing about the titillating topic in his two-decade retirement either (1974-1994). But it is what the candid wife of a good friend claims that Nixon did that's the crux of this truly amazing nonfiction tale...

---

1. Russell Baker, "A Very Wretched Relationship," *New York Books*, April 4, 2013.
2. Salla, Michael, ed., "SOM1-01 - Special Operations Manual / Extraterrestrial Entities and Technology, Recovery and Disposal," *bibliotecapleyades.net*, December, 1996.
3. Zack White, "Astrobiologist: 'Surely we will meet humans from other worlds,' mysterioussociety.com, November 24, 2021. 8
4. Admin, "It's Official: Scientists Discovered A 'Second Earth' *Ideas for Tips* www.ideasfortips.life/its-official-researchers-have-discovered-a-second-earth
5. Wikipedia contributors, "Linda Moulton Howe," *Wikipedia*.
6. Linda Moulton Howe, "Maze of Deception,", *earthfiles.com*.
7. Wikipedia contributors, "Central Intelligence Agency," *Wikipedia*.

8. Wikipedia contributors, "Roswell incident," *Wikipedia*.
9. Wikipedia contributors, "Project Blue Book," *Wikipedia*.
10. Wikipedia, Linda Moulton Howe.
11. Wikipedia contributors. "Area 51," *Wikipedia*.
12. Wikipedia contributors, "J. Edgar Hoover," *Wikipedia*.
13. Also, for more information, see a 2015 publication entitled *UFOs and the White House: What Did Our President Know and When Did They Know It?* This book was authored by C. Ronald Garner, a respected UFO researcher.
14. Wikipedia contributors, "NASA," *Wikipedia*.
15. Wikipedia contributors, "Apollo program," *Wikipedia*.
16. Heathcliff Peters, *"UFOs and US Presidents: US Presidents Talks About UFOs,"* Astral *Citizens*, February 2022.
17. Wikipedia, "Apollo Program."
18. Richard Nixon, "NASA statement/speech," *nasa.gov.*, January 5, 1972.
19. Wikipedia contributor, "Ronald Reagan," *Wikipedia*.
20. Howe, "Maze of Deception."
21. Wikipedia contributors, "Camp David," *Wikipedia*.
22. Steve Hammons, "Alleged Briefing to President Reagan on UFOS," *AmericanChronicle*, November 27, 2007.
23. "Aztec, New Mexico UFO Crash Recovery 1948," *Noufors*.
24. "Presidential Daily Diary, May 1970" *Richard Nixon Museum and Library*.
25. Wikipedia contributors, Mamie Eisenhower, *Wikipedia*.
26. "Nixon Presidential Daily" July 1970.

CHAPTER ONE

NIXON AND GLEASON: IMPORTANT BACKGROUND DATA

"Damn hush money! How are we going to...how do we get the stuff?"

President Richard Milhous Nixon has long been rumored to have traveled to an American military base in February 1973 to view the physical evidence of otherworldly visitation—much like his former mentor President Dwight D. Eisenhower, did years before, in February 1954. Unlike Eisenhower, Nixon brought along a local golf buddy—who happened to be world-famous comedian Jackie Gleason, a stalwart South Florida resident and UFO enthusiast. Upon arriving home from this meeting at Homestead Air Force Base that night, a traumatized Gleason spilled the proverbial beans to his wife and then clammed up for the rest of his life. Together, he said, he and the president had scrutinized dead extraterrestrials.[1]

This unusual but electrifying story is so old it has grown whiskers, as they say, but, despite some falsehoods injected into the story by attention-seeking UFO buffs, the heart of the legend might well be true. It is time to separate the truth from lies and find out what *really* happened during this "close encounter of the Florida kind."

To begin, let's set the table for the crux of the amazing tale with facts, not fantasy...

To stay at his "Winter White House" in Key Biscayne, Florida,[2] just outside Miami, Mr. Nixon almost always flew aboard Air Force One to Homestead Air Force Base. He really was in and out of there a lot. Homestead AFB was an important military installation situated at 360 Coral Sea Drive in Dade County, Florida.[3] The base was located thirty-seven miles south of the metro Miami area, near the Atlantic Ocean.[4] The arriving president would normally spend only a few minutes on the ground there before he and his party would board a waiting Air Force helicopter. They would then be choppered north—in about fifteen minutes or less—to his surprisingly modest vacation home near Biscayne Bay. A large landing pad was eventually created, near Nixon's waterfront estate, for handy convenience. Nixon made numerous trips like this at taxpayer expense, requiring the protection of the Secret Service and local law enforcement personnel.

Mr. Nixon probably spent more time away from the White House than any previous (or future) U.S. president. On his trips to Key Biscayne, the quirky chief executive would go through long stretches of relative silence; perhaps he was brooding or pondering important matters. His thoughts were likely loftier at times than other souls around him as he wondered how to pull together the friction-filled elements of the modern world into peaceful coexistence. Sensitive to criticism, Nixon urged his team to strike back hard at any perceived slights, and he often plotted vengefully in private to undermine or spy on his political enemies—which caused his eventual undoing.

At his main waterfront home on Bay Lane, the president would hold court with various visiting dignitaries, family, friends, and staff. Everything was carefully arranged for Nixon to be catered to at the estate; everything he desired could be imported. The White House press pool and local news reporters were kept at arm's length, lodged at a Miami hotel, unable to view at close range any activity in the president's well-guarded beach community. Most traveling White

House aides stayed at a Key Biscayne hotel. For safety's sake, whenever Nixon was relaxing at his Bay Lane home, southernmost Key Biscayne was considered a no-fly zone, and two Coast Guard boats patrolled the nearby restricted waters and Nixon's private beach.[5] Many a security guard strolled the compound, eyes peeled for any kind of potential trouble or threat to the nation's commander-in-chief. Apparently, none occurred.

For Nixon, the critical portal to and from this idyllic vacation site was Homestead AFB. Decades earlier, the military facility was a key site for the American world war effort on the East Coast, from its inception in 1942 to a devastating hurricane just weeks after the end of World War II in the late summer of 1945. Homestead was reactivated a decade later and served as a landing, refueling, and takeoff site for jets, airplanes, helicopters, and at times Air Force One. Over the decades, the airbase built up more modern offices, barracks, hangars, advanced radio technology, storage sheds, and labs until it was nearly wiped off the map by a major hurricane in August 1992. Reopening after two years and $100 million in renovation work, the installation was back on track in April 1994, officially dubbed "Homestead Air Reserve Station." It was further renovated in 2015.[6]

To emphasize an important point, Homestead was no ordinary airfield. The American military maintained Naval Security Group activity at the base, transmitting often encrypted messages to planes, ships, and land-based operations in the area as well as intercepting some enemy messages. The U.S. Army was also participating in coded data transmission at Homestead, along with the Air Force and likely the Coast Guard as well, since the Atlantic Ocean was so close by, just beyond a mile or so of cultivated farmland. They were monitoring the seas and humid skies for Russian subs, ships, and planes. Remember, the '70s were part of the Cold War era, with Americans in uniform on their guard against unfriendly communist nations, especially the far-left Cuban dictator Fidel Castro (1926-2016). His neighboring "red" government posed a threat, coddling Soviet soldiers and diplomats just 100 miles to the south, close enough to Florida's shores to make United States military and intelligence personnel nervous.

Plus, over the recent decades, there had been a few brief, but exciting UFO sightings off the coast, some in what would later be dubbed the "Bermuda Triangle." Military missions to scout that seemingly tumultuous area for unusual, unexplained craft or missing ships and planes often began at Homestead.

All of these factors combined mean that top-notch Secret Service agents, military intelligence personnel, and CIA operatives were usually housed at the well-guarded base, working there daily or at least in and out on a regular basis, on missions amid pretty tight security. Meanwhile, highly trained and armed personnel made up the bulk of the population in and around the base. A favorite place to hang out in those days was a pub called "The Sandbar," near a gated entrance, a checkpoint that stopped incoming and outgoing traffic. Plus, base personnel had to watch out daily for some dangerous unwanted visitors: alligators. This threat was most common each April, when they came up a nearby canal to sunbathe, perhaps mate, and look for food.[7]

How important was Homestead to Richard Nixon? Records show that in his first term alone, the president traveled there (to access his Key Biscayne compound) a whopping *fifty-five* times. He spent 118 days of his presidency at his waterfront estate. Each time, he depended upon the Homestead personnel to land, fuel, and protect his presidential plane, as well as the family, friends, and aides who arrived to visit the awkward chief executive. Nixon even arranged to have returning Vietnam War veterans flown into the base to be reunited with their anxious families in a made-for-TV media event, even though a U.S. West Coast airbase would have been a much quicker and easier reunion site for all concerned since they were coming back from Asia. These televised reunions were likely intended to promote Mr. Nixon as a great peacemaker in late 1972 and early 1973.[8]

So obviously, no unscheduled, uninvited civilian could just waltz

PAUL BLAKE SMITH

into Homestead Air Force Base any time they felt like it. This was a tightly wrapped military installation with some secretive goings-on behind its chain-link fencing. Its nearby town of Homestead, Florida, consisted of about 14,000 citizens in 1973, and most of that population was based around serving the installation's needs and surrounding agri-business.[9] Evidently, unexplained UFO sightings in the area were becoming commonplace, continuing into the twenty-first century.[10]

When Nixon visited his one-story Biscayne bungalow, he'd hole up there for days at a time, unwinding, reading, and golfing in the laid-back community. He would wade in the surf, walk the white sand beaches, and go boating with his low-key Cuban-American friend from next door, Charles Gregory "Bebe" Rebozo (1912-1998).[11] Stays were clearly for relaxation purposes, to relieve the tension and stress of governing for a president trying to handle a faltering economy, a failing war effort in Vietnam, and the daily Cold War struggle around the globe

Bebe Rebozo was a prized chum, always exuding calm but with little to say to anyone. Nixon aides would remark that divorced Mr. Rebozo was "the perfect companion for a man who likes solitude because being with Bebe can be almost as good as being alone."[12] How trusted and close was Mr. Rebozo to Dick Nixon? Crimemagazine.com, airing Nixon's various mafia ties, put it this way: "Rebozo came in and out of the White House as he pleased, without being logged in by the Secret Service. Though he had no government job, Rebozo had his own private office and phone number in the executive mansion. When he traveled on Air Force One, which was frequently, Bebe donned a blue flight jacket bearing the presidential seal and his name."[13] Secret Service agents compared notes years later about the Nixon-Rebozo friendship and discovered that during Florida coastal boat trips, beach walks, or just hanging out together quite often, neither man spoke a word! They were both evidently lost in thought but very comfortable with each other's company. Bebe Rebozo was famous for his silence; he gave almost no media interviews and never issued a tell-all book, taking his intimate presidential secrets with him to his grave.

A high-level aide close to Nixon recalled much later that very little government work was actually handled at Nixon's air-conditioned "Southern White House." Loafing, eating, gossiping, golfing, swimming, sunning, napping, reading, and watching old Hollywood movies from a projector in the evening were the usual pastimes when Nixon vacationed at the modest house.[14] A swimming pool, which cost the public $13,600, was installed but sat mostly ignored when the president wasn't in town and often even when he was. Reading consisted of top-secret military and government reports, which were understandably "eyes only." Highly classified briefing reports were mysteries to most of his aides, who were not authorized to review them. Nixon did not read actual books or newspapers. Television was of no interest, and neither were contemporary movies. His favorite yellow legal pad sat nearby for jotting notes that would be brought up in meetings and later utilized in the books he wrote.

Key Biscayne is, in fact, an island connected to Miami in 1947 by the completion of the four-mile Rickenbacker Causeway. This opened the small strip of land to developers and greater human habitation. Nixon's properties located there may have been purchased with his own money, obtained from a Florida politico in late 1968, but his funding was pieced together by local mafia-connected individuals associated with shady banker Rebozo. Then federal funds from U.S. taxpayers were utilized to renovate the compound homes, dredge the bay near the boat dock, and build the concrete helicopter pad (which alone cost $400,000). A neighbor recalled decades later that "lots of very serious-looking men were everywhere," with security agents, policemen, and military personnel roaming the properties.[15]

To add to the convenience and security of the Biscayne presidential compound, the Secret Service rented a house nearby (468 Bay Lane) for their residential quarters. A close-by White House Communications Agency office was established in another house down the street. Special alarms and phone lines were installed along with two "guard gates" at the road entrance to the gated community, which wasn't all that upscale even when updated. Visitors who got past the two checkpoints might have been surprised to see that the president's twin homes on the cul-de-sac were modest affairs made largely of cinder blocks cemented together, almost like Legos, but it was a far shorter flight from the White House than the Nixon's' more palatial San Clemente, California, estate. The early '70s were a sleepier, more laid-back time in Florida. Since that time, Miami and the narrow Biscayne Island have experienced tremendous commercial growth, spoiling the old, easier-going, less developed atmosphere.

Richard Nixon's first visit as the nation's chief executive to his new Florida waterfront estate occurred in early February 1969, and White House records show that his second, only a month later, featured a phone call conversation with crosstown Jackie Gleason. Digitized logs show that four months later, Nixon returned to his cul-de-sac compound and attended a four-hour golf date at the Country Club of Miami with Gleason.[16] This meeting took place on Sunday, July 6, 1969, two weeks before the historic Apollo moon landing. Strangely—suspiciously?—the list of passengers traveling that afternoon with the president and the great comedy star was removed from Nixon's official logs. This seemingly innocent and fun golf match was very likely coordinated through phone calls to Gleason's longtime, trusted secretary.

Could the instantly recognizable president *really* have left his beachfront house in the dark of night and traveled to Homestead in February 1973 to quietly show off alien bodies to a pal? It seems like a pretty wild, weird story that is now nearly an "urban legend." But while Nixon was known for being a bit odd at times, he was widely known for being a clever, ruthless schemer, going to great lengths in private to achieve his goals. He would not balk at working through intermediaries for weeks or months in advance to get what he wanted. He accomplished much through careful planning. His Homestead trip with Gleason fits that description: it was likely prearranged after behind-the-scenes negotiations with third parties. Not a spur-of-the-moment act at all.

To fully understand the zeitgeist going on in the early '70s, we have to try to grasp the sense of power and elitism that was pervasive in South Florida. It seems that just about all the characters involved in or around the Nixon-Gleason extraterrestrial story seem to have made a beeline for that part of the peninsula. In the '60s and '70s, Miami rivaled New York City and Washington D.C. as a hub of important American business and pleasure of all sorts. Don't believe it? Let's look at a "Top Ten List" of key figures that flocked to those balmy climes as a great center of American power back in the day...

1. President Richard M. Nixon first vacationed in Key Biscayne in 1951. He returned sporadically, then purchased his own house in early 1969 at 500 Bay Lane, the official residential address of the Winter White House. Mr. Nixon also utilized 516 Bay Lane next door as his office. The First Couple's next-door neighbor (490 Bay Lane) was banker buddy Bebe Rebozo, who had ties to at least two of the Watergate burglars.

2. President John F. Kennedy[17] (1917-1963) and the wealthy Kennedy family kept at least two beachfront estates in nearby Palm Beach for many decades. Just after the 1960 election, victorious, vacationing JFK met defeated Nixon at a hotel on Key Biscayne. Plus, Kennedy's last weekend alive was spent visiting various South Florida locales while staying at his beach house, utilizing Homestead Airbase for arrivals and departures. British author Timothy Good stated in a 2007 book that he developed an inside source (or two) who told him that in 1961 President Kennedy "expressed the desire to see the alien bodies" that were recovered from a tragic extraterrestrial

crash (the precise year and site went unnamed). According to Good, it was arranged for the young commander-in-chief *to visit a military airbase in Florida to secretly view the bodies of the otherworldly cadavers.*[18]

3. FBI Director J. Edgar Hoover (1895-1972) and his close underling Clyde Anderson Tolson (1900-1975) vacationed together in Miami every holiday time during their government tenure, enjoying frequent visits to Hialeah Park's racetrack for petty wagering.

4. Meyer Lansky (1902-1983), the notorious mafia boss who had ties to Nixon, Rebozo, and even Hoover, was based out of Miami for decades. At times he shared his territory with gangland's powerful Santos Trafficante, Jr. (1914-1987)—who was also an associate of Rebozo. Fellow mobster Johnny Roselli (1905-1976) was a frequent visitor to the area and was even found dead there, his mutilated body discovered floating in an oil drum in a local bay. It is believed that mob asset and future assassin Jack Ruby (1911-1967) also made trips to Miami—and may have even been known to congressman Nixon in the late '40s.

5. The Dulles brothers kept a South Florida home. This is where former Secretary of State John Foster Dulles (1888-1959)—then serving under President Eisenhower but also well known to Nixon—once recuperated from cancer surgery and where his brother, former CIA Director Allen Welsh Dulles (1892-1969), vacationed. Allen Dulles and Vice President Nixon may well have plotted foreign political overthrows and assassinations together in the '50s while in D.C. and Miami. Also, the CIA's Deputy Director from 1972 to 1976, Vernon A. Walters (1917-2002), lived in West Palm Beach. He kept a framed picture of his lovely beach house on the wall of his Langley, Virginia, office. Why? "I told them this was what was waiting [for me] if anyone squeezed me too hard."[19]

6. James R. "Jimmy" Hoffa (1913-1975), the President of the Teamsters, spent some of his time living and working out of an upscale Miami hotel suite, greeting visiting Labor leaders and mafia figures there. Hoffa was eventually replaced by Frank E. Fitzsimmons (1908-1981), who was sworn in as the Teamsters union president in Miami—with Richard Nixon present. The official AFL-CIO headquarters was also located in Miami Beach.

7. E. Howard Hunt (1918-2007), once a CIA employee, Nixon aide, and the Watergate break-in manager, kept an upscale estate—featuring a stable for up to six horses—in Key Biscayne (11337 NE 8th Ct Biscayne Park). Hunt's abode was ritzy for an undercover operative, and this becomes a small factor later in our story. He frequently huddled in the area with his fellow "White House Plumbers"—shadowy operatives often working for the Central Intelligence Agency. These right-wing agents trained in South Florida for the failed 1961 Cuban Bay of Pigs invasion. In fact, the CIA's largest station outside the D.C. area was located in Miami, mostly for coordinating anti-Castro activities in the Caribbean and maintaining ties to the then-powerful mob.[20]

8. Florida Senator Edward J. Gurney (1914-1996) was urged by fellow Republican Nixon to run in 1970. Gurney won and was soon mired in scandal. He was eventually indicted for influence peddling in a messy case surrounding loan improprieties in Coral Gables, just a few miles from Nixon's house. Both Nixon and Gurney resigned from office in disgrace in 1974.

9. Howard R. Hughes (1905-1976), the shadowy billionaire industrialist who contributed to many political campaigns—including Nixon's—to manipulate matters behind the scenes, also maintained a home in Coral

Gables, although he likely didn't spend much time there by the early '70s.

10. John Herbert "Jackie" Gleason (1916-1987), the famous comedy star, moved to Miami in 1964 and stayed there until his death at age seventy-one. He brought his entire TV production with him, which drew big-name celebrity guests from all over. Gleason was delighted to learn in mid-1973 that his old flame, Marilyn Taylor Horwich (1925-2019), had recently moved to the area to be closer to her sister, who was already living there. "When Jackie learned that mom had moved down there and had been widowed, he put on a full-court press. The phone would ring, and he pursued and rekindled the romance with mom," recalled Marilyn's adult son in 2019. Gleason ran a celebrity pro-am golf tournament in suburban Lauderhill that brought many stars from various fields to visit, including President Nixon.[21]

As we can see, the Miami area was like a glamorous, color-splashed magnet, pulling all manner of Americans into its warm breezes and cool vibe. This included major corporations, sporting events, TV and film productions, and various conventions. By February 1973, three Major League Baseball franchises were utilizing local stadiums for their spring training regimens and games. Football coach Don Shula and the now-legendary Miami Dolphins teams of the early '70s were all the rage, winning three straight AFC Championships and two Super Bowls. Records show that President Nixon used to call Shula and a few NFL players just to talk football now and then.

There are still other famous and influential personalities involved with South Florida, such as retired U.S. Senator George A. Smathers (1913-2007). He was a Miami native and a close friend to Nixon, even before he sold Nixon his Key Biscayne property. Governor Reubin O'Donovan Askew (1928-2014) lived in the area, and Gleason welcomed him as a guest while co-hosting a national talk show in Miami in late 1972. Once out of office (1971-1979), Askew joined a local law firm. The list of the powerful who visited or dwelt in the Miami area continues, but time and space are limited.

It cannot be emphasized enough that the NASA space program was also based out of South Florida, up the coast from Miami, so naturally many American astronauts lived in the area. Plus, various showbiz figures would visit South Florida just for fun or to take part in an entertainment project.

Okay, just one more famous name: ex-Beatle John Ono Lennon (1940-1980) visited South Florida in the '60s and '70s, eventually purchasing a waterfront vacation home—dubbed "El Solano" ("The East Wind")—in Palm Beach. The British songwriter had told a Palm Beach reporter during a 1974 visit: "I don't really want to leave Palm Beach, I'd like to own a piece of it."[22] And he soon did. As we will discuss in Chapter Seven, Lennon seems to have a strange connection to Nixon and UFOs as well. Nixon himself was also a visitor to Palm Beach in the same general time frame as Lennon, staying as a guest at 1055 N. Ocean Boulevard, thanks to his elderly friend, New York businessman Elmer H. Bobst (1884-1978). Nixon had his own entire guest wing in Elmer's 6,667-square-foot beachfront mansion, located not all that far from Mar-a-Lago (meaning "Sea to Lake"), the eventual landing site for another New York City business executive Donald J. Trump (1946-). The future president purchased it in 1982 after visiting Miami/Palm Beach many times. White House records for July 7, 1974, reveal that Nixon and Rebozo helicptered in from Key Biscayne to look over the now-famous Mar-a-Lago estate as a possible new presidential retreat for hosting visiting foreign dignitaries. Nixon resigned, however, just one month later, and the ornate property lay relatively fallow for eight years.[23]

Not far away was a coastal home for Nixon's choice for RNC Chairman, George H. W. Bush (1924-2018), and his young sons (one a future president, like his dad, and the other Florida's future governor).

Clearly, South Florida was a sunny, swingin' site for movers and shakers of all sorts year-round. And hopelessly square, Dick Nixon was somehow at center stage.

Now let's focus on Mr. Nixon's famous golfing partner, Jackie Gleason...

Millions of fans the world over referred to him routinely as "The Great One." Professionally, he was a supremely entertaining and gifted man. Almost mind-numbingly so. Each week on his CBS variety show, Jackie Gleason moved from monologues to magic to mime to music. He acted in sketches, slipping from comedy to pathos in seconds flat, then he raced to the next segment where he might conduct an orchestra, chat with a high-profile guest, belt out a song, or do some stand-up jokes. He flung himself across the television stage, running, sliding, dancing, and cartwheeling through physical stunts that left him sweaty, breathless, and bruised but left his audience and critics alike with amazement, amusement, and enjoyment. Mega-popular Gleason fleshed out original, unforgettable characters; did spot-on impersonations; employed healthy doses of slapstick; and even dabbled with the trumpet. He was, at times, his own choreographer, producer, director, and set designer. Fireball Jackie was frequently his program's orchestra conductor. He was, after all, a composer who whipped up and released almost forty albums of mood music. And all of this while barely glancing at a script the day of the show and rarely rehearsing! Gleason utilized his photographic memory, plus his improvisation skills and an overall sense of just plain fun, to bring his show to life.

Whether it was comedy or drama, The Great One galloped through each taxing performance as if he'd been doing this every day for forty years. As a result, *The Jackie Gleason Show* was a '50s smash hit. Instead of truly ending, it was reshaped and returned in different formats for the Columbia Broadcast System as the '60s commenced. By 1970, there probably wasn't an American alive who hadn't at least heard of Jackie Gleason, watched his television production, or seen him in Hollywood movies. "Superstar" was an apt title. Acknowledging his large ego, he even routinely referred to himself as "The Great Gleason."

Fans also chuckled throughout the syndicated sitcom Gleason created and starred in, *The Honeymooners*. But they were seeing only a fraction of what he could accomplish on a stage. He proved far more than the short-fused but goodhearted "Ralph Kramden," the bumbling bus driver character in that CBS spin-off show, yet that is what he is best known for to this day. He truly earned his nickname and reputation as perhaps the greatest entertainer of all time, at least during his tenure on his variety show. No one in showbiz history ever did more in an hour. Gleason could master *anything*, and he knew it. CBS executives rewarded him with an appropriately oversized contract. Despite his love of spending, millions of dollars piled up in Jackie's bank accounts, a fact that cannot be overlooked as we delve further into the Nixon-Gleason ET encounter.

Over the course of his career, Jackie Gleason performed on night-club stages; Hollywood movie soundstages; radio stations; Broadway stages; and television studio sets, creating and honing his own humor and original characters (although later he hired writers to help). According to biographer William Henry III, Gleason issued high salary demands and requested outrageous perks, such as insisting upon the longest limousine in all showbiz, if not all of New York City.[24] He was #1 in the ratings and wanted to be #1 in *life*. In everything, he expected the very best, including access to the finest clubs for golfing, drinking, and even accessing inside knowledge, especially in the field of mysticism. Thus, The Great One also became a Freemason, some say rising to the highest level, or 33rd degree, within that secretive fraternal organization.[25]

Jackie Gleason was also a brilliant billiards buff, a voracious book reader (of course), and—according to a relative—an amateur ham radio operator. "He listened to airplanes flying over at the airport" via his home radio setups, his stepson recalled in 2018. Gleason became an expert and used these radios to communicate with people all around the globe, his third wife's son remembered fondly.[26]

Nixon and Gleason *could* have first met when visiting New York City or Miami in the '50s, but if and when that meeting took place is unknown. We do know that Nixon moved to The Big Apple in 1963, and for at least a year, he and Gleason were Republican big-city pals. They both escaped at times to South Florida, socializing there mostly while out on the links. Apart from a game on the golf course, a quick beach walk, or a boat ride, neither man spent much time outdoors. By 1967, the two were more regularly noted by the press as using the electric carts at Miami area country club courses. Nixon understood that he needed companionship, someone to bounce ideas and opinions off of. It was perfectly natural for him to fall into the company of Gleason since both celebs were essentially loners otherwise. Only one habit of Gleason's—smoking five to six packs of cigarettes per day—would have been disdained by Nixon (who never indulged). The duo had every reason to bond and no reason to ever reveal each other's intimate, shared secrets. Theirs was a private world of enormous success and exclusivity.

Although it was not widely known at the time, Gleason obsessively collected and read *hundreds and hundreds* of books, magazine articles, newsletters, and newspaper stories on the supernatural, including material on life beyond planet Earth. In fact, the subject of "flying saucers" and "little green men"—common terms in the '40s and '50s—nearly *consumed* Jackie during his downtime. The entertainer filled more and more bookshelves in his New York City apartment. His *Honeymooners* co-star, actress Audrey Meadows (1922-1996), recalled seeing the startling parapsychology library there.[27] In 1964, the collection was boxed up and shipped to his new Miami home, where hundreds more books were added over the next two decades. When he died in 1987, Jackie's massive collection was donated by his widow to the University of Miami, where the donation can still be viewed in a Special Collection room—over 1,700 publications![28]

One man wrote online in July 2013: "Having worked as a night manager of the Doubleday Bookstore in Miami Beach, Lincoln Mall in the late '70s, I can tell you firsthand that I received many requests for books from Jackie Gleason by phone, asking for the newest books on psychic/paranormal phenomenon, and the UFO mystery. He was obviously very interested in these two areas of research."[29] Gleason's stepson recalled how a box of mostly paranormal books would be delivered each week to their Lauderhill residence, and Jackie eagerly devoured them all right up to the end.

TV writer/producer Leonard B. Stern (1922-2011) spoke on camera of his friendship with Gleason: "As he got older, he became increasingly withdrawn. He was interested in the supernatural and the psychic. He became a student of the occult."[30] Gleason biographer William Henry III wrote: "Jackie Gleason had a lifelong fascination with the supernatural. He would spend small fortunes on everything from financing psychic research to buying a sealed box said to contain actual ectoplasm, the spirit of life itself. He would contact everyone from back-alley charlatans to serious researchers like J.B. Rhine of Duke University."

So, this is another interesting point to bear in mind: Jackie "spent small fortunes" to learn the truth about paranormal matters.

To top all of this off, in 1954, Gleason personally designed—working with architect Robert Cika—his own "spaceship house," some forty miles outside New York City.[31] One cannot imagine somebody becoming more obsessed with the idea of extraterrestrial visitation than this. *It was as if Gleason, in his thirties, wanted to live inside an alien craft.* Something really spurred him into action in 1954.

"Round Rock Hill" was the innocuous name he gave to his unique property in Westchester County. The main building and two nearby structures—a garage and a tool shed—were almost perfectly circular, with glass and silver metal roofs that, when viewed from the air, looked as though advanced aliens had descended into the thick woods. The address was 196 Furnace Dock Road in Cortlandt Manor, located in the forested suburbs of Peekskill, an obscure town of about 18,700 people, according to the 1960 census. A large portion of the main room's ceiling was glass, allowing Gleason to install large,

PAUL BLAKE SMITH

high-powered telescopes for scanning the heavens. The place even had a functional Tesla coil that could emit long sparks as well as electromagnetic radio waves, possibly for attempted contact with star people.

At this point, one may wonder how Jackie Gleason ever got interested in the works of inventor Nikola Tesla (1856-1943), a man who once admitted to attempting to use his technology to contact extraterrestrials as early as 1899.[32] While the newly married comic toured clubs and theaters all over the Big Apple in his early twenties, Gleason lived near where Tesla retired. The increasingly eccentric and frail mechanical engineer was spent his eighties holed up at the New Yorker Hotel on 8th Avenue (Suite #3327), obsessively "feeding pigeons while occasionally meeting dignitaries," according to *Wikipedia*. There is, then, a possibility the two men met. By early 1941, Jackie separated from his first wife and daughter and turned to Hollywood for film work, so it seems unlikely the rising performer ever contacted the legendary scientist—unless they both attended the same masonic lodge. This is unknown, but it evidently wasn't until the early '50s that the newly rich and famous TV star began delving into his pricey private passion for paranormal publications and arcane points of view, years after penniless Nikola's death.

Jackie Gleason's amazing spaceship-like property was finally completed in 1959 at a total cost of at least $650,000, which equals more than five million bucks in today's world. It was so unique that it was featured in a photo-filled April 1960 issue of *Popular Mechanics*. An often-overlooked feature was, well, an overlook. That is, Gleason chose to build on the side of a steep 175-foot elevation, giving his progressive pad's floor-to-ceiling windowed walls a grand view, as if occupants could feel like passengers inside a hovering saucer, looking down upon the earth.

Was there a cosmic incident—any specific run-in with aliens— that fired Jackie's imagination? By his own admission, Gleason had not even seen a UFO at this time! Could it be that ET enthusiast Jackie learned about the February 19, 1954, alien landing at Edwards

Airbase to meet with President Dwight Eisenhower? It is looking increasingly likely because high-profile Jackie had plenty of contacts, including ET authors and bigwigs in the military and government (see Chapter Four). People who wouldn't normally talk of such matters might well have blabbed to a world-famous TV star who lived in a futuristic UFO house—especially one who generously financed supernatural research.

Supposedly, Jackie Gleason dubbed the main house in Peekskill "The Mother Ship," and his guest house, garage, and tool shed were "The Scout Ships." But it really wasn't his *home*, nor was it anyones. He only hosted an occasional party there for guests willing to drive far out of their way. In the rare case of his sleeping overnight there, the superstar would walk across the lawn alone to bed down in a "normal" house that was also situated on the nine-acre property. In reality, the "Round House" was nearly worthless, like a "white elephant." Most of Jackie's existence when not at the CBS broadcast studio focused on boozing it up in Manhattan bars and reading alone in his upscale apartment.

In her 1994 autobiography, *Love, Alice,* actress Audrey Meadows mentions visiting the spaceship house and discloses the fact that Gleason was an inept driver, even during daylight hours. Pedestrians went scrambling for their lives whenever the comic roared his expensive car toward his destination. Perhaps his mind was focused on comedy, wine, women, and song. Riding along as Gleason steered rather ineptly, chatted away, and smoked incessantly became a bit of a nightmare, Meadows reported. It wasn't long after, she said, that Jackie wisely opted for a chauffeur and long, expensive limousines, allowing him to think, talk, laugh, and freely see the sights as he puffed and guzzled in the back seat. The Great One rarely drove anything again except a golf cart: a precaution that likely saved his own life.

Biographers discovered years later that Jackie Gleason was known to engage a few folks—famous or not—in passionate discussions on extraterrestrial visitation, often over drinks in a bar or nightclub. Gleason surprisingly tended to side against "contactees" of the era, people who claimed to have met and flown in spaceships with friendly aliens to Venus or Mars, then returned safely to tell or write about it. The beloved actor was more accepting of reported sightings of unusual craft that performed at extremely high speeds, and yet he apparently had never experienced such a thing himself. In a May 21, 1955, interview granted to *TV Guide*, Jackie Gleason admitted, "I've never seen a flying saucer anywhere personally." However, he explained he had been reading plenty about them and had spoken to UFO experts and authors whenever possible, spending far more time reading books and magazines about aliens than scripts and treatments for movie roles or TV productions.

Jackie Gleason always experienced problems sleeping through the night. Insomnia was an enemy, but fascinating metaphysical books, magazines, newsletters, and periodical clippings were his allies. He was aided by overnight talk radio in New York City, especially station WOR at 1440 Broadway, with its paranormal-themed programs. Roused by the topics he heard discussed on the airwaves by host "Long John" Nebel (1911-1978), the restless Gleason would leave his apartment in the middle of the night and take a taxi or limo to the studio to sit in as a special, honored guest of the tall, thin radio man. At other times, Jackie would simply call into the show for a chat. Later, he would even write the Introduction to a biography on Nebel.[33]

A key event took place one night on the air with knowledgeable Nebel: "On one show, Gleason offered $100,000 to anyone with physical proof of aliens visiting Earth. Gleason later upped the amount to one million dollars, but it was never claimed."[34] *A million bucks!* And he wasn't kidding, either!

It wasn't just talk. Jackie could financially back up this offer. He made quite a fortune in his day. Years later, he told an interviewer he was making up to $15 million *per season* from CBS. The Great One was mighty generous, after all; he boasted of his namesake golf tournament's $260,000 purse as the richest of any match on the pro tour. So, a cool mil for solid ET proof was no problem![35]

Here we arrive upon a critical point: *Gleason passionately desired hard, indisputable evidence and offered an enormous sum of money for it.*

It is likely the TV star's pal Richard Nixon had heard obsessive Gleason's offer several times over the years. Is this what caused Nixon to act boldly one night in 1973 by bringing Jackie to a normally off-limits airbase? It would have been quite the believable, understandable motivation for Nixon to show off extraterrestrial bodies in return for a fat check. Why else would Nixon take a big risk on exposing a top-secret project to a hard-drinking, easily recognized civilian who never spent a minute serving in the military or government?

An equally important factor to consider: Jackie Gleason had to know when making his stunning offer that likely no private citizen possessed the power and ability to own ET hardware or corpses— but he sure suspected certain powerful figures within the American military and government *did*. Did Gleason bait Commander-in-Chief Nixon on purpose? If so, he succeeded admirably. When playing pool or golf for money, Jackie often half-jokingly referred to his opponents as "pigeons." He would place bets and take their cash after winning. Did Gleason "pluck" Nixon in this way? Only to pay *him* money? Gleason wanted the ultimate trophy, worth more to him than money or material objects. Hard proof would satisfy his tremendous curiosity and obsession once and for all. He would thus become even *more* special, with unique insider information and status above all others.

Still, why would Richard Nixon want a million dollars? Surely, he had his own financing, right? By early 1973, he no longer needed to finance election campaigns.

Nixon biographers would note in later years the various underhanded ways the politician sought and received funding, often under the table and skirting around the limits of campaign laws. If exposed, illegal contributions would have sunk "Tricky Dick," but if

Gleason was able to funnel his prize money to Nixon through a false name, dummy corporation, or discreetly via a trusted operative, it would not be surprising in the least. Since many such donations were often poorly recorded or not logged at all, this exchange could have been done in 1973 and remained hidden to this very day.

Often Richard Nixon's pal Rebozo handled shady political donations, some even from the criminal underworld. *Wikipedia*: "By the 1960s, FBI agents monitoring the mafia had identified Bebe Rebozo as a 'non-member associate of organized crime figures.'" Much of the seedy underside of the Nixon cronyism was still not known to the public by February 1973. It seems assured that Nixon would have introduced Rebozo to Gleason at some point in those heady Miami/Biscayne years, money matters notwithstanding. But there is still another factor about Richard Nixon to ponder regarding early 1973.

The Watergate Hotel, Apartment, and Office complex in Washington D.C. was burglarized repeatedly in the spring of 1972 by President Nixon's underlings, nicknamed "Plumbers" (as they were low-level operatives imported to plug administrative leaks to the press). While some historians are unsure of Nixon's involvement, others feel certain he ordered the break-ins. It remains a somewhat mystery to this day. While on trial, the arrested henchmen in late 1972 and early 1973 had legal defense bills to pay and needed income for their families to survive on with regular bills to pay—especially as inflation kept climbing. In short, it is safe to assume they were demanding "hush money" to pay the bills, with a promise to keep quiet in return.

Criminally charged E. Howard Hunt, in particular, was actually *blackmailing* the president of the United States to get funding, and Hunt knew where the bodies were buried—perhaps even extraterrestrial ones. Howard Hunt had recently lost his wife in a plane crash and had that ritzy Miami home to keep up and pay off, the one with the stable for six horses. Plus, he had his D.C. home, his kids, pets, hobbies, and attorney fees to cover. Supposedly to land the filthy lucre, Hunt also pressured CIA superiors for money as well. This got both Nixon and Central Intelligence leadership upset with him, to say the least.[36] But Mr. Hunt may have had them over a barrel, utilizing some special leverage: *he allegedly knew a startling state secret about the extraterrestrial monitoring of our planet.* Watergate attorney Douglas Caddy (1938-) learned this directly from his client in 1974. Just before the espionage "expert" surrendered to authorities to begin serving his Watergate prison sentence, Caddy asked him the real reason why President Kennedy was assassinated. Caddy recalled to this author that Howard Hunt replied, "It was because he wanted to give away our greatest secret to the Soviet Union...The alien presence" on Earth. This knowledge alone was worthy of pressuring higher-ups for money, lest it "accidentally" slip to the press. Nixon was caught on his Oval Office tapes saying around this time: "This fellow Hunt...will uncover a lot of things...you open that scab...It would be very bad to have this fellow Hunt [talk], he knows too much."[37] Now, we may know more of precisely what he meant.

An attorney for the original seven arrested Watergate break-in figures, Mr. Caddy, was then, and remains now, a serious, accomplished person with excellent credentials. He attended Georgetown University School of Foreign Service (B.S.) and New York University School of Law (J.D.) and remains a member of the Texas state and D.C. bars.

Did Hunt know about the secret of what lay behind the locked, guarded doors at Homestead Air Force Base? It's certainly possible. He used to serve in the Army Air Corps. He lived and worked (for the CIA) in South Florida, in fact, just a short drive from Nixon's place and Homestead. He worked his way up the CIA ladder through many connections, and at one point, became an executive assistant to legendary agency director Allen Dulles.

In the end, Hunt's financial extortion may have been an inadvertent catalyst for Nixon to grudgingly reveal to Gleason the prize behind door number one at Homestead.

Thus, President Nixon, in February 1973, was caught in a vise and needed money wherever he could get it. The press was slowly piecing together the sordid Watergate break-in story, and some reporters would likely have offered tempting payments to the burglars or their lawyers for hot tips or tell-all interviews. It was also greatly feared in the Oval Office that some of the Plumbers who worked for Nixon's White House might sell out and flip—as the president's own lawyer John Dean did that late April 1973—by turning state's evidence in a legal deal. The statute of limitations on prosecution for the crimes of the burglars was five years following their June 1972 arrests. Thus, nearly five years' worth of money needed to be raised—and *fast*.

Historycollection.com reports: "The papers and tapes held in the Nixon Presidential Library and the later testimony of thousands of individuals inside the administration and outside of government provides overwhelming evidence that Nixon was not only aware of the fundraising and its illicit use, in many instances he directed where some of the money was to be spent.[38] Following the arrest of the Watergate burglars, for example, Nixon called his top aide, H. R. "Bob" Haldeman (1926-1993), and suggested that he have Bebe Rebozo start a fund for their defense in Miami. The slush fund money could then be deposited in the defense fund." As a *Time* magazine reporter once said, "Bebe would do anything for Nixon. He'd lie in front of a train for him."[39] Thus, we see secrecy-loving Rebozo (and likely his less-than-reputable bank) was the collector of the illicit fundraising, making it even more probable that Gleason was hit up for some dough...and perhaps Bebe would even take part in the nocturnal Homestead caper with Jackie? More on that possibility later.

By January and February of 1973, Nixon was likely sweating bullets, anxious to put together secret, untraceable slush funds and salvage his image as the "Law and Order President." That phrase was starting to sound like a joke, less believable by the week. A January 1973 audiotape from Nixon's Oval Office conversations revealed the president was anxiously pondering aloud the irksome problem. He irritably told an aide (on tape): "Damn hush money! How are we going to...how do we get the stuff?"[40] It was a terrible hurdle to overcome, for Nixon desperately wanted his public facade kept clean. He and his top men clearly couldn't figure out how to come up with big money donations while operating under intensifying congressional and media scrutiny. Remember, this revealing conversation took place just one month before the president's planned visit to Key Biscayne, which was arranged partly to appear at pal Jackie Gleason's Inverrary golf tournament.

What to do?

Biographers have noted that by March 21, 1973, Nixon's huge funding issue was suddenly softening quite a bit. White House attorney John Dean recalled decades later telling the president on this specific date the need for one million dollars for "defense funds" (hush money) was "for openers."[41] It would need to be "washed" and quietly dispersed to the Watergate accused criminals by a third party. President Nixon, this time calmly replied (on tape): "We could get that." And then added a minute later: "You could get a million dollars and you could get it in cash. I know where it could be gotten. I mean, it's not easy, but it could be done."

How did Mr. Nixon go from vexed and perplexed over enormous fundraising to confident and calm between January and March of 1973? Why was he suddenly sure of obtaining at least one million dollars in cash? That was an enormous sum in those days.

Who could have agreed to discreetly provide the funds within that rather narrow time frame? What reliable, firm supporter of the troubled president had at least a million bucks in cash to hand over, with no questions asked?

The payoff would doubtlessly have been handled by a reliable source like Rebozo—who often visited the White House without being logged in by the Secret Service—or Nixon's lawyer, Herbert W. Kalmbach (1921-2017). Kalmbach also represented the entertainment production juggernaut MCA—which had ties to Jackie Gleason.[42] In just one deal in the '50s, for example, MCA paid Gleason two million dollars for the rights to old *Honeymooners* episodes, which was considered a bargain then. By the 1973 Watergate mess, Nixon used Kalmbach to handle cash payments, dispersing it to the accused burglars (via a private detective as a helpful bagman). Kalmbach later served jail time for his testimony-admitted crimes but generally kept quiet about the details of these shady payoffs.[43]

Another way of potentially funneling money to Nixon by Gleason could have been through the shifty president's former Commerce Department official who dispensed illegal campaign funds as recently as 1970. That particular funding scheme became the subject of a peripheral Watergate investigation but was not discussed much in the press for some reason. It would have been a clever way of disguising entertainer Jackie's contributions (if he made any). Why? The ex-government operative involved was named Jack Gleason![44]

Admittedly, there is no smoking gun document (or returned, cashed check) that links Gleason's money to Nixon's fund for desperately gathered hush money. It is speculative, but the links of the chain are there. We know Jackie Gleason was quite wealthy and previously quite willing to help his favorite Republican politico. It is also likely he personally knew Herb Kalmbach. In such a scenario, Jackie could maintain his presidential friendship and his own high-profile standing in society, even the prestige of his celebrity-filled pro-am golf tournament, by having the American chief executive agree to make an appearance. Nixon would, in turn, provide Gleason with the critical, indisputable proof of ET visitation he longed for.

All of the motives for Gleason to fork over the cash after viewing the goods, at last, were there. All the motives for Nixon to ask for, and perhaps keep pressing for, the million dollars were there in early 1973, too. Touring handy Homestead AFB one night was simply the logical thing to do for both men.

A seemingly little-known fact is that President Nixon sweet-talked Gleason's showbiz friend Francis Albert "Frank" Sinatra (1915-1998) to come out of retirement that spring of 1973 and sing at the White House at a state dinner for the prime minister of Italy. Sinatra obliged and even kicked in a personal $50,000 contribution to Nixon's piggy bank. At least, that's the figure investigators were able to uncover, but there might have been more in the usual way of under-the-table "campaign donations."[45] Frank also passed along an "unrecorded contribution" of $100,000 from an imprisoned mafioso who promptly got a presidential pardon in return. Devious deals, funneled funds, and shady shenanigans were par for the course for an increasingly beleaguered president in 1973. Shaking down wealthy celebrity friends and mobsters in return for pricey presidential favors was no problem and was only uncovered during congressional Watergate committee hearings and federal investigations. Remember: Nixon had already won re-election; what "campaign" were these donors supposedly contributing to?

Gaining Sinatra's love and money was critical to Nixon by early 1973. As thesmokinggun.com put it in 2010: "White House aides plotted the 'seduction' of Frank Sinatra, who was viewed as a source of 'massive financial resources,' and a man 'who controls a great number of celebrities, entertainers and other public figures.'" Gleason and Sinatra were old friends from '40s New York City and some showbiz projects, getting together whenever "Ol' Blue Eyes" visited Miami. Broadcaster Larry King (1933-2021), of later CNN fame, got a job in Miami radio in 1957 and quickly landed an interview with Sinatra, who openly discussed his friendship with Jackie Gleason on the air.[46]

Showing loyal Gleason indisputable proof of ETs was probably considered unthinkable by Nixon during the first four years of his presidency. But by February 1973, Tricky Dick was so eager to drum up cash he not only thought about it but apparently pulled it off and kept it relatively quiet. In theory, Gleason was not eager to discuss it either, since he had ponied up a pretty penny to make it happen, with a secret, illegal political contribution. Talking publicly about it at any time might open an old wound better left healed. But again, this is speculation, albeit quite logical and reasonable to project.

There was another factor to consider in Richard Nixon's decision to break some security codes and reveal to his comedy friend the goods within a top security military airbase. February 19, 1973, was just five days away from Jackie Gleason's 57th birthday. *What to get his Florida friend who already had everything?*

By 1973, Jackie Gleason was doubtlessly feeling his age thanks to his aforementioned drinking, smoking, overeating, and loafing while in retirement. He could afford to rest on his laurels. He was still receiving residuals from his past efforts on the small screen. His now-ended *Jackie Gleason Show* had once been the second highest-rated TV show in the country. As mentioned, his popular variety program spawned *The Honeymooners*, a simple comedy sketch at first that was later produced as a half-hour sitcom. This black-and-white classic is, of course, still in repeats to this day, earning tidy revenue for Gleason's estate. One of its most charming episodes—first airing on December 31, 1955—was entitled "The Man From Space," where Gleason, as beleaguered Ralph Kramden, creates a metallic alien costume for a party![47]

In 1964, the Columbia Broadcast System pitched an upgraded, more modern variety show format for Jackie. He agreed, but only on the condition that he could produce the weekly program in Miami instead of New York City, so he could golf year-round. It was a seemingly outrageous suggestion, but the treasured entertainer was so popular and such a past moneymaker for CBS that the notion was approved. Gleason packed his belongings and sold his flying saucer house to CBS executives as part of the negotiated deal. "And *awaaaaay* we go!" as Jackie would shout—or even sing—enthusiastically on his program.

In September 1964, still deathly afraid of flying—seemingly odd for a spaceship buff—Gleason took a train down the East Coast with his entire production team in tow. He settled in and adapted to a new lifestyle. His resulting Miami TV production was a smash, just as he promised it would be. By 1965, The Great Gleason had purchased a large house on Alton Road in Miami Beach and a second home, a whopping 9,000-square-foot ranch-style estate, at the

Country Club of Miami (a golf course community in Hialeah). Media images show that while there in 1965, he golfed with his pal Nixon.[48] This new home created a convenient eleven-mile limo drive to his studio, the Miami Jackie Gleason Theater (now the Fillmore). That revamped entertainment site with nearly 3,000 seats was located sixteen miles from Nixon's place on Biscayne Bay. It wasn't far from the 1968 Republican Party convention hall, either (also utilized in the summer of 1972). Jackie's variety show chugged along, garnering Top Ten ratings in "The Sun and Fun Capitol of the World," as it was advertised from the fall of 1964 to the spring of 1970. "How sweet it is!" had become Gleason's weekly show motto, and in his private life too, eventually wearing on people around him with its banal repetition.

In 1971, Gleason moved once more to "The Hills of Inverrary," a lush new country club (East Course) community at 4830 Inverrary Boulevard.[49] Jackie's home within the gated community was situated at 3425 Willow Wood Road. The sprawling two-story "Glea Manor" became his final home, boasting 14 rooms and over 6,000 square feet of space for living, entertaining, playing pool, and accessing the nearby golf course. Jackie had purchased three lots total and carefully supervised the design and construction of his custom-made domicile, which means he carefully arranged for the five different bars within. No more wacky Round House for the more mature Gleason. Glea Manor was a contemporary, ranch-style design that blended in well with its immediate upscale neighborhood.[50]

Jackie, of course, enjoyed reading his treasured metaphysical books within his new pad's massive, custom-built library. To help fill it, he also lined some of the sturdy shelves with untouched law books—something suggested by law school grad Nixon, perhaps? A room upstairs was filled with more than a dozen ham radios. Gleason often holed up and listened in on air traffic conversations and long-distance radio operators from around the world, his stepson recalled many years later.[51] Knowing him, Jackie was probably also searching the dials for NASA space program transmissions and even communiques from actual space aliens. He may have even been sending out his own signals in hopes of communicating with any orbiting races. As discussed in *President Eisenhower's Close Encounters*, high-frequency radio transmissions were used to contact friendly ETs who allegedly communicated with U.S. military officials to negotiate a landing site and peaceful meeting with America's commander-in-chief. Is that something Jackie had learned and hoped to do on his own? Knowing his obsession with ET visitation, why else would Gleason spend his private downtime alone, fiddling with such radio equipment? If he was attempting to summon and lure outer space visitors, where could they possibly land for a meeting at his convenience? Well, there was a flat golf course right outside his door, albeit studded with palm trees...but also a special flat helicopter landing pad, too. Again, this is conjecture, but it is a fairly reasonable conclusion for the grand-thinking Gleason.

Another idea: was Gleason at his ham radio dials hoping to over-hear some ongoing secret alien-military radio exchanges from Homestead AFB? This is all speculative, of course, but intriguing thoughts nonetheless. There's a likely link for all of this extraterres-trial radio angle...

In his heyday, Jackie Gleason met with UFO/ET authors in person and quizzed them at length. A key figure for this would undoubtedly have been George Hunt Williamson (1926-1986). Williamson was a former military pilot who claimed he began making ham radio contact with aliens as far back as the early '50s—by copying, he said, what the U.S. government was doing in private! A few months after President Eisenhower's covert ET contact at Edwards Airbase on February 19, 1954, Williamson was quoted as telling a Michigan lecture audience (relayed in unarianwisdom.com, among others): "The government has the story. They have also made radio contact with saucers. Whether they will ever give out this information, we do not know. They may wait until we know all about it and then confirm it. There's a project known as 'MQ707' at Edwards Air Force Base, which is a project for telecommunication with saucers [via alien occupants]. They contact these craft and attempt to get them to land."[52] Williamson then put some of the ET messages he received in his mid-1954 book, *The Saucers Speak!*. Sure enough, this 127-page book is listed as part of the Jackie Gleason Collection, now kept at the University of Miami. That Gleason knew Williamson and his radio contact stories seems assured, so once again, it is not difficult at all to believe that Jackie was giving high-frequency contact a try himself in his Lauderhill radio room.

Was there also such a radio room within Gleason's Peekskill UFO house, the one with the Tesla coil? Could there be a tie-in in attempting ET contact via the technology developed by that scientist? MysteriousUniverse.org notes: "In an article for *Collier's Weekly* in 1901, Tesla would make the claim that he had listened in on actual alien communications at his lab in Colorado Springs in 1899. This was an era in which both he and Italian inventor Guglielmo Marconi were pioneering the push into radio technology with their ground-breaking discoveries, and one night Tesla would be testing out a unique radio antenna designed to monitor thunderstorms he claimed that he had eavesdropped into communications by other-worldly alien intelligences...Through all of this, Tesla supposedly actually invented new antennae towers and equipment specifically for the purpose of continuing his eavesdropping sessions on the aliens."[53] Knowing ET-obsessed Jackie as we do now, his Tesla coils and radio sets all seem to connect nicely. Tesla's attempted contact with any alien races in the vicinity of our solar system through his 1899 power transmission tower test in Colorado was mentioned as semi-successful in a 2017-leaked Defense Intelligence Agency document dated January 1989.[54] ETs apparently received Nikola's signal, the report noted and tried to signal back, but he was unable to fathom their response.

At his South Florida golf course manor, Jackie could invite over his celebrity friends, like Sinatra or presidents Nixon and Ford, and entertain them with plush comfort, from the thick shag carpeting to the padded furniture and extra-long dining table. In fact, the kitchen and dining area was so large that one observer recalled later that it greatly resembled a restaurant. A wraparound driveway featured a hotel-like lobby canopy extending from the front door. A huge marlin was stuffed and mounted on a living room wall after Gleason snagged him while trying his hand at deep sea fishing. Jackie sure knew how to bait a line and be patient—possibly like his offer of a million dollars for ET proof that Nixon went for. Whatever the case, life was grand indeed in the guarded, pampered community.

By 1971, Gleason agreed to sponsor a CBS-televised yearly golf tournament right outside his windows. Each February, he hosted a collection of pro and amateur golfers, celebrity performers, and politicos, sometimes holding court with them over drinks around his enticing swimming pool. Thick surrounding foliage and towering palm trees helped to muzzle noise and keep the press and public at bay. The property was actually not far from the busy Florida Turnpike but nestled safely within secure fencing and entry gates. It's a good thing, too, since Miami had the second-highest crime rate in the country.

Thus, it was in mid-1964 that CBS bought and controlled the Peekskill UFO house. A discreet, professional realtor handled the unusual estate for the esteemed television network, renting it out to a series of wealthy clients over the coming decades. Tenants included rock star David Bowie (1947-2016), of "Space Oddity" and "Star Man" fame. Privately, Bowie was obsessed with the subject of extraterrestrials and said he had seen multiple UFOs from an observatory, according to his friends and biographers.[55] Obviously, Jackie's spaceship house with its Tesla coil was a perfect match for the young "glam rock" singer. Whether or not Bowie ever met or telephoned Gleason is unknown. They would have been a shockingly diverse pair who had one riveting subject in common! Bowie was so wild for Nikola Tesla—and began to actually *resemble* him as he matured—he even portrayed the brilliant, quirky inventor in a 2006 movie.[56]

Only rarely did Jackie Gleason return to New York City for

nostalgic visits. One of Mr. Gleason's biographers—Hollywood gossip columnist James Bacon—interviewed the performer's journalist-friend Robert Considine (1906-1975), a UFO skeptic who told Bacon about a remarkable statement Jackie uttered during an argument the two were having in the late '60s in a New York City bar. "Four U.S. presidents have personally told me about UFOs," Gleason confidently informed Considine, likely referencing new President Nixon as one of the chief executives.[57] As relayed in greyfalcon.us., the reporter recalled that a well-decorated, retired U.S. Air Force general who once worked under President Eisenhower—Emmett E. O'Donnell, Jr. (1906-1971)—overheard the Gleason-Considine tavern conversation that night and blurted out: "Jackie's right." O'Donnell, also a Brooklyn native, had been stationed at Wright Field in Ohio after WWII, the site of so many tantalizing rumors of crashed UFO recovery examinations at his post: Air Material Command. Gleason also insisted there had been "small UFO sightings on both sides during World War II," which might indicate he had previously spoken to President Eisenhower, who commanded Allied troops as the top general in Europe.

Gleason was known for his bluntness and candor but definitely not for creative embellishments. As one biographer from thelifeandtimesofhollywood.com noted: "Performers tend to be terrific liars, masters of putting up facades that have nothing to do with their personal lives, but Jackie meant what he said."[58] Gleason was never a spinner of yarns. Having a rough life for his first thirty years had grounded him. In his private life, he didn't have time for fantasies; he wanted cold hard facts. He read his nonfiction books and periodicals voraciously, ignoring works of fiction. Similarly, Richard Nixon read daily briefing documents and government reports to consume his time—not fiction.

Finally, by the mid- '70s, Jackie Gleason candidly confessed that while he was living in Florida, he had his own unidentified flying object glimpses in daylight. The late author Timothy Green Beckley (1942-2021) once stated that the entertainer "had sighted UFOs on at

PAUL BLAKE SMITH

least two occasions that he was willing to admit to in public." Both events happened near Miami and were clear and convincing. Gleason recalled to Beckley: "These were definitely not objects made on our planet. They weren't secret weapons but were solid craft."[59] The Great One said that "on both occasions, the UFOs reflected the rays of the sun and were low enough for me to determine that they could not be explained by ordinary means." His startling interview statement on the two separate UFO incidents even became a question for the NBC game show *Hollywood Squares*. These special but likely brief encounters were not the hard, tangible proof that he craved most of all. Gleason wanted something he could touch or study. Perhaps to Jackie, the sightings were icing on the cake if they occurred after Homestead.

While life in "The Sunshine State" was seemingly idyllic, both Nixon and Gleason presented themselves as clean-cut and respectable "law and order" family men enjoying the good life. However, both were often dark, brooding, foul-mouthed, and disagreeable. They were husbands and fathers, controlling perfectionists with tempers, and always cleverly plotting the next step to stay ahead in their careers. The two men were, in reality, nearly identical in their personalities. But there are even *more* startling similarities. So...let's set out another "Top Ten List" of comparisons between Nixon and Gleason:

1. Both Nixon and Gleason lost a younger brother to disease while they grew up in nearly impoverished conditions on opposite coasts.
2. As a young man, Nixon did some community theater acting in tiny Yorba Linda, California, and an existing 1937 program shows he played the part of a district attorney in a Whittier stage play. As a young man, Jackie Gleason was all about showbiz. He grew up in Brooklyn, New York, and honed a comedy act for the stage and later for movies and television. When he was nine years old,

Nixon's family moved to Whittier, California, about thirty miles from Hollywood, and he returned there after WWII. Gleason moved to Hollywood to act in films after World War II. For a short while in their early adulthood, Nixon and Gleason lived only a matter of some twenty-five miles from each other.

3. Nixon disliked exercise, perspired excessively, and suffered from phlebitis. Gleason disliked exercise, perspired excessively, and suffered from phlebitis. Both took golf carts when hitting the links and limos when hitting the town. Both men would have felt right at home at Homestead AFB since a golf course was installed there in 1960.

4. Nixon moved to New York City after the two worst blows of his life (to that point): losing the 1960 presidential election and then the 1962 gubernatorial race in California. He served as a lawyer in a Big Apple law firm for a few years. Gleason had moved from Hollywood back to New York City in the early '50s and remained there for over a decade. His worst professional blow (to that point) was suffered in 1960 when his TV show was canceled.

5. Nixon visited Miami many times and finally bought a house in nearby Key Biscayne in 1969. In 1964, Gleason moved to and lived in the Miami area before buying a house there in 1971. Nixon enjoyed boat trips—in Washington aboard the presidential yacht *The Sequoia*—sometimes off the Miami coast with Bebe Rebozo in his houseboat, *The Coco Lobo*. In mid-1972, the yacht *Volga 70 Hydrofoil* was gifted to Nixon by a Russian ambassador, and this was also used on occasion in South Florida. Meanwhile, Gleason owned a 70-foot, extremely plush 1970 Chris-Craft 60 yacht named *Savoy* that he utilized on occasion off the Miami coast.

6. Nixon admired FBI Director J. Edgar Hoover and applied to be an agent for the bureau in 1937 but was turned down. Gleason admired Hoover and did some informing to the FBI in his prime. An FBI document dated July 29, 1974, described the entertainer as a "Special Agent Contact" of the Miami Division who had been "added to Christmas card list" and was a "long-time admirer and supporter of the FBI."[60]

7. Nixon was an openly conservative Republican. Gleason was quietly so, but he "came out" publicly in the fall of 1968 to contribute to Nixon's second presidential campaign with a TV special to promote his friend's candidacy. Jackie taped a one-minute-long statement, more personal than political, which opened a televised Madison Square Garden rally for Nixon in New York City that aired on Halloween night that year.[61]

8. Nixon was an insomniac. Gleason was an insomniac. Both men stayed up late or woke up in the middle of the night. When they could not sleep, they both spent their time reading nonfiction, including all about the U.S. space program.

9. Both men were drinkers, but Nixon only imbibed in the evening. Both were lousy drivers and rarely got behind the wheel of a vehicle. Both employed longtime personal secretaries, lawyers, and accountants to help their professional lives run more smoothly.

10. Nixon fathered two daughters, Tricia and Julie, in the '40s. Gleason fathered two daughters, Geraldine and Linda, in the '40s.

With these facts in mind, it seems genuinely plausible that, as U.S. president, Richard M. Nixon would take Jackie Gleason into his confidence. They were bonded buddies with matching backgrounds and pastimes, almost astoundingly so. Even if Gleason was not a constant confidante, Nixon would likely feel safe meeting this kindred spirit at Homestead Airbase one night in 1973.

After his service in the U.S. Navy in World War II and completing Duke University law school, Nixon practiced law as an attorney. He turned his socially awkward life around by boldly throwing his hat into the political ring. He soon became a U.S. representative from southern California; a U.S. senator; a controversial vice president in the '50s under Eisenhower; and a recurring candidate for the White House in the '60s. As America's 37th president, he deliberately bugged his own offices in order to capture conversations, supposedly to improve his memory of events because he planned to write his memoirs someday.[62] White House audio recordings that were released to the public caught him swearing and scheming revenge on critics, which clashed with his carefully crafted public image of a wholesome Quaker who often consulted pastors. One Oval Office tape transcript from 1971 featured a bitter conversation with an aide regarding the increasingly popular but controversial new CBS TV sitcom *All in the Family*. Nixon said of the actor who portrayed the fictional conservative character Archie Bunker: "He looks like Jackie Gleason." And why not? ABC executives passed on the show in 1970; they had originally wanted Gleason in the situational comedy's lead role since he was a big Nixon supporter on and off the small screen.[63] Still, the tapes show Nixon hated the program and likely didn't watch much more.

In early 1973, Richard Nixon was at the height of his fame and approval ratings. It was just over three months since his monumental landslide victory at the polls. Although the June 1972 Watergate break-in by shady men working for Nixon's top advisers was a notable sore spot, no one at the time really suspected or accused Nixon of engineering the caper or its coverup. When arriving anywhere, he went that first half of the year; the president was met by dignitaries and treated like triumphant royalty. Florida, whose constituents voted solidly for Nixon, was a shining example. He overwhelmingly won the state with 71.91% of the vote, carrying all of

Florida's 67 counties and 17 electoral votes. David T. Kennedy, Miami's mayor, even joined "Democrats for Nixon" in 1972. Nixon's popularity poll figures rose even higher after January 15, 1973. That's when he publicly cited progress in peace negotiations and announced the suspension of offensive action in Vietnam. On January 23, the president declared that a peace accord had been reached to end the increasingly unpopular war. On February 11, the first American POWs were released from Vietnam, and uniformed personnel were coming home to tearful family reunions on airbase runways as the television cameras captured the images for the evening news. Nixon's favorability ratings rocketed upwards.[64]

Another factor to consider in Nixon's choice to expose private citizen Gleason to the truth about alien visitation was a general lack of oversight or governmental pressure to remain silent on the subject. By February 19, 1973, almost all of Mr. Nixon's peers were either deceased or retired, leaving him completely in charge. He really could get away with almost anything now. Let's look at why, in more detail, Nixon was free at last to act boldly that mid-February without fear of consequences...

1. Former President Dwight D. Eisenhower, Nixon's political godfather and one-time governmental boss died in March 1969.
2. Former President Lyndon B. Johnson, Nixon's predecessor, died just after Richard's re-inauguration in late January 1973.
3. Former President Harry S Truman, Nixon's political enemy from the '50s, died in December 1972.
4. Thomas E. Dewey, Nixon's political mentor and two-time Republican Party nominee for president, died in March 1971.
5. Allen W. Dulles, the longtime director of the CIA (and a subsequent intel think tank in D.C.), died in January 1969.

6. Deputy Director Charles P. Cabell, Dulles' knowledgeable and powerful CIA underling, died in May 1971. Cabell, by the way, had his own UFO/ET history. Plus, one of the top officials in the CIA during the Dulles/Cabell years, C. Tracy Barnes, died of a heart attack on February 18, 1972. Both Cabell and Barnes were former Air Force officers with military intelligence training.

7. Admiral Sidney W. Souers, the first Director of the CIA and an original member of the UFO-focused MJ-12 committee, died in January 1973. Souers was educated at the University of Miami. There were, in fact, only a few original members of that covert committee left by February 1973. Plus, Nixon's personal White House science adviser, Edward David, resigned that January, so the commander-in-chief then abolished the position entirely, along with the decades-old President's Science Advisory Committee.[65]

8. Longtime FBI Director J. Edgar Hoover—the most knowledgeable regarding UFO crashes—died in May 1972.[66]

9. U.S. Representative T. Hale Boggs, the Majority Leader of the House of Representatives (and Warren Commission member), died in October 1972. As a powerful Democrat, Boggs opposed most of Nixon's political agenda, but he perished in a mysterious airplane accident in Alaska. His body was never found.

10. Frank Costello, a mafioso so powerful he was referred to as the "Prime Minister of the Underworld," died on February 18, 1973, during Nixon's idyll in the Miami area.

Additionally, top nosy journalists—used to scoring big scoops days or even weeks after notable events—had also, by February 1973, passed away. This list included Edward R. Murrow in 1965, Hedda Hopper in 1966, Frank Edwards in 1967, Drew Pearson in 1969, and

Louella Parsons and Walter Winchell in 1972. Additionally, retired TV newsman Chet Huntley was ill with cancer in 1973, as was Ed Sullivan. Both men died of the dreaded disease in 1974. All would have been thrilled with the exciting story of a top entertainer teaming up with a president to do *anything*.

Obviously, it's an astonishing number of coincidental deaths that left President Nixon by mid-February 1973 answerable to, well, *no one*. It's as if the heavens opened wide and let only "Tricky Dick" through, for a while anyway. If anyone in the military, federal government, or intelligence branches objected to a brazen breach of security by inspecting some highly classified, top-secret alien artifacts with a civilian at a guarded U.S. Air Force base, President Nixon's response would have been, *"I'm in charge as America's commander-in-chief. Who are you going to complain to?"*

One extra note: when attending Duke law school in North Carolina during the Great Depression, loner Dick Nixon surprisingly joined a fraternity. Businessinsider.com reported: "Founded in 1913, The Order of the Red Friars was a semi-secret society at Duke University. New members were initiated, or "tapped" by a member of the Order donned in a red hood and robe...Duke University's library lists Nixon as a member. The Order voluntarily disbanded in 1971."[67] Thus, the president was, by early 1973, not even bound by any sort of secret fraternal order's lifelong code of conduct—no matter how long ago or semi-seriously it was taken.

One source of UFO/ET information over the past seven decades has been the seriously secretive Central Intelligence Agency. In his first term, Nixon's CIA chief had been Richard M. Helms (1913-2002). He and Nixon had a bit of a love-hate relationship; ten days after winning re-election in the fall of 1972, the president made the decision to can Helms and replace him with a brand-new director. By the new year, Nixon transferred Helms into an ambassadorship to Iran, getting him not only out of the way but out of the country and continent entirely. Nixon had never been very keen on the CIA. As villagevoice.com put it in 2011: "The *New York Times* has reported that it has been Nixon's determination since taking office to either seize political control of the CIA or to cripple the agency and transfer its intelligence functions to other agencies, such as the National Security Agency or the Defense Intelligence Agency, over which he is known to have complete control. The firing of Helms and a subsequent purge of more than 1000 CIA employees have been seen as the first moves Nixon has made in this direction." This may explain more why theories have sprung up—including Nixon's—that CIA members had infiltrated his team's Watergate break-in plan and botched it on purpose; this was done to blow up his presidency and humiliate him. Retaliation, in other words, against Nixon's years of control. And it worked—just not as swiftly as some CIA personnel involved had hoped.

Richard Helms' last day at the helm of the CIA was set for February 14, 1973, but was inexplicably moved up by Nixon to February 2.[68] Did this move show the president's premeditation for a visit to Homestead? With powerful and knowledgeable Helms gone and the president's handpicked successor in place *before* February 19, Nixon could have freely toured a top-security laboratory on any military airbase without intelligence community resistance or blowback.

Victor Leo Marchetti Jr. (1929-2018), CIA Director Helms' assistant at Central Intelligence, spoke out in 1979, a decade after completing his intel tenure (1955-1969). Marchetti summed up: "My theory is that we have indeed been contacted—perhaps even visited —by extraterrestrial beings, and the U.S. government, in collusion with other national powers of the Earth, is determined to keep this information from the general public...UFOs are considered sensitive activities."[69] The CIA apparently knew plenty then, and perhaps they know even more today. In late January 1973, outgoing Helms and his secretary reportedly shredded or destroyed "four thousand pages of transcripts" from the director's personal office voice-activated taping system, along with "all personal records from six and a half years," according to a Nixon biographer in 2012. Was any of it UFO/ET data?[70]

PAUL BLAKE SMITH

Yet another factor motivating emboldened Nixon to brazenly act to please Jackie Gleason was that top military adviser Army Brigadier General Robert Ludwig Schulz (1907-1984) was let go in late January 1973. Schulz was once President Eisenhower's longtime personal aide who stuck with Ike into his retirement until Nixon hired him in early 1969 to act as his liaison to the former American presidents. But as of February 1973, there were none left, so Schultz was pushed into retirement, possibly because he knew plenty about past ET contact and would have wanted it kept hushed. A January 16, 1967, letter from General Schulz to dogged UFO researcher John Alva Keel (1930-2009) remains of interest.[71] It has the military aide to the ex-president telling Keel, "There is no basis in fact to the statements you present" regarding "the rumored UFO landing at Muroc [Edwards] AFB, 1954." Eisenhower was still keeping the lid on that story thirteen years afterward and pushed the burden of that secret on his assistant Schulz. What else was Ike going to do? Tell a UFO investigator the highly classified truth and blow the amazing contact story sky-high?

It's all as if "the perfect storm" set in, so to speak, with powerful politicos and popular personalities out of the way by February 1973. The right conditions allowed the ET examination to occur, and there was no one able to stop it. Remember Nixon's motto to cover his schemes: "If a president does it, that means it's not illegal."

Oval Office records show that the day before he left the White House for Florida—Thursday, February 15, 1973—the chief executive must have been pretty pumped up about the vacation, starting a virtual game of "phone tag" that evening. Nixon first called his pal Bebe Rebozo in Key Biscayne at 3:02.[72] Then, after a little state business, he called his daughter in Jacksonville. He went in for a quick haircut by the White House barber, then came back to his office and called her again at 6:24. The president then tried to telephone comedian Leslie Townes "Bob" Hope (1903-2003), one of Jackie Gleason's best friends and golfing buddies. Hope was scheduled to play in the nearing Inverrary tournament, but Nixon could not reach him. A few minutes later, he called Hope again and got through for eleven minutes of chit-chat. When that wrapped up, at 6:47, he tried to phone popular golfer Arnold Palmer, who was in Miami readying to play in Gleason's pro-am but failed. Later, at 7:02, Nixon connected and spent a couple of minutes in discussion with Palmer. Then the chief executive called Rebozo at the Key Biscayne compound one more time at 7:14. A few minutes later, he called his daughter in Jacksonville yet again. The president was like an excited teenager the night before the prom—focused like a laser beam on Florida and his impending activities there.

It was as if Nixon could hardly wait to get down to Miami and have some fun.

---

1.   , "Jackie Gleason Claims Presidents Told Him UFOs are Real," *Alien UFO Sightings*.
2.   Wikipedia contributors, "Key Biscayne,' *Wikipedia*.
3.   Wikipedia contributors, "Miami-Dade County, Florida," *Wikipedia*.
4.   Wikipedia contributors, "Homestead Air Reserve Base," *Wikipedia*, last updated July 2022.
5.   Sean McCaughan, "Nixon Winter White House, Private Beach, Helipad Adjacent," *Curbed Miami*," May 22, 2012.
6.   Wikipedia contributors, "Homestead Air Reserve Base," *Wikipedia*.
7.   Various first-hand recollections, via: "Homestead Air Force Base Survivors Group" Facebook page.
8.   "'Mr. Peacemaker' Nixon Is Welcomed in Florida," *New York Times*, January 27, 1973.
9.   Wikipedia contributors, "Homestead, Florida," *Wikipedia* July 28, 2022.
10. "UFO Sighting in Homestead, Florida (United States) on Friday 15 October 2010" *UFO Hunters*.
11. Wikipedia contributors, "Bebe Rebozo," *Wikipedia*.
12. William Saffire, "Before The Fall," *Belmont Tower Books*, 1975
13. Don Fulsom, "Gangster in the White House," *Crime Magazine*, September 11, 2009.
14. Dave Rolland, "Richard Nixon and Key Biscayne," *Jitney Books*, April 9, 2020.
15. Phillip Shabecoff, "Secret Service Director Says That Most of $1.9-Million Spent on Nixon's Homes Was for Security," *The New York Times*, June 28, 1973.
16. "Presidential Daily Diary," July 1969.
17. Wikipedia contributors, "John F. Kennedy," *Wikipedia*.
18. Timothy Good, "Need To know," *Pegasus Books*, paperback edition, November 2007
19. Henry Applebaum, "Vernon Walters - Renaissance Man," *Studies in Intelligence*, Volume 46, 2002.
20. Howard Jones, "A Beach-Head Too Far?" *Lessons Not Learned at the Bay of Pigs*, August 28, 2008.

21. Jeff Shain, "Flashback: Jackie Gleason's Inverrary Classic," *Pro Golf Weekly*, February 22, 2018.
22. Elaine Raffel, "A Slice of Beatle History Hits the Palm Beach Market," *Second Shelters*, May 13, 2020.
23. Antonio Fins, "Richard Nixon toured Mar-a-Lago a month before he resigned presidency," *The Palm Beach Post*, February 18, 2019.
24. Christina Stoehr, "Biography reveals Jackie Gleason's many flaws" *Baltimore Sun*, July 18, 1992.
25. Source: high-ranking U.S. West Coast Freemason who asked this author not to disclose his identity
26. Stephanie Nolasco, "Jackie Gleason 'embraced' lasting success on 'The Honeymooners,' never regretted playing Ralph Kramden," *Fox News*, January 1, 2019.
27. Audrey Meadows, Joe Daily, "Love, Alice: My Life as a Honeymooner," *Crown Publishers*, September 1994
28. "The Jackie Gleason Collection," *University of Miami Libraries, Special Collections,*, Florida.
29. Lobosco, David, "A Trip Down Memory Lane: Jackie Gleason and UFO," *greatentertainersarchives* , August 1, 2011.
30. Foundation Interviews, "Leonard Stern on Jackie Gleason on 'The Honeymooners,'" *YouTube* video, 4:29, August 2016.
31. Luke Stangel, "Jackie Gleason's Spaceship-Like House Is Listed for $12M," *Realtor.com*, August 6, 2018.
32. Brent Swancer, "The Strange Story of Nikola Tesla and the Aliens," *mysteriousuniverse.org,*, January 19, 2021.
33. Donald Bain, "Long John Nebel: Radio Talk King, Master Salesman, and Magnificent Charlatan," *MacMillan Books*, January 1974.
34. Wikipedia contributors, "Long John Nebel," *Wikipedia* August 2017.
35. Winnie Muriuki, "Jackie Gleason Net Worth 2022: Age, Height, Weight, Wife, Kids, Bio-Wiki," *Wealthy Persons*.
36. Bob Woodward and Carl Bernstein, "Nixon Debated Paying Blackmail, Clemency: 'Keep Cap on Bottle,'" *The Washington Post*, May 1, 1974.
37. Samuel Rushay, "Listening to Nixon: An Archivist's Recollections on His Work with the White House Tapes," *National Archives*, 2007.
38. Larry Holzwarth, "10 Crimes of the Nixon Administration," *historycollection.com*, March 27, 2018.
39. Jonathan Poletti, "Was Richard Nixon Gay? Let's Look at the Facts," *medium.com*, April 30, 2009.
40. Douglas Brinkley and Luke Nichter, *The Nixon Tapes: 1973*, Houghton Mifflin Harcourt, September 2015
41. "You could get a million dollars," *Miller Center*, March 21, 1973.
42. Wikipedia contributors, "Herbert W. Kalmbach," *Wikipedia*.
43. Anthony Ripley, "Kalmbach Pleads Guilty to 2 Campaign Charges: May Be Jaworski Witness," *The New York Times*, February 26, 1974.
44. UPI, "Nixon Aide Guilty on Political Fund," *The New York Times*, 1974 November 16.
45. Don Fulsom, "The Mob's President: Richard Nixon's Secret Ties to the Mafia," *Crime Magazine*, February 5, 2006.
46. Eric Meisfjord, "The Truth About Larry King And Jackie Gleason's Relationship," *Grunge*, January 23, 2021.

47. *The Honeymooners* 1955, Season 1, Episode 14, "The Man from Space"
48. "1965 Press Photo Jackie Gleason and Richard Nixon golfing in Miami, FL." *eBay*.
49. "The Hills of Inverrary, COA in Lauderhill, Florida."
50. Peter Burke, "Jackie Gleason's former Lauderhill home for sale" *Local10*, February 25, 2016.
51. Stephanie Nolasco, "Jackie Gleason 'embraced' lasting success," *Fox News*, January 1, 2019.
52. George H. Williamson, "A Message From Our Space Brothers," *bibliotecapleyades*, June 21, 1954.
53. Brett Swancer, "The Strange Story of Nikola Tesla and the Aliens," *My Inventions and Other Writings*, Penguin Random House, 2011.
54. "Ultra-top-secret-MTD, DIA report," January 1989
55. Brett Swancer, "David Bowie and the Music of Space, Aliens and UFOs," *mysteriousuniverse*.
56. "The Prestige (2006) - David Bowie as Tesla."
57. Jame Bacon, "Foreword," *How Sweet It Is: The Jackie Gleason Story*, St. Martin's Press, June 1, 1986, Foreword by Jackie Gleason.
58. Frank Kelly, "The Great Drunk: Lushing Large with Jackie Gleason," *Modern Drunk Magazine*.August 2002.
59. Timothy G. Beckley, "And Away We Go... The Night Jackie Gleason Saw the Corpses of the Little Men from Mars,"*UFO Digest*," June 19, 2015.
60. According to the eventually-released report, Gleason kept in touch at times with Miami FBI Special Agent Kenneth W. Whittaker
61. Jack Doyle, "Richard Nixon and television," *The Pop History Dig*, March 2018.
62. Wikipedia contributors, "Nixon White House tapes," *Wikipedia*.
63. Katherine G, "Things You Might Not Know About 'All In The Family'," *Fame10*, April 11, 2017.
64. David Coleman, "Nixon's Presidential Approval Ratings" *History in Pieces*.
65. Richard D. Lyons, "Science Adviser to Nixon Leaving for Industry Job" *The New York Times* January 3. 1973.
66. HelmerReenberg, "May 2, 1972 - President Richard Nixon's Remarks on the Death of FBI Director J. Edgar Hoover," *Bing* video.
67. Aine Caine and Abby Jackson, "20 US presidents who belonged to shadowy secret societies," *Insider*, February 19, 2018.
68. Thomas Powers, "The Rise and Fall of Richard Helms," *Rolling Stone magazine*, December 16, 1976.
69. Chet Dembeck, "Former CIA Analyst Claims Intelligence Agencies Have Proof ET Exists - But Hide," *Unknown Boundaries*, June 3, 2022.
70. "Inside the Department of Dirty Tricks," *The Atlantic*, August 1, 1979.
71. The released letter is on stationary headed: "Office of Dwight D. Eisenhower" in "Gettysburg, Pennsylvania."
72. "Presidential Daily Diary," *Richard Nixon Museum and Library,*

PAUL BLAKE SMITH

CHAPTER TWO

MID-FEBRUARY 1973

"He would also make claims of aliens being present on Earth, that he had been present on a military base 'when they brought one in!'"

White House logs[1] show that on Friday, February 16, 1973, President Nixon—along with the First Lady—flew from Washington to an airbase in Jacksonville, Florida. Not long afterward, near 4:00 p.m., he was off to Homestead Air Force Base, south of Miami. We don't know who made this flight with the president as *this page of his digitized official records was strangely and suspiciously expunged.* The names of those who flew with the chief executive to Homestead and again when the Florida idyll was over have been removed from internet-access files. Such a list would likely have told us the name of one or more military officials who were imported by the president to help grease the wheels of the planned covert extraterrestrial review at the airbase.

Before continuing, let's bear in mind what respected British UFO author Timothy Good (1942-) discussed with a U.S. military officer once stationed at a Florida airbase—Tyndall AFB, near Panama City Beach—when that source said of recovered alien artifacts: "I hear they move this stuff around."[2] In other words, we can assume ET evidence was studied at various off-limits laboratories at different military bases, at private corporate headquarters; and at classified government installations. In that way, a wide variety of different doctors, scientists, military brass, intelligence officers, and researchers could scrutinize it, working with different equipment and updated test data while keeping foreign spies off-balance and unaware of their top-secret activity. In such a mobile, shifting plan, the U.S. government could then absorb a diversity of opinions on the otherworldly bodies and hardware to learn as much as possible. They could also independently verify other previous findings and keep the covert "shell game" moving around. The critical ET studies would also have been shifted from base to base in order to throw off and foil the press, inquisitive congressmen, possible military squealers, and the curious general public. Shuffling and reshuffling the deck, as it were.

Did President Nixon order that covertly retrieved alien corpses be gathered for ongoing examinations at his beloved Homestead Airbase? As mentioned, Nixon was rather famous for this sort of self-absorbed demand. Both the 1968 and 1972 Republican Party conventions were held in Miami, for example, just a short drive from Nixon's Biscayne Bay home. Aides and cabinet members, friends and family, and foreign dignitaries all had to fly to Miami just to meet with Nixon during these long South Florida interludes. Reels of Hollywood movies for Nixon's projector, food and drink, government files, and luxury items were all brought to the president when he was lounging in South Florida. Why not actual ET bodies too?

Perhaps only *one* figure in the Nixon administration needed to be alerted in advance of the president's plan to sneak with normally unauthorized civilian Gleason to Homestead AFB. The only conceivable hurdle might have been U.S. Secretary of the Air Force Robert C. Seamans Jr. (1918-2008).[3] Seamens was no stranger to space studies. From 1948 to 1958, he served on technical committees of the National Advisory Committee for Aeronautics. He then worked for

PAUL BLAKE SMITH

NASA in the '60s and was also a National Delegate in the "Advisory Group for Aerospace Research and Development for NATO" from 1966 to 1969. In July 1968, he was appointed to a visiting professorship at MIT in the Department of Aeronautics and Astronautics. During that tenure, he acted as a consultant to the Administrator of NASA. That's when Nixon brought him on board with the exalted USAF post, where he stayed until his retirement in May 1973.

Air Force One landed at Homestead AFB that Friday, February 16, around 4:45 p.m. After introductions on the runway, the president and his immediate party boarded his "Marine One" helicopter for the short flight to his Key Biscayne bungalow. Once settled in at 500 Bay Lane by 5:07, with his secretary working next door (within 516 Bay Lane), existing logs show that martini-sipping Nixon went for a dip in his pool, tended to some office duties, ate a meal with family and pal Rebozo, and watched an old movie on a projector screen with his invited guests. Then it was time for bed, perhaps a little jet lag setting in for the busy leader.

That February was a remarkably quiet one for America. There was little going on in the news or sports world. There were no pressing crises or growing news events absorbing the country— minus the Watergate scandal, and public interest in that was still rather mild. The Olympics were held the year before. Baseball training camps were starting to fill up in the Sunshine State and elsewhere. The NFL's season was over, with the Super Bowl having been played a month earlier. So, there were no great sporting events on television, just a little hockey and basketball. Nixon was a fan of both the NFL and MLB and often called players and coaches for a quick chat, mostly to show off his knowledge of sports. It was the dullest, quietest time of the entire year.

On Saturday morning, February 17, President Nixon tended to undescribed matters at his "Winter White House" then toured a public park. At 11:00 a.m., he and Bebe Rebozo went "motoring" with the president's personal physician to a public recreation area, where they strolled the grounds with the First Couple's daughter and son-in-law. Then they got back in the limo and were taken first through the grounds of the local country club's golf course, then to Rebozo's Key Biscayne Bank and Trust Company. The group toured Bebe's offices for about fifteen minutes and then departed for home. The president set his mind on more unspecified business at his 516 Bay Lane office. He had lunch before he was driven back to the local golf club to play nine holes with buddy Bebe and his White House doctor.

Hang on a sec. Was the president feeling ill? Why bring along your doctor to South Florida? Nixon used to brag he was so healthy he didn't even get headaches, and his physician was once quoted as saying that he was barely needed for much more than the occasional common cold. Is it possible he, too, felt the need to get away from it all and enjoy some sunshine and green fairways on a relaxing wintertime vacation? Significant or not, this White House physician used to attend to President Eisenhower's health—and he golfed with him, too. The doctor and Rebozo now hit the palm-tree-filled links with the leader of the free world, away from Nixon's relatives, the public, and the press, able to speak openly on any subject—a possible important factor for later.

After golfing, President Nixon went home (without his doctor) and attended to some more office work next door, then took his party out to eat at a local restaurant. After that, it was time for another old movie on their projector when they got home. Then it was bedtime. Remarkably, none of the entourage tended to watch any television programming or go out on the town.

The next day, Sunday, February 18, Nixon leisurely engaged in more mundane business, including a boat ride on the calm Atlantic and some phone calls made to White House aides from his office. Then he and Rebozo flew by helicopter to Key Largo, where they toured Bebe's vacation home. The duo flew back that evening and soon enjoyed another old Hollywood movie on the screen before going to bed.

Meanwhile, across the metro area, Jackie Gleason was probably busy handling preparations for his televised pro-am golf tournament, scheduled to commence the next day in Lauderhill. Gleason was well-suited to the task of keeping all the visiting celebrities, local dignitaries, and PGA officials happy, fed, lubricated, and entertained.

Finally, Monday, February 19, 1973—the big day!—arrived.

It was the anniversary of the birth of the legendary Polish astronomer Nicolaus Copernicus (1493-1543),[4] who first fully grasped and publicly espoused that Earth revolved around the sun, a controversial and dangerous stance in his day. Copernicus spent much of his life studying planets and stars and wrote *Six Books Concerning the Revolutions of the Heavenly Orbs*, which eventually changed the world of science forever. A Frenchman named Charles Messier (1730-1817),[5] another pioneering astronomer, chose this specific date in 1771 to add observed galaxy clusters to his official catalog, which would eventually be the first to establish for our world a systematic examination of nebulae and star groups in outer space. Both men inevitably inspired others to ponder the notion of lifeforms in other parts of the incredibly vast universe, well beyond our planet.

The American president began his day the usual way, rising, showering, shaving, dressing, and seating himself at the breakfast table by 8:35 a.m. That Monday's high temperature would top off at only 64 degrees, with light breezes, 97% humidity at most, and some light precipitation on and off all day.

Between 9:00 and 9:30 a.m., the president placed two calls to his aides in Washington. Then an hour is left unrecorded. By 10:37, he had strolled to the nearby helipad on the Biscayne Bay and boarded his chopper for a short flight to Haulover Beach, Bal Harbor. Oddly, the list of Marine One passengers who went with the president has been removed from the official digitized records. Upon arriving, Nixon slipped into his waiting limo and was driven the short distance to the Americana Hotel to greet U.S. labor leaders. The AFL-CIO was having a large-scale convention at the site. When there, the chief executive even met with the assembled media, an unusually congenial moment for the normally press-loathing president.

By 11:46 a.m., Mr. Nixon vamoosed and motored back to Haulover Beach, where he boarded his waiting helicopter. It was time to go see his old pal, Jackie Gleason. Inverrary Country Club was the next stop.

Having the chopper route set like this shows premeditation and the president's desire to avoid an obtrusive motorcade through the metro area during lunch hour. It would have been some 21 miles by limousine from the Americana Hotel to the Country Club to meet Jackie Gleason. The chopper ride took 17 minutes, including boarding and landing times. Obviously, the president's visit was not a spur-of-the-moment decision.

We can see that outer space occupied Richard Nixon's mind, at least briefly, during his Florida vacation; the president "signed a senate resolution designating the manned spacecraft center in Houston as the 'Lyndon B. Johnson Space Center.'" This was noted in a newspaper report for that very day, issued from Key Biscayne by a dutiful press service reporter, doing his best to cover Nixon's visit at arm's length.[6]

In 1971, Jackie Gleason agreed to lend his name to a new professional-amateur golf tournament, which began a year later. In 1973, the fun began with celebrity-only action on Monday, February 19. It finished with big-name pros swinging from Thursday to Sunday (the final two days airing on CBS television). The famous amateurs consisted mostly of old showbiz cronies like Morey Amsterdam, Jack Carter, Mickey Rooney, Forrest Tucker, Fred MacMurray, and Gleason's familiar golfing buddy Bob Hope. Some of the NFL Super Bowl Champion Miami Dolphins were there, along with some of Gleason's favorite aging New York Yankee stars of the '50s.[7] Jackie was very much in his element and just a short golf cart ride away from his backyard patio. No telling how many high-profile stars were in and out of Glea Manor that weekend. *How sweet it was.*

Compared to Nixon's modest Biscayne neighborhood, Gleason's

life of luxury at exclusive Inverrary was enviable and lavish. Nixon's Monday stopover was meant to be the *public* highlight for both the politico and the comic, if not the entire tournament. In those days, a sitting president didn't play golf on live television. It wasn't considered dignified. If Nixon had a bad day on the links, it would have been most embarrassing in front of spectators, reporters, and commentators.

Records show that at 12:10 that Monday, Nixon's helicopter flew directly to the Inverrary Golf and Country Club landing site near the links. Once again, *the White House list of passengers for this aerial ride was mysteriously removed from the president's official daily records.* The document might have shown the name of a USAF official or presidential aide who could have briefed Jackie Gleason on his Homestead journey that would occur later.

One eyewitness riding with Nixon—aide Stephen B. Bull (1941-) —vividly recalled to this author in 2017[8] seeing eager Jackie Gleason steer a white golf cart right up to the presidential helicopter while its blades were still whirring. Grinning Gleason almost got scalped. "I thought for sure Jackie was going to be decapitated on the spot," Bull remembered to this author with a chuckle. What the aide witnessed may have been extremely important. It was a "dry run" for later that night for a planned, covert operation. Nixon and his Marine One pilot were demonstrating the ability to land not far away from Glea Manor and later depart efficiently. The veteran pilot now had the experience, the proper coordinates, and the moxy. And Gleason was, in effect, measuring how he could walk up to the chopper to enter it or at least greet it—something he'd be doing later that night.

White House logs show Nixon and Gleason chatted for two minutes as they climbed into an electric golf cart and got settled, with Jackie at the wheel. Bystanders whipped out their cameras. The media took some snapshots for the next twenty minutes, providing photos that can still be viewed online today. Nixon sported his usual dark blue suit and necktie. Gleason wore a white trench coat to ward off the occasional light mist coming down, plus a colorful paisley shirt, open at the collar, with a dark sports jacket and lighter slacks. It could be that both men had on these same clothes that night when clandestine adventure was afoot.

The two smiling celebrity friends buzzed across the lush green course in the cart. They were followed by two security agents in their own golf vehicle and a presidential secretary taking notes of the people and times involved. The duo finally got out and "addressed guests" at a tall, thin stand with two microphones—again, showing this visit was prearranged—at 12:20 p.m. The president began his remarks with the usual awkwardness. According to inverraryclassic.-com, he looked over the celebrity golfers and blurted out, "I'm delighted to be here. I understand you don't start playing [with professionals] until Thursday, except for the celebrities. Do you call that playing?" Gleason must have been rattled but kept his cool, replying, "Only when the girls are here."[9]

The crowd laughed, then quieted respectfully. The president informed them he was visiting to help Jackie and the famous golfers promote the Boys Club of America, which was to receive some of the proceeds of the event. Plus, Gleason and Hope had set a $25,000 wager, which was donated to charity as well. Gleason won. Nixon also relayed a little self-promotion, telling all that the U.S. under his leadership had achieved its Vietnam objective, which was to prevent a Communist takeover of South Vietnam by force. This proved to be remarkably inaccurate as Communist North Vietnamese forces took over that country within two years and maintain control to this day.

Nixon and Gleason then sparred lightheartedly with the press, helping to make the start of the "PGA Jackie Gleason Inverrary National Airlines Golf Classic" a great success. So much so, Country Club ownership even renamed its entire main course "The Great One" in Jackie's honor. Interestingly, a famous name not from the field of sports, showbiz, or the media was in the mix of amateur golfers that Monday, someone who *may* have figured in ET matters around this time.

Former United States Air Force pilot, astronaut, and aerospace engineer Leroy Gordon Cooper, Jr. (1927-2004)[10] was taking his swings that day. Cooper had previously orbited the moon twice and was a high-ranking Freemason. He was granted an *honorary* 33rd degree, Scottish Rites. According to a masonic source for this author, so was Jackie Gleason. This undoubtedly created a special bond that Nixon did not share because he was not a mason nor a part of any other secretive organization after college (although he did twice visit the mysterious Bohemian Grove society in Northern California[11]). Cooper was an esteemed member of Carbondale Masonic Lodge #82 in Colorado; nearly all astronauts are said to have been well-connected brother masons and even left a Freemason's "deputation" on the moon for any visitors to view.

In his creative work, Jackie Gleason made sure to include some references to the Freemasons in earnest or parody. For example, Gleason explored a "Raccoon Lodge" membership for the characters Ralph Kramden and Ed Norton in *The Honeymooners*. In the fall of 1969, a Gleason variety show episode featured an opening song-and-dance number with men wearing suits and masonic red fezzes. This was Jackie's private world, and it was that of Gordon Cooper as well. Secret brotherhood meetings, secret handshakes, secret code words, and just plain *secrets*.[12]

Lieutenant Colonel Gordon Cooper kept silent to the public on the subject of alien visitation until he got out of the space program and completed his military service. Then he talked openly about several UFO sightings he experienced during his military career. During his sixth space mission, for instance, Cooper reported a specific flying object which quickly approached his capsule, then soared away.[13] NASA refused to respond to questions about the incident. Gordon maintained until his death in 2004 that the United States government had long been engaged in a large-scale UFO/ET cover-up. In a letter to Ambassador George Ashley Griffith of Grenada via the United Nations in New York, dated September 9, 1978, the former astronaut candidly wrote: "For many years I have lived with a secret, in a secrecy imposed on all specialists and astronauts. I can now reveal that every day, in the USA, our radar instruments capture objects of form and composition unknown to us...I feel that we need to have a top-level, coordinated program to scientifically collect and analyze data from all over the Earth concerning any type of encounter, and to determine how best to interface with these visitors in a friendly fashion."

The secretive space program trained USAF pilots like Gordon Cooper at Edwards Airbase, the remote desert site of President Eisenhower's close encounter of February 19, 1954. Cooper said that on May 3, 1957, he had a film crew set up a camera on the dry lakebed near the Edwards facilities, then took off. His men came back to him later that day with an incredible story captured on film: a flying saucer landing. It was clearly a silvery disc, which eventually took off "at a sharp angle" at a very high rate of speed. Cooper said he watched the impressive UFO footage, then had it sent to the Pentagon in Washington. He never heard back about it. He also said that while serving in Germany in 1951, he had personally witnessed some UFOs on consecutive nights while piloting his Air Force jet.[14] Cooper declared in his candid letter for the United Nations ambassador: "I believe these extraterrestrial vehicles and their crew are visiting this planet from other planets."

Little wonder Master Mason Gleason invited Master Mason Cooper to his golf tournament! One now must ponder the possibility that Cooper was at Homestead Airbase the night of, or the day after, the Nixon-Gleason encounter, which could have been only *part* of the show at the base that mysterious Monday night. Consider this...

British author Timothy Good once transcribed an audiotape made for an interview transcript featuring a person said to have been Leroy Gordon Cooper. It was turned into a mid-1973 magazine article. Keep in mind that Cooper had retired from the space program a year after the first moon landing, in July 1970, and was interviewed in the spring of 1973, while at a "UFO congress" in New York. The subsequent article (by writer J. L. Ferrando) was printed in French, which Good had translated into English by a friend.[15] Civilian

Cooper is quoted as saying the following often-overlooked statement within that article:

"I was furthermore a witness to an extraordinary phenomenon, here on this planet Earth. It happened a few months ago in Florida. There I saw with my own eyes a defined area of ground consumed by flames, with four indentations left by a flying object, which had descended in the middle of a field. Beings had left the craft, there were traces to prove this. They seemed to have studied topography; they had collected soil samples. And eventually returned to where they had come from, disappearing at an enormous speed...I happen to know that authorities did just about everything to keep this incident from the press and TV, in fear of a panicky reaction by the public."

It seems as though L. Gordon Cooper was saying he did not *witness* the alien encounter himself, only that he saw its aftermath: the visibly altered ground. He was told what took place there by someone else, apparently someone high up in the military or the federal government. Obviously, Cooper was informed by someone with substantial clearance to talk of such classified secrets.

This revelation was risky. Gordon Cooper may not have been relying too much on the pension and health care plan provided by the Air Force and NASA. He had his own income from business endeavors. However, he needed to keep his reputation sterling by not blabbing shocking state secrets or edging into what was still considered by some as "UFO nut country" in the '70s. He had to financially support himself and his family, so his comments were likely reserved and carefully considered beforehand. In 1973, he also had a personal and professional reputation to maintain if he wished to keep his new position as a design consultant to American motor companies, such as Ford. According to *Wikipedia*: "Cooper was president of his own consulting firm, Gordon Cooper & Associates, Inc., which was involved in technical projects ranging from airline and aerospace fields to land and hotel development. From 1973 to 1975, he worked for the Walt Disney Company as the vice president of research and development for Epcot Center." It is clear now that Gordon had an extra reason for being in the Sunshine State and was therefore available for Jackie Gleason's golf tournament. Cooper had connections all over the place—just like Nixon.

Looking back on September 9, 1968, the national news media recorded NASA's Gordon Cooper giving then-candidate Richard Nixon and his family a tour of the Manned Spacecraft Center in Houston, Texas.[16] There was a possible solid start to a friendship. The president went on to host many an astronaut at his 1600 Pennsylvania Avenue address in D.C. He was likely eager to be associated with the successful Apollo program, to pump up his public image with voters as a trusted leader in coordinating NASA's space ambitions.

Now then...if we can trust the mid-1973 UFO article's translation into English and Gordon Cooper's memory of what he witnessed and add up all the known facts...we can see some very eerie parallels to the Nixon-Gleason encounter developing...

1. Cooper was not only working in Florida in 1973, but he was also definitely at Jackie Gleason's tournament, if not a guest at Glea Manor itself. Since the opening round on Monday ended that late afternoon, he could have been around the house or at least in the neighborhood that night, available for a hush-hush local journey.

2. Cooper was a popular former U.S. Air Force pilot who was familiar with airbases around the country, likely including Homestead AFB. As a famous NASA astronaut and respected, daring test pilot, he would have been welcomed with open arms any time in 1973.

3. Cooper said in his 1973 New York interview that he was "in Florida" to witness the ground where an actual ET event had just recently taken place out in a "field." Was this an *air*field? Was the landing site out on one of the landing strips at Homestead?

4. In that same interview, Cooper said he learned that aliens had arrived in their spaceship and set down at the unspecified Florida site in 1973 and left evidence behind that he personally witnessed. He *had* to have been nearby quickly for this, and he had to have learned this very sensitive information from a well-placed source since he said the government worked hard to keep the incident hushed up. Somebody *very* high up had tipped him off and perhaps even invited or escorted him to the scene to take a close look.

5. Cooper indicated that the 1973 Florida extraterrestrials felt it was important to land, get out, move about at the site, and supposedly scoop up some dirt to take home. Was that all they wanted? Perhaps. Were the off-world visitors actually landing to meet Air Force personnel and perhaps the American president? This seems like a far more worthy excuse to land and take a chance on being discovered.

6. Cooper was friends with Jackie Gleason—a fellow Freemason—and with Nixon as well. Did this give Gordon an advantage on being invited to inspect the landing site, whether it was at Homestead or not? Inquisitive Gleason likely knew that Cooper had seen UFOs in person in 1951 and on film in 1957 and then while in space in the late '60s. Jackie Gleason liked and trusted Gordon Cooper enough to invite him to his golf tournament, above all other astronauts. Perhaps he was looking for an opportunity to quiz Cooper more closely on recent contact events?

7. Cooper reported in the spring of 1973 that the Florida landing event took place "a few months earlier." Maybe Monday night, February 19? It certainly fits within the time frame given by the ex-astronaut.

8. Cooper would have been at the mercy of the federal government for some of his livelihood in 1973 and likely gave only a few incomplete memories at the UFO convention of the recent incident on purpose. What was he holding back? Telling more might have endangered his bank account, reputation, and lifestyle—if not his life.

9. Cooper knew that the ETs left the scene of the landing "at an enormous speed" after digging in the dirt, but how did he know this? Such information must have come from an actual eyewitness to the departure or from someone with additional information. Again, could Cooper have been given this data via a well-placed, well-informed figure— like Gleason or Nixon? Or via Homestead personnel?

10. Cooper also said he knew that the military and government were working hard to keep news of aliens and landings away from the media and the public, supposedly to avoid a resulting "panic." He recounted that he and fellow astronauts were sworn to secrecy over sensitive things they saw or heard. After the covert Nixon-Gleason affair, Jackie apparently told his wife the very same thing. She strongly suspected that he had solemnly sworn an oath to keep quiet about what he saw.

In 1978, guest Gordon Cooper surprised the TV studio audience at *The Merv Griffin Show* by stating flatly that ETs and UFOs were quite real, a fact that was being squelched by the American government. A 2017 ufoinsight.com article by Marcus Lowth on Gordon Cooper recalled: "He would speak of the covering up of information by NASA and other arms of government...He would also make claims of aliens being present on Earth. He made the statement that he had been present on a military base 'when they brought one in!'"[17]

Wow!

"Brought one in." Was Cooper referencing the mid-February 1973

Homestead AFB case? Was "one" a recovered ET airship or an actual alien body?

The website bd-updates.com has aired their opinion of how Gordon Cooper privately admitted he knew more than he ever let on in public. The site explained how the late ex-astronaut had once been asked about an alien spaceship that had allegedly crash-landed in America. "Cooper continued by stating that, based on the various UFO contact and abduction reports he had been privy to, he was convinced that the occupants of this crashed UFO were 'probably not that different from what we are'—that they are almost entirely humanoid." Researcher Lee Spiegel, stunned by what Cooper had alleged on national radio, called Cooper's office the following morning.[18] Spiegel recalled, "Cooper admitted to me that he could have revealed more on the air, but he decided not to play his entire hand because he felt certain that some 'official eyebrows were going to get raised.'"

Returning to 1973, Cooper had his 46th birthday coming up on March 6. What to give as a gift for a man who had been into space and expressed such an interest in extraterrestrial life?

L. Gordon Cooper seems to have had the means, motive, and opportunity to have participated in the secret presidential airbase visit. He would have possessed the prior experience, background, official clearance, and the calm acceptance of understanding ET visitation. As a brother mason, Gleason would naturally have left Cooper out of the account to his wife to protect his identity and participation. However, this is purely speculative. Overall, the famous ex-astronaut desired that everyone on Earth know that we humans are not alone, and that he had seen alien visitation for himself. Yet he never said a word in recorded appearances and interviews about going to Homestead Airbase that fateful night, so we cannot count on his participation, yet we cannot rule it out, either.

Gordon Cooper's presence at the pro-am golf event is indisputable, but it is far from the only subject of interest here. Now let's return to the Monday, February 19, 1973, pro-am golf event...

At 12:30 p.m., Gleason and Nixon climbed back into their golf cart, chatting away. Indeed, this might have been the happiest day of Gleason's entire life, even without an ET encounter planned later on that night. He was really in his element.

Two Secret Service agents followed closely in their own electric cart. At one point, the famous duo stopped, and newsmen, like ABC's Tom Jariel (1934-), in the vicinity closed in, microphones held out. Photographers snapped away. Golfers tried to concentrate on their game but likely stopped to watch and chuckle as Gleason turned on the charm. Nearby, Bob Hope and Gordon Cooper might have felt some small amount of jealousy. Finally, after a brief question-and-answer time, Jackie hit the accelerator, and they zipped across the course, headed toward the chopper landing site.

There was only a little time for private conversation as the duo pulled away from the gallery and the press. An astounding 40,000 people attended the tournament, according to news reports, and one pro noted that this total was more than the most recent prestigious U.S. Open. Finding quiet time to discuss private matters wouldn't be easy.

It is speculative, but it makes sense that if Nixon asked Gleason: "Is your one million dollar offer for hard proof of alien life still valid, Jackie?" Gleason would have replied affirmatively. The president probably made a firm request: "Then be ready for a surprise tonight. I'm sending a chopper to that pad tonight at about 9:00 to pick you up. Tell no one but be ready to go on a little trip. Can't tell you where. Just don't tell anyone."

Again, this is only a *supposed* scenario, but it is a logical probability based on what we know. It was all that needed to be said, taking less than a minute.

Eventually, at the Inverrary helipad, the entertainer saw the politician off as he headed back to his Key Biscayne compound. The digitized page for the list of passengers going with Nixon was again mysteriously removed from his online presidential records. His trip across the city took 22 minutes. Upon landing on the Biscayne helipad, the president went straight to his 516 Bay Lane office, not his residence, and taped a prepared national radio address on mundane matters to air on February 22. Finally, he had lunch at 1:30 p.m.

We can see that Nixon played no actual golf that day. In fact, there were no golf clubs or bag in that fringed-roof, white electric cart. The whole get-together took only twenty minutes, from 12:10 to 12:30. It seemed innocuous. The amateur golfers got on with their swings for another four hours. Gleason was here and there that gray afternoon and in the days to come, according to home movie footage. By late Sunday afternoon, the pro-am wrapped up on CBS's afternoon schedule, and Jackie awarded the first prize trophy and a check to winner Lee Trevino (1939-). Gleason undoubtedly glad-handed course officials, pro golfers, country club bigwigs, and any remaining invited celebrity pals during that wrap-up on Sunday. Meanwhile, White House logs show a gap between 2:21 and 5:40 p.m. for Richard Nixon on that Sunday, February 25, 1973. Was he watching the final round of the Gleason tournament on television while holed up in his Executive Office Building space? He often skipped the Oval Office for this more private setting across the narrow street.

In returning to that late Monday afternoon, February 19, we can imagine the scene as the sun set and the opening-day crowds and press melted away. The celebs were wrapping up and heading to the clubhouse. It was getting dark, so Gleason went home—a short golf cart ride—to rest, eat dinner, have a drink, and look after any house guests. After the hectic past few days of readying the televised tournament, it was seemingly a quiet evening at Glea Manor at last. Did recovering Jackie Gleason settle back and read one of his paranormal books? He had so many to peruse in his massive library collection, and more would come in by way of his secretarial assistant and by mail.

In order to keep his personal address away from strangers, Jackie Gleason may well have maintained a business office to receive books and periodicals in the mail. "Way back in the mid-1960s, I got a letter in the mail from *Jackie Gleason Productions*, Hollywood, Florida, ordering a copy of a mimeographed booklet I had put together relating to UFOs," recalled author Timothy Green Beckley.[19] "This, to me, was confirmation of what I had heard rumors about for a long time, that The Great One was personally involved in researching UFOs."

If Gleason had been tipped off to his destination later that night, he might have selected just such a book to prepare emotionally.

Meanwhile, President Nixon spoke on the phone to aides around this same time of the evening and placed a one-minute call to his neighbor, Rebozo. No other activity was recorded until dinnertime, held from 6:30 to 7:00 p.m., with Bebe as a guest. After that? *Nothing*. Well, a quick one-minute phone call, supposedly from Nixon to his young aide just down the street, occurred at 8:36 p.m. However, the lack of records is not proof of anything. It should be noted that presidents can order their printed official schedules to be scrubbed or altered in any manner they want.

Other than that brief telephone chat, no activity was allowed to be entered into the official logs after 7:00 that night. Where did Mr. Nixon go? What was he doing that night? Why was a message inserted into his records at this point stating that a restricted document had been removed?

Whatever the reason, it had to have been awfully important, for it was rare indeed for the daily presidential appointment records to have been cut out like this. Researchers getting at the truth of a controversial night in UFO/ET history have been carefully—if not *deliberately*—thwarted.

That's it in the official White House logs until the following morning. Nixon's exact official whereabouts from 7:00 p.m. until 8:19 a.m. the next day remain lost to history, apparently.

As the evening hours went by, Jackie Gleason was left on his own and seemed to disappear from view, if not from the house entirely.

The stage was now set, and the mysterious drama of a lifetime was about to unfold.

PAUL BLAKE SMITH

1. Nixon Library.
2. Timothy Good, "Need to Know," January, 2006.
3. Wikipedia contributors, "Robert Seamans," *Wikipedia*.
4. Wikipedia contributors, "Nicolaus Copernicus," *Wikipedia*.
5. Wikipedia contributors, "Charles Messier," *Wikipedia*.
6. "Houston Space Center Is Named For Johnson," *The New York Times*, February 19, 1973.
7. Complete list found in president's daily diary in *nixon.gov* records for February 1973
8. Telephone interview with Stephen Bull, May 20, 2018.
9. Gerhard Peters and John Woolley, ""Informal Remarks at the Jackie Gleason Inverrary Classic, Lauderhill, Florida," *The American Presidency Project*.
10. Wikipedia contributors, "Gordon Cooper," *Wikipedia*.
11. "What did Richard Nixon say about Bohemian Grove?" NSN Search response.
12. Wikipedia contributors, "Freemasonry," *Wikipedia*.
13. "Major Gordon Cooper, USA Astronaut, and UFOs," *UFO Evidence*, October 4, 2004.
14. Marcus Lowth, "The UFO Conspiracy Revelations of NASA Astronaut Gordon Cooper," *UFO Insight*, March 27, 2017.
15. "Astronauts and UFOs: Reports and Statements by USA Astronauts," *UFOlogie*, undated.
16. Alex Stuckey, "Listen: Apollo 11 Crew Now Isolated From Everyone Except Nixon," *Houston Chronicle,* July 4, 2019.
17. Lowth, Marcus, "UFO Insight," 2017.
18. El Toro, "Gordon Cooper & UFOs: An Astronaut Speaks Out About Aliens," *Newcarz*, March 14, 2022.
19. Timothy G. Beckley, "And Away We Go: The Night Jackie Gleason Saw The Corpses of Little Green Men From Mars," *UFO Digest*, June 19, 2015.

CHAPTER THREE

BEV'S TALE

"Actually seeing the bodies of those aliens was the final proof."

For the main foundation of the entire Nixon-Gleason saga, we have to go straight to its original source: a former country club office secretary and the telling—and selling?—of her story to a well-known supermarket tabloid. That doesn't exactly inspire confidence right off, but it may still be true since it was repeated without any real changes twenty years later for nothing in return.

For many decades, the *National Enquirer* has reigned as the king of sensationalist journalism.[1] It was transformed in 1967 from a crime-and-violence weekly in New York City to a parade of celebrity gossip and paranormal claims for the nation. Undoubtedly, it became a Jackie Gleason favorite since few other publications were willing to print supernatural stories, and he snapped up whatever he could find on that subject. In 1971, the *Enquirer*'s national headquarters were moved south to Lantana, Florida, just 37 miles from Jackie Gleason's new house in Lauderhill[2]. The *Enquirer* likely arrived by mail to the Gleason home or may have come via his Hollywood, Florida, office. Perhaps Jackie's wife and even his household staff flipped through the tabloid. [3]

Beverly "Bev" McKittrick Gleason (1934-) was the superstar's second wife, wed a mere ten days after his 1970 divorce. Beverly was from Baltimore, Maryland, and ended up a Miami country club secretary. She first met Jackie in 1968, and they began a whirlwind courtship. The couple were married in London, England, at a registrar's office on July 4, 1970. They held a more religious ceremony in Miami that September. Quiet and short-haired (unusual for that era), with no experience in show business, Bev was a rather odd choice for the boisterous, creative entertainer. The two resided, with her little schnauzer, in one fine Miami home, then another: "Glea Manor," on Willow Wood Road, in Lauderhill. [4]

After a few years, it became obvious the marriage was a mistake. To make matters worse for Gleason, showbiz was changing, moving toward a new, grittier youth culture. Jackie's movies and fading comedy-variety format were on their way out. By 1973, why bother to push oneself anymore? Gleason was, by then, an older man with gray hair (when not dyed), aches and pains, weight problems, and unshakable addictions that were affecting his overall health. He had made his fortune, and his talent and legend were assured. It was time for leisure. This left "The Great One" without many showbiz projects to work on and perhaps frustrated by the many changes of the '70s.

Sometimes idleness and closeness can suffocate a couple. Despite having more time together in the same house, the Gleasons drifted apart. Jackie was becoming more and more of a loner, hanging around reading, watching TV, and chatting with business agents and old cronies on the phone while chain-smoking, eating, and boozing. He had his mood swings, for sure. Beverly apparently went shopping a great deal and ran up some bills.

Thus, in mid-1974, Mrs. Gleason was on the outs. Disgruntled Jackie wanted a divorce and formally filed for one that September; they just weren't a loving couple anymore. At first, he moved out of

Glea Manor in order to be closer to his ex-girlfriend, according to a 1975 *People* magazine article. He even announced his engagement to be married to his new/old flame, leaving his actual spouse, Beverly, stunned. She contested the divorce, hoping for a reunion after Jackie calmed down and realized he had acted impulsively. She was right, in a sense. "On December 20, he moved back without warning," Beverly informed *People*.[5] "We lived as man and wife" once again in very late 1974 at the two-million-dollar estate. Jackie had cleaned up his excessive drinking, remarkably, after he seemingly had finally put much of the shock of February 19, 1973, behind him. Sadly, more squabbling commenced, and Jackie soon moved into his own Glea guest bedroom. *People* noted that the main issue between the couple was money; Beverly alleged her wealthy husband had given her "only two hundred dollars" since December 1, 1974, and carefully noted that his total worth was "$3.5 million." The 1975 magazine article mentioned Beverly was "short on cash" but "long on credit," owing five-figure totals on her bank accounts.

By mid-1974, Beverly was low on cash, unemployed, and flushed with free time as her marriage had gone sour. Jackie was out of the house a lot, spending time with his old flame. Bev grew more desperate.

Many years previously—1946, in fact—Jackie Gleason met and fell in love with Marilyn Taylor, sister of June Taylor (1917-2004), a choreographer on Gleason's old variety show. The TV star wanted to marry Marilyn, but his first wife, Genevieve Halford Gleason, was Catholic and refused to grant a divorce for nearly 15 years. Marilyn married someone else, and they produced a son, Craig Horwich, an attorney who co-owns and operates "Jackie Gleason Enterprises," along with Gleason's daughters, according to a 2018 news article.[6] When Marilyn's husband died, she took their son to Miami, not far from Gleason, to live closer to her sister. By mid-1974, Jackie was calling on widowed Marilyn, "the love of his life," in nearby Hallandale, Florida. Nobly, their reignited love affair was apparently not consummated until after Jackie's divorce a year and a half later.

The problem from Bev's point of view was that she was essentially flying solo and in need of money. The parties had dried up. There were no more celebrity guests. No more free rounds of golf in handy electric carts. There was not even much food or drink left at the manor since Jackie had cut off her credit. What to do?

By 1974, Beverly had a plan to raise some cash. She called upon the most astonishing story she had ever heard, one she knew the public would like to hear. Something that her estranged husband once told her. Something that would fit right into the tabloids he perused.

The entire saga of the Nixon-Gleason alien encounter was first introduced to the public when the estranged Mrs. Gleason rather brazenly and indiscreetly spoke to a print reporter in the late summer of 1974. Nixon had just resigned as president, out of power and out of favor with the public. Meanwhile, Mr. Gleason was out on the town.

"Out with your new lady, are you? Well, I'll show you," might have been her new attitude. Beverly decided to mention to the tabloid journalist that her hubby was deeply interested in the paranormal and considered himself a leading expert on Extra Sensory Perception, hypnosis, and UFOs. In fact, he had told her a shocking tale just the year before. She claimed that Jackie informed her that President Nixon had shown him the corpses of aliens at an American military installation. "It was just the one statement," Beverly recalled many years later of this 1974 interview.

It was a bombshell revelation with national security implications.

One problem with this account is that decades later, Beverly repeatedly claimed the name of this publication was *Esquire*, a slick, color, monthly magazine—not a weekly, black-and-white supermarket tabloid. According to Bev, Jackie's photograph was even on the cover of the *Esquire* issue. A careful review of 1974 issues of *Esquire* shows no Jackie Gleason cover nor any major article on him.[7] Did Bev remember the wrong magazine?

Sure enough, a check of 1974 *National Enquirer* issues reveals one edition—September 8—headlined by a large black-and-white cover photo of a Hollywood actress alongside some brief descriptions of what's inside. One headline states: "Jackie Gleason: I'm the Greatest Believer in ESP in America." The article inside was apparently about Gleason's once-hidden, intense interest in psychic phenomena and evidently included his shocking mention of a president-guided inspection of deceased celestial visitors.[8]

It was almost a full decade later when Jackie's photo appeared on the cover in a similar *Enquirer* story, this time *written* by Bev, so it seems obvious the former Mrs. Gleason was incorrect in her recall of the 1974 media revelation. But let's face it, *"Esquire"* does sound like *"Enquirer."* It was and is an understandable mistake. In one extra note on how this memory merge could have happened, the 1974 *Enquirer* article mentioning Jackie Gleason was listed under a larger banner atop the page: "AMAZING UFO SIGHTING...Seen by 2 Veteran Airline Pilots and Tracked by Airport Radar." This article had nothing to do with the Gleason piece, but it could have helped confuse anyone looking back afterward.

In the early '70s, the *Enquirer* paid as much as $2,500 or more for information on celebrities. Bev certainly had a connection to a celebrity and a story to tell. Importantly, she *felt* Jackie was being genuine in his startling otherworldly account. This belief leads us to the second motivating reason for Beverly. In 1972, the *Enquirer* had put together a special "Blue Ribbon Panel" of UFO experts, including the esteemed researcher Dr. J. Allen Hynek (1910-1986). The tabloid decided to offer a reward of $50,000 for "the first person who can prove that a UFO came from outer space and is not a natural phenomenon."[9] This sounds like Gleason's on-air offer when asking for ET proof as far back as the '50s. The magazine further asserted: "The *Enquirer* also offers up to $10,000 each year to anyone judged by the panel to have supplied the most scientifically valuable evidence on UFOs." Could Bev have been reaching for either prize—and some further headlines—by talking to a reporter in 1974?

Telling a titillating tabloid a tantalizing tale would bring the ex-secretary a little extra time in the spotlight instead of her husband for a change. *She* would be the interviewee, for once, the center of attention. Beverly wanted her spouse back; she wanted him to forgive their differences and acrimony. She retained faint hopes that somehow their marriage could be saved, she admitted later. In his final extensive interview, Jackie pointed to finances as being a factor in Bev's actions. While reminiscing for *Playboy* (August 1986), Gleason summed up: "Well, what would you do if you were a woman married to a wealthy guy, and a divorce was coming up? You'd want to get some of the money." His sympathetic *Playboy* interviewer stated that "in the press," the actor's estranged wife was "very hostile over the split."

In 2003, as recorded in presidentialufo.com and theblackvault.com,[10] Beverly recalled a sincerely shaken "Jack" (as she routinely referred to Gleason) after the 1973 airbase visit account: "I bought the story, hook, line, and sinker...He was very convincing." The TV legend was visibly drained, pale, and physically slumped in the last hour of that long, eventful day. While he was an actor, used to putting on grand performances, what purpose would such a charade serve? He *could* have made up a different, much more conventional story—such as being out drinking with the boys—if he wanted to. He could have changed or recanted his story later—but the entertainer didn't.

When the resulting *National Enquirer* issue came out in September 1974, voracious reader Jackie Gleason saw it and exploded. He'd been squealed on, in a sense. His most precious secret was now out, albeit undetailed. He had previously moved out of Glea Manor but heatedly phoned Beverly there to say in explicit terms he was *most* displeased she had spilled the extraterrestrial Nixonian beans.

"After the interview was published, Jackie was upset" about the ET claim going public, Beverly recollected. "We were on the verge of divorce, but everything was okay until it came out" in the tabloid.

When Gleason saw the article, "that just finished everything" as far as their marriage was concerned, she remembered sadly. Jackie pushed angrily and aggressively that mid-September for a legal divorce settlement—and got it in less than two years.

During all of this, Jackie Gleason was still a "Special Agent Contact" of the FBI, on the agency's annual Christmas card list. He always strove to maintain a good relationship with the federal government—Nixon in office or not—including the FBI (even with J. Edgar Hoover dead). It was embarrassing for him to have the White House and the Justice Department find out he leaked one of the biggest sworn secrets in American history right after he had been let in on it. A *"blaaa-ber-mouth!"*—as he had famously bellowed in *The Honeymooners*.

In a move that puzzled everyone, Gleason refused public comment when asked about the stunning story over the next weeks, months, and years. The superstar knew that the tabloid controversy would only gain more attention if he said anything. Patience and time would let the claim fade from the headlines. If the wild story *wasn't* true, he could have easily quashed it with an interview or press release saying so. He even moved back in with Beverly, as mentioned, but it didn't last. By December 1974, he had settled in his own guest room and decided to boot Beverly out two months later. His February 1975 Inverrary Golf Tournament on CBS was coming up again, and new U.S. President Gerald Ford was expected to play on camera along with many other well-known celebrities. Party-hosting and socializing were of prime importance now. Was it possible another covert airbase visit was in store, this time for Jackie and Jerry? Perhaps in Gleason's mind—in his hopes and dreams. The superstar wanted Beverly to pack up and leave Glea Manor. She had betrayed him by blabbing about the secret 1973 airbase encounter, and perhaps he felt she could not be trusted if it were to happen again.

Jackie had Beverly's membership at the Inverrary Country Club revoked just one week before the big February 1975 pro-am and, according to the *People* article, had a founding member of that organization ask her to move out of the upscale golf course home. Feeling that Jackie simply wanted his new/old flame, Marilyn Taylor, to act as tournament hostess, "I'm not leaving" was Bev's defiant response.[11] It was awkward that week as Mr. Gleason teamed with Ford, while Miss Taylor hovered around, and Mrs. Gleason still camped in Glea Manor. That awkwardness was perhaps becoming familiar. Jackie celebrated his 59th birthday with Marilyn on February 26, 1975, and attended a ritzy presidential reception that week in full view of the press and the public. President Ford evidently did little else in the Miami area but golf with Gleason and take off, digitized White House logs show.

In the ensuing weeks and months, Jackie kept urging his Miami-based lawyer, Hugo L. Black, Jr. (1922-2013), to not only get the divorce finalized but to respond candidly to Beverly's revealing statements in the press. "She said she'd try to embarrass Jackie if he didn't do what she wanted," the attorney told *People*. "And what she wanted was a two-million-dollar settlement," something the entertainer was definitely *not* in the mood to agree to. In the meantime, Mrs. Gleason eventually relented and packed her belongings, moving away from Inverrary entirely. Evidently patient, Marilyn Taylor did not move right in, however, and maintained her own residence for a while.

Divorce was legally granted and signed by both parties in November 1975, and things settled down for several years. Just as the divorce paperwork's ink dried, Marilyn wed still-eager Jackie and moved into Glea Manor, establishing a good married life together, hosting parties, celebrity guests, and golf outings galore. Jackie was now a stepdad and toned down his excesses a bit to set a good example for his new family.

Nine years passed relatively quietly for both The Great One and his ex.

Then, in mid-1983, Beverly McKittrick returned. She had decided to write her memoirs, focusing mainly on her memorable time with

PAUL BLAKE SMITH

The Great One. The '80s were becoming more of a brutally candid, tell-all era in show business, with book publishers, magazine editors, and talk show hosts tackling—or shamelessly exploiting—once-intimate matters. Bev knew she still had a great story. Her famous ex-husband wouldn't publicly discuss it, so why not? Bev would need a publisher for her planned book, and she began looking for a way to publicize it even before she began typing it.

Wisely or not, Beverly went back to the familiar *National Enquirer*, perhaps naively thinking her ex-husband would not care by now. True, he had long since moved on, gotten remarried, and was a big movie star all over again. Jackie remained in his gorgeous golf course home at Inverrary, now with lovely wife, Marilyn. Bev's move to dig up the past once more and type up the amazing February 1973 ET account—and other private inside information on Jackie—would likely provide her with some much-needed extra income.

Possibly she was inspired by a May 17, 1983, *National Enquirer* cover story with a front-page color photo of her ex-husband along with the teasing headline: "Hospitalized Jackie Gleason Ignores Doctor's Warning—May Lose Leg." Did someone else close to the remarried entertainer leak details about his personal life? Jackie's health woes were mounting, and it appears an inside source decided to go for the money and reveal some details about The Great One's private medical issues, undoubtedly without permission. Beverly was no longer part of Jackie's world since their 1975 divorce, so it was likely not her.

Having been a secretary accustomed to drawing up documents...and having read some of Jackie's books, scripts, and magazines...Beverly McKittrick knew how to piece together a fascinating showbiz tale. She likely received assistance from an *Enquirer* editor or reporter along the way. The neat, one-page article with splashy photos indicates some professional shaping of the story.

In an article printed in the August 16, 1983, *Enquirer*, Beverly recalled in her own words the amazing extraterrestrial matter at Homestead Airbase once again, in a little more detail than back in

1974.[12] This time, the *Enquirer* did indeed feature a color photo of Jackie on the cover with the blurb: "Ex-Wife Reveals...Jackie Gleason Saw Bodies of Space Aliens At Air Force Base." This was undoubtedly the magazine photo and cover story that Beverly seems to have misremembered when interviewed about it twenty years later.

The article was all part of Beverly's upcoming book on Jackie Gleason; the publication admitted up front, one that, unfortunately, never materialized. The *Enquirer* noted before the article began that they repeatedly attempted to call Jackie Gleason for an interview to confirm or deny Bev's allegations. Few celebrities in those days ever spoke directly to the famous yellow journalism sheet, so Gleason was in a bit of a bind. He continued to ignore the story and refused all comment.

"I'll never forget the night in 1973 when my famous husband slumped white-faced in an armchair," Bev began for her 1983 *Enquirer* exposé. She had been worried, as the memorable incident happened at about 11:30 p.m. when Jackie finally arrived home physically and emotionally shaken. Beverly was seated in the living room and said she heard the front door being unlocked and opened, apparently causing her to jump to her feet. She was glad that her husband was home since only he had a key. What she learned next shocked her, especially since it involved the president of the United States.

Beverly admitted in 2003 she was not sure *how* that specific night's meeting was set up, but that previous hook-ups between Nixon and Gleason had been arranged by an aide to the president and Jackie's discreet secretary, so she believed it likely this method had been utilized once again. But how did the comic get to Homestead AFB? It would have been a long car trip of over fifty miles through the darkened mean streets of Miami and its suburbs, and he would have needed a knowledgeable, patient chauffeur. But wait! Beverly never said that Jackie was *driven* there. She only wrote that she had heard his key unlocking the front door but said nothing about hearing a car's motor, voices outside, or a car door.

How could The Great Gleason travel to an airbase with the usual luxury and convenience he was accustomed to and arrive back home so quietly?

The simplest answer: *via helicopter.* A helicopter could have picked him up at the very same nearby helipad on the Inverrary course that Nixon had utilized in his official Marine One chopper that day. Was Nixon present for the aerial trip to Inverrary again that night? Possibly. It was dark, and no one was expecting it. This was a quick, top-secret mission, and the helicopter held communications gear that all presidents must be near when traveling. It is also possible that Nixon flew directly from Key Biscayne to Homestead on Marine One and waited there while a nondescript military helicopter was dispatched to Lauderhill.

All Jackie had to do was walk or perhaps drive an electric golf cart from his house to the helipad. And awaaaaaay we go!

The fifty-seven-mile journey (by car) from Inverrary to Homestead probably took only half an hour by air. Even though Jackie was not fond of flying, this was different. This was a high-level luxury chopper flight, possibly seated next to the President of the United States and a Secret Service agent or two. Heady stuff. Jackie was likely giddy with excitement that they were pulling off this trip without the rest of the world knowing what was going on. No media, no fans, and no Inverrary residents knew what that helicopter in the dark was all about.

"When I arrived at the base, I was given a heavily armed military escort," Jackie told Beverly, probably referencing the point at which his helicopter landed on a Homestead runway or on a special chopper landing area (which Nixon utilized every visit). Notice how the comic did not say, "When we drove up to the front gate." He never mentioned any sort of hour-long drive through Miami. So, we can reasonably assume that a special team of military men surrounded The Great One as he stepped out of the helicopter, its whirring blades winding down in the darkness. He and Nixon merely removed their seat belts and stepped out onto the airbase runway. Military vehicles waited nearby. Greetings and identifications were exchanged. Gleason then recalled that from this point, he was "driven to a building in a remote area."

Once at the special building—possibly a medical laboratory or military morgue—the vehicles were parked near the front door, where another armed guard was stationed. "We had to pass a guard at the door, then were shown into a large room." This indicates it was probably not a cavernous airplane hangar.

Presumably, some of the military escort stopped outside the structure and stood guard. That's when the Great One received the fulfillment of a nearly lifelong dream.

When Beverly asked Jackie, flopped in an armchair near midnight at Glea Manor, what precisely had left him in such a visibly disturbed state, he told her he had just inspected something genuinely incredible and shocking.

He explained that he had just scrutinized four corpses of deceased off-world creatures. "I've seen the bodies of some aliens from outer space," was how Jackie initially put it to Beverly, direct and to the point.

In the 1983 *Enquirer* article, Bev admitted smiling at this surprising revelation, thinking at first it was a joke. However, Jackie's subdued demeanor, wavering voice, and unusually pasty skin tone sobered her up quickly. He looked "haggard," she recalled in 1983. Shaken and most stirred. This would have been nearly impossible to pull off in an acting performance. Gleason was clearly emotionally rattled by something.

"His reply stunned me," Bev recalled. Who could have been expecting such a response several hours after his nationally televised celebrity golf tournament had begun right outside? Mrs. Gleason was probably expecting Jackie to confess that he had been out hobnobbing with some of the visiting stars. Perhaps he had been at the Inverrary clubhouse or at a local watering hole tying one on. That would have been a far more believable explanation for his absence that night.

Jackie wanted to immediately assure his smiling spouse that he was dead serious about what he had just experienced. He warned her in no uncertain terms: "It's top secret, only a few people know."

To Gleason's photographic memory, the haunting image of the dead alien bodies was not only substantial and real but also quite lasting, sticking in his mind for the rest of his life. That night, the troubled actor undoubtedly reached for his old vices: his cigarettes, lighter, and a glass of booze. It had been a momentous evening, and he had reached the pinnacle of his two decades of metaphysical research.

Was there a Secret Service presence at the base? Jackie Gleason evidently did not say, but if Nixon was involved in any way, he likely had at least one agent present. An outside yet seemingly fitting choice would have been Treasury/Secret Service Agent John Eastland Gleason (1935-2014). Despite the startling coincidence, Agent Gleason was born and raised in rural Mississippi and was evidently no relation to the famous Brooklyn-born comic.

If there is a standout among the Secret Service men to have participated in high-level high jinks, it is a high-ranking Treasury agent named Arthur Lincoln Godfrey (1921-2002). Godfrey was said to have been "unusually close" to Nixon, so much so that he flew to California to visit the ex-president in his retirement. The unlikely duo once attended an auto race together. A camera buff, "Rawhide" Godfrey took photos on freelance assignments and eventually became the official photographer of his fellow former Secret Service agents. After his time in the Treasury Department, Art Godfrey went to work in the press office of the vice president once Gerald Ford became America's commander-in-chief. Truly, Godfrey was tall, tough, tight-lipped, and trusted. He died in 2002 of kidney failure[13] and was buried with honors at Arlington National Cemetery.[14]

In February 1955, Art Godfrey was one of the agents on a list of those who accompanied President Eisenhower to Holloman Airbase in New Mexico to covertly meet humanoid aliens there as a kind of follow-up to his 1954 encounter in California—in which Godfrey also might have been involved with trip security. A year after

Nixon's 1973 airbase odyssey and not long after the twentieth anniversary of Eisenhower's first summit—privately renegotiated by Nixon again in 1974 South Florida—Godfrey retired. Godfrey soon got a job offer from none other than Bebe Rebozo. This is surprising because almost *no one* got close to the tight-knit, tight-lipped Nixon and Rebozo—at times, not even their spouses. Godfrey seems to have shared quite a private bond with the conservative duo.

Before retirement, Agent Arthur Godfrey had achieved the rank of "shift leader" and also undertook Secret Service "advance planning" in the White House, working with U.S. presidents and their top staffers to set out well-guarded itineraries for trips. This included arranging and coordinating the proper security for journeys involving limousines, helicopters, and airplanes, some of which were kept secret from the public. Godfrey likely made *dozens* of trips to Homestead Airbase, accompanying every president from Truman to Nixon.

Agent Godfrey was deeply respected. He is described in an online bio as courageously "having served in the U.S. Army in Europe during WWII, and his decorations included a Silver Star, Bronze Star, and Purple Heart. He received the Silver Star for rescuing a soldier and carrying him back to friendly lines in Italy while under enemy fire. He was the recipient of the Treasury Department's Albert Gallatin Award," a reward upon "the retirement or death of a Treasury employee who has served 20 years or more and whose record reflects loyalty to duty."

One could search but seemingly never find a more qualified and worthy agent than this upstanding individual. In 1973, Art Godfrey celebrated his 52nd birthday on February 12, two weeks ahead of The Great One; what would have made a memorable "present" or reward for his service?

The record of Nixon's traveling companions to Key Biscayne that February 1973 was deleted from his presidential library's digitized files. However, it is a logical conclusion to reach that Arthur L.

Godfrey was assigned to go along for protection, especially on the 19th. But was he with Nixon aboard Marine One?

Furthermore, was astronaut L. Gordon Cooper participating that night? There's one problem in pinning down astronaut Cooper: *he never said a word in public that he was Gleason or Nixon's secret escort to or from Homestead.* Because the Homestead encounter is a legendary story in UFO circles and Cooper openly copped to UFO/ET stories in public, his silence here is unexpected. On the other hand, he was a Freemason, accustomed to keeping deep, encoded secrets. Professional driver and bodyguard Art Godfrey also intrigues. He passed away at age 81 in May 2002 without commenting on Nixon's private behavior or nocturnal excursions. His wife, Betty, left this world the following January. Four years earlier, Bebe Rebozo had passed away, but still, Art said nothing. Another possible side-story is that Rebozo *might* have been present during the February 19 visit to Homestead...

As we've seen, banker Charles "Bebe" Rebozo was *deeply* trusted by Richard Nixon. He was a former airline steward who grew up in the Miami area, so he knew local roadways quite well. Records show he ate dinner with Nixon at the president's Key Biscayne home that Monday night, from 6:35 to 7:00 p.m. What he did afterward will probably never be known for certain. However, Nixon's loyal White House aides were wary of Rebozo and his habit of driving the commander-in-chief around on whims. Just a few days before leaving for Florida, on February 13, a Nixon aide wrote a White House memo on how dreadful a driver Rebozo was and how he should *not* be escorting the president anywhere by automobile. Possibly this meant driving anyone else of importance to the president, so once again, we can more reasonably lean on the helicopter presumption for traveling that night. The memo was only recently discovered within Nixon's presidential library. Although initially unpublished, it can be seen now as a candid view on how Bebe's driving was considered "dangerous" and too fast, despite his having once been specially trained behind the wheel by the Secret Service.[15] The memo also mentioned that a helicopter had to be dispatched to follow Rebozo and Nixon after they took off on a road trip during a recent vacation in Florida, showing us how remarkably unlikely it was the president simply drove away from home, let alone to Gleason's house, that Monday night, February 19, 1973.

Meanwhile, there's another possibility for participation that night: Major General Walter R. Tkach[16] (1917-1989), Nixon's trusted White House physician. He participated in the Florida trip, for some unknown reason. Walt Tkach was first President Eisenhower's assistant physician, obviously a trusted military man of great integrity and healthcare knowledge. Could his very presence in Key Biscayne have been due to his needed medical-science expertise for examining bodies—perhaps *alien bodies*—and not the generally healthy president?

Dr. Tkach would have fit right in on a secure military base with dead ETs held in a kind of morgue or medical exam room. A top-notch Army medic turned Air Force surgeon, Tkach's opinion on alien physiology—and perhaps on Gleason's emotional and physical state—might have been considered quite important that February 1973. Walt had served in the U.S. Air Force in various medical positions and had previously become—most interestingly!—a member of the "Aerospace Medical Association." His was a commanding presence of high rank and bearing. On the other hand, he was likely unfamiliar with the area and Gleason's home. It is conceivable that the USAF aerospace doctor went along to the alien lab at Homestead AFB by traveling with Nixon directly by chopper. His educated surgical opinions on the physiology of the ETs would have been priceless. What is more, physicians are accustomed to keeping secrets as part of usual doctor-patient privacy agreements.

Who else might have played a role in the airbase subterfuge, perhaps even without knowing the real intent of sneaking around after hours that Monday night?

Logs show President Nixon's Press Secretary, Ronald L. Ziegler[17] (1939-2003), was along on the Biscayne trip. However, Zeigler was more likely to have been involved in keeping the media occupied and distracted at the Sheraton Four Ambassadors Hotel that night. This would have been an important part of the plan, first implemented by President Eisenhower two decades earlier, and Ron had no "need to know."

Nixon's USAF pilot Major William Shaw (1931-2016), was also around with free time on his hands. Shaw had retired as the president's Marine One helicopter co-pilot days before. Right there, at Homestead, he had posed for photos shaking hands with Nixon on Friday, February 16, 1973. No longer a part of the Executive Flight Detachment, Bill Shaw would have had the free time necessary to participate in a plot to get either Nixon or Gleason to the airbase without any fuss or fanfare. William Shaw had impressive USAF credentials and was familiar with much of the region, including the airbase and how to access it. Plus, Shaw originally worked on the flight crew handling Air Force One for President Eisenhower in 1958.[18] He spent his final years in South Florida and was buried in Palm Beach County.

Brigadier General David Emmett Rippetoe, Jr. (1925-1990) was likely on the Homestead runway to welcome any VIP visitors that night. Rippetoe became the Vice Commander of the 31st Tactical Fighter Wing, Tactical Air Command, at Homestead AFB in August 1970. David assumed top command of the unit in May 1971.[19] He was promoted to brigadier general on February 1, 1973. After experiencing the rigors of Southeast Asia, Rippetoe's squadron had been moved during Nixon's first term to Homestead and dubbed either the "31st Tactical Fighter Wing" or the "31st Civil Engineer Squadron." We should bear in mind that in 1968, according to his official USAF biography, Rippetoe became chief of the "Space Division in the Office of the Deputy Chief of Staff, Operations." What kind of *space* matters did he attend to just before Homestead? This question, left hanging in the air, lends credence to the idea that there was something going on at the base beyond mere alien corpse viewing.

Rippetoe retired June 1, 1979, and died November 19, 1990, apparently not revealing a thing publicly regarding Nixon and Gleason's nocturnal base tour. He was buried in Central Florida.[20]

Alonzo J. "Lon" Walter, Jr. (1928-) should also have been nearby. In June 1971, Walter became vice commander and later assumed full command of the 31st wing group at Homestead.[21] Walter was promoted to Brigadier General on July 1, 1974. At one point in the '60s, Walter was one of 32 semi-finalists in NASA's search for astronauts to train for space missions. In November 1966, he was assigned as the Plans Officer at the Aerospace Studies Institute at Maxwell Air Force Base. So, once again, the men in charge at Homestead had *outer space* education—not just jet flight instruction.

Walter retired in 1979 as the Deputy Director of Operations, J-3, National Military Command Center, Organization of the Joint Chiefs of Staff, Washington, D.C. Whether he has passed on as of this writing is a mystery.

Note: there was yet another "vice wing commander" at Homestead AFB: Colonel William Deming. White House records show he spent about ten minutes on a base runway with arriving President Nixon on January 12, 1973.[22] Not much else is known about him.

Any of these individuals could have been involved with ET programs and the Nixon-Gleason visit. If so, they have honored a pledge to keep silent for the rest of their days. Yet...this remains speculative. There are some logical assumptions, but we are still fuzzy on their possible participation.

Now, before we go any further, let's ask ourselves exactly *where* the alien bodies at Homestead originally came from. That is: where were the "four dead creatures" discovered, then preserved before being transferred for a top-secret examination at Homestead? After all, the South Florida installation had to get them from *somewhere*.

The best bet is Wright-Patterson Air Force Base near Dayton, Ohio. As mysteriousuniverse.com put it: "For years, it has been rumored that at Wright-Patterson, there exists a highly classified (and decidedly off-limits) series of rooms, aircraft hangars, and underground chambers, where the preserved remains of a number of dead alien creatures are stored."[23] Supposedly, the "Air Material Command, Foreign Technology Division" handles this otherworldly material in their "Blue Lab." According to the 2019 research of UFO co-authors Thomas J. Carey and Donald R. Schmitt, the Blue Lab at Wright-Patterson possessed ET cadavers and would "loan" them "to other airbases around the country throughout the years" for the purpose of diversifying medical examinations.[24] The authors included a USAF source who told his sons, for instance, that 1947 Roswell crash "bodies later went to a base in Florida."

In early 2016, UFO/ET author Raymond Szymanski described his first days on the job at Wright-Patterson AFB in January 1973. "When a mentor named Al introduced him to the Avionics Laboratory's Management Operations Office by asking, 'Have you heard about our aliens?' He said that in 1947 there was a crash down in Roswell, and they brought the machines and the aliens here for inspection and said they keep them in secret tunnels under the base." Szymanski admitted he never actually saw the ET bodies but said he had dozens of conversations with people at the base who knew the big interplanetary secret, and no one ever denied it to him.[25]

It appears Wright-Patterson was where dead aliens were imported for study by us, and Nevada's top security S-4 site was where live ETs dropped by to study us.

UFO researcher/author Leonard H. Stringfield (1920-1994) once passed along this enticing tale: "Charles Wilhelm got the story from a friend in the Army Reserve whose father worked with Project Blue Book at Wright-Patterson Field and held high security clearance. On his deathbed, he related to his son that he had seen two disc-shaped craft, one intact and one damaged, and four preserved, small alien bodies 'packed in chemicals' being examined in secret" at the Ohio base.[26] In 2012, Stringfield's research papers were donated to the Mutual UFO Network, a national investigative group of citizens, and within their pages was Jackie Gleason's contact information.

It is by now a familiar phrase: *four preserved, small alien bodies.* And what did Jackie Gleason say he saw? *Four preserved, small alien bodies.* Not big corpses, not memorably mangled ones, and not poorly maintained or decaying bodies.

Now get this: Homestead's Walter Alonzo had a 20-year-old daughter at the time of the Nixon-Gleason encounter. Terry Lee Walter (1952-), now retired from the U.S. Air Force herself (in 2010), was commissioned as a second lieutenant after college graduation in 1974 and went on to serve with great honor and distinction.[27] Where did she end up? As the Vice Commander of the USAF Air Materiel Command at Wright-Patterson Airbase!

Was this a case of like father, like daughter?

It would be great to find out the truth about the Homestead cosmic corpses from Terry today, but the idea that she'd spill top-secret and highly classified data held dear for many decades is too much to ask. Terry Walter was a mere college student in 1973 in Baton Rouge, Louisiana. It is not likely she was visiting Miami that February. She may never have been told about the otherworldly cadavers. Plus, she was supposedly only involved in logistical preparations for war planning at Wright-Patterson. She was the Director of Logistics there from August 2001 to December 2003 and likely had nothing directly to do with ET evidence. But she sure might have heard things!

Would Wright-Patterson AFB have okayed and obeyed an order to send a cargo plane bearing some of their highly prized and scrutinized crash victims? Undoubtedly, when the command came in from the highest source in the land—the president—they would have. Ironically, in 1944, U.S. Navy enlistee Richard M. Nixon was placed in charge of loading and unloading cargo planes in Papua New Guinea, during his WWII stint in the Pacific.[28] He knew how to empty military aircraft and carefully set up such crated items in airbase hangars and storage areas away from prying eyes from personal experience.

If the 1973 ETs were brought to South Florida, it's likely the armed military intelligence personnel at Homestead that night had set things up in advance and were standing by, eager to see their president but inwardly puzzled as to why TV's Ralph Kramden was

PAUL BLAKE SMITH

at their top security installation. It was unexpected at any hour, frankly. Instantly recognizable, Jackie Gleason was popular and beloved, sure, but a *civilian entertainer with no past military history or clearance,* no discernible "need to know," and probably no orders or papers to present to base officials? This must have seemed unimaginable.

Therefore, we can assume the top brass that greeted The Great Gleason on the base runway that night were tipped off in advance that he was coming with special permission granted by the commander-in-chief. Their orders were probably to greet this Master Mason cordially and respectfully, drive him over to that special base building, and remain silent about it—forever.

So, let's get back to the plot: with Jackie taken inside that secure special building via the guarded front door and escorted into a large room within what was likely a USAF Aerospace Medical Laboratory...

The sight Jackie beheld shook him up for the rest of his life (fourteen and a half years). The extraterrestrial cadavers would continue to haunt him. According to Beverly's account, "there were the aliens, lying on four separate tables." Presumably, therefore, Gleason saw four separate deceased entities from another world, stretched out on four flat medical examination tables.

Note: paranormal researcher and author Linda Moulton Howe's information asserts that at least two glass-windowed display cases of dead aliens were also present that night, set up against a wall *vertically.*[29] However, if Gleason included this detail in his discussion with Beverly, she evidently never said so.

Did Jackie immediately realize what he was staring at? It had to have nearly floored him as he absorbed the incredible sight. We can imagine his first response. A chill down his spine? His knees buckling a bit? Goosebumps? Did he think, perhaps, that he was being pranked?

More importantly: what *exactly* did the four outer space creatures look like?

"They were tiny, only about two feet tall. With small bald heads and disproportionately large ears," Bev recalled of her famous husband's description.

Very strange indeed! Almost all other ET eyewitnesses indicate that alien visitors are about four or five feet in height and, in some rare cases, up to *seven* feet tall. But *two*? The Homestead bodies were leprechaun-like, doubtlessly dwarfed by examining tables that had been built for ill or deceased human adults.

The smallish extraterrestrials had large *ears*. Certainly, this detail does not match with the MO41 crash, the Roswell event in 1947, or the 1954 Edwards Airbase encounter with President Eisenhower. However, it was a quite notable feature.

The reality of the situation must have come home to Gleason after a few moments of inspection. These strange corpses were not human, nor fakes. Perhaps shock washed over him: his face going pale and goosebumps emerging.

A near match for the Homestead aliens can be found within a controversial story from Sunday, August 21, 1955. That's when eleven members of the rural Sutton family fled their simple country home in a panic late at night.[30] The clan found their way in the dark from their farm to the Hopkinsville, Kentucky, police station with quite a story to tell.

The southwestern Kentucky family anxiously and earnestly alleged they had just engaged in a tense gun battle with some strange outer space creatures. The inquisitive ETs didn't fire back, but they wandered around the Sutton property, playfully peeking in windows and doorways. The unnerved men of the Sutton crew grabbed their shotguns and blasted away at them. They apparently hit their targets, at times, with no effect. The Suttons estimated that there might have been as many as ten to fifteen creatures.

The extraterrestrials were said to have been about two feet tall and gray in color. Frustratingly, the local media dubbed them "little green men," and this misinformation stuck and "went viral," as we say today. "Little green men" became a catchphrase one might hear to this day. These ETs allegedly sported noticeably *large, pointy ears.*

PAUL BLAKE SMITH

They had thin arms and legs with chesty bodies. They also featured glowing, yellow-rimmed eyes and no noses on their bald heads. The elf-like aliens sported a line, or thin slit, in place of a mouth. They wore what looked to be a type of metal plating.

Those disproportionately large ears provide a memorable detail that stands out for the Suttons, Gleason, and us today. It is a specific description that also matches what the Broad Haven schoolchildren in England saw in 1977[31]—and what many others in France reported seeing in 1954.[32] The kids recalled seeing "pointy-eared goblin-like creatures."

In 1978, movie director Steven Spielberg planned a sequel to his smash hit *Close Encounters of the Third Kind*. It was supposed to be called *Night Skies*[33] and feature the 1955 Kentucky ETs who looked like impish "gremlins"—the title of a 1984 movie that Spielberg produced, with creatures strongly resembling what Gleason and the rural Kentucky family reported seeing. UFO expert Dr. J. Allen Hynek personally informed Spielberg about the little alien creatures from 1955, and, knowing Jackie Gleason, he was likely aware of the amazing allegation too. However, Spielberg ditched the film idea and soon turned to directing a taller, more cuddly cinema creation: *E.T., The Extraterrestrial.*[34]

A pair of responding Kentucky police officers who journeyed to the Sutton property early that August morning mentioned hearing that the "little men" had reappeared around 3:30 a.m., and yet the cops only found greatly agitated Sutton family members clutching their guns. However, some local policemen also reported seeing three disc-like aerial vehicles earlier that summer. One cop said, "I know I saw them. And if I saw them, the [Sutton] story certainly could be true." In 1955, the Suttons also claimed to have witnessed a metallic disc parked in their backyard near the woods. One or two eyewitnesses agreed, claiming to have seen it land quietly.

Like the undamaged Kentucky ETs from mid-1955, Gleason did not recall to his wife any visible injuries on the four creatures he inspected at Homestead. Yet "they must have been dead for some time because they'd been embalmed," Gleason allegedly noted to his wife. How did he learn that? Someone in the know must have informed him during this scrutiny. At least, from this detail, we can assume that the four little humanoids were well-preserved and natural-looking—not decaying, with exposed inner organs or bones. If they had truly been embalmed, how long they had been in America's possession is anyone's guess.

Many questions arise. Did Jackie *touch* the entities? Did he pick one up and squeeze it, perhaps believing at first that it was a doll? Did the ETs sport any clothing? Have teeth or hair? Fingers and toes? Have gender differences? How did they die? In short, there are many questions and no answers to relay.

Human cadavers can be examined, inside and out, and then stitched back together before postmortem embalming. Had this been done with the tiny ETs? Jackie did not recollect seeing surgical stitches or open cuts in the skin of the Homestead space beings, and he had that amazing photographic memory. However, we must recall that we're relying on Beverly McKittrick Gleason's ten-year-old memory of their late-night conversation, edited to fit within a one-page *National Enquirer* article.

According to Bev's 1983 tabloid article, Jackie told her that Monday night: "No one would tell me the full details, but a spacecraft has obviously crashed near here." That's a bit of a leap to a conclusion since an alien craft could have crashed *anywhere* on earth, and the deceased could have been moved around the nation in the hushed aftermath. If the ET bodies were undamaged, it may not have been a traumatic spaceship crash that killed them. Perhaps the cause of death was a virus or asphyxiation, a result of the off-world beings stepping out of their safe vehicle and being unable to cope with our atmosphere.

Plus, "*no one* would tell me..." confirms that Gleason was not alone and asked questions of those around him at the Homestead facility.

The aforementioned American Army's *Special Operations Manual*

PAUL BLAKE SMITH

1-01, dated April 1954, was leaked some decades after its printing. It is truly a blockbuster document, with shocking details and instructions for its military intelligence personnel. It mentioned crash recoveries and how to package the ET corpses without the public learning the truth, even if it meant lying to the press and the populace in covering their tracks. It was for the overall good of the nation. At least four different races of extraterrestrials were said to have been encountered by recovery teams as of 1954. None of the races described in the manual's pages closely matched the Gleason description or the Hopkinsville, Kentucky, case. Overall, the shocking manual did not say that four known species were *all* that had been discovered as of 1954. The booklet's text asserted that various alien corpses were to be taken by special Army teams to the "W-P Blue Lab," near Dayton, Ohio, the same site mentioned earlier.

Additionally, a once-classified *Operation Majestic* briefing document from the Defense Intelligence Agency—dated January 1989 and leaked to radio hostess Heather Wade in 2017—made some reference to the American government's collection of dead aliens and their crash-landed spaceships. It states: "The remains of seven flying crafts and the bodies of twenty-seven deceased non-human beings have been recovered as of this briefing data, and are at present being studied by MAJIC-12 scientists." We see that Majestic operatives were not only discovering amazing crashes but also *still* examining the retrieved specimens in presumably top-secret laboratories—perhaps just like Homestead AFB's remote building.

Gleason's close examination of the bodies probably took only a few minutes. He had to have been weak in the knees but held up well enough to make it back outside, past the guard, with the strength to lift his right arm. It was (most likely) time to take a solemn oath of secrecy for life. "This did not happen, you know nothing of these matters here," he was undoubtedly warned before departing.

At this point, Jackie Gleason was most likely driven back to the helicopter and taken straight home. First, to Lauderhill's golf course chopper pad, then he likely made it back to his house via his golf cart since he didn't like to walk anywhere.

The absolute truth on ET visitation had been *right there* before Jackie's eyes, yet the poor soul couldn't take any snapshots or notes —let alone sneak home any hard proof as a souvenir. His hosts wouldn't tell him any great details about the circumstances of the aliens. Jackie Gleason was somberly sworn to uphold a promise of silence. It seems logical to conclude he was somewhat dazed and frustrated on the ride home, probably lighting up cigarette after cigarette, lost in thought. More than likely, they sent Gleason home with just an Air Force helicopter pilot who later flew back alone to the base from Inverrary.

Once at his front door, the shaken comic searched his pockets for his house key. If he had, for example, driven himself home, parked his car, and entered his Inverrary house by way of the garage, one would assume the interior doors were left unlocked. Gleason would only need a key to open the *front* door. Photos show Glea Manor had a built-in garage.

Emotional Jackie stepped in from the foyer and made his way to the living room, likely with one eye already on the bar. He flopped into his comfy armchair, Beverly recollected, white-faced and spent. Under questioning, Jackie promptly spilled his guts. Mrs. Gleason must have run the gamut of emotions as she listened to the slight tremble in his voice and stared at his blanched face. *This was no joke.*

Visibly upset, Gleason proceeded to blurt out nearly everything he had just been warned to keep to himself. *That's* how rattled he was. He had that darn photographic memory, and he'd never forget those creepy dead ETs. The vivid experience was locked in his mind, *tormenting* him for years to come.

When his evening's recount was finished, Gleason undoubtedly swigged back quite a shot of booze and inhaled deeply on a ciggie, lost in thought. Beverly must have been shocked, too.

To make matters worse, Jackie grew increasingly embittered, Beverly recalled in her 1983 *Enquirer* article. He began railing aloud.

PAUL BLAKE SMITH

The blasted government! Why wouldn't they admit the truth? Why wouldn't they release at least *some* exciting facts and artifacts to the American people? Damn it all! *Why* the great secrecy? The reality angered and flustered Jackie greatly, Beverly said. He soon had trouble eating meals, sleeping, and focusing. Working seemed out of the question as he couldn't concentrate during the days, weeks, and months to come. Beverly noticed that Jackie began to smoke and drink more heavily. It is possible his excesses were an attempt to put the chilling sights at Homestead out of his photographic mind or allay his frustration at the government's policy of staying mum or outright ridiculing UFO eyewitness accounts in America.

All in all, the situation didn't help the couple's marriage. Within a year, they split up.

But John Herbert "Jackie" Gleason had his hard proof and shocking truth at last. That, at least, was a great relief. The question of ET visitation was now answered beyond a doubt. His lifelong quest for the facts was resolved.

Nearing midnight on February 19, 1973, Jackie emphasized to Beverly that he *wasn't* lying or joking. "I swear it's true and I'll never forget it. Ever." He *meant* it, *every word*, it dawned on Mrs. Gleason.

That night, and in the days and nights to come, The Great Gleason became, at times, upbeat and excited. He was feeling privileged to have gone through a special experience that no other civilian (and few military or government representatives) had. He was often "giddy," Bev recalled. "It was something that had a profound effect on him," she remembered. Before long, though, his emotions would race back in the opposite direction again, furious and frustrated with the feds. "They know all about them," Jackie would thunder angrily, but the military and the government "keep denying that they exist and painting people who believe in them as idiots!"

When one ponders this deeply emotional reaction, it seems impossible to dismiss Jackie Gleason's story as an impromptu, flimsy, or fictional excuse for his absence one evening.

At some point after his revelation to Beverly, Jackie stood up and trudged off to bed. It had been an incredibly long, wearying day—likely the most remarkable and memorable of his entire life. His celebrity golf tournament was just getting underway, and he was expected back out on the course the next morning with a smile and a swing.

Naturally, Jackie experienced great trouble sleeping, which was actually par for the course for the longtime insomniac. But this was worse. All of his books, his talent, his showbiz memories, his smarts, his liquor...he'd need them all to get through the lonely dark hours that night and in the nights to come. Maybe he could speak out and defy his oath? No. He just *couldn't*. It might put his or his wife's life at risk. It could even endanger his two daughters from his first marriage.

The emotional entertainer was still babbling on about the experience for days, Beverly wrote. This is another strong indication he had not related some sort of tall tale to Beverly. Jackie continued to stew, growing increasingly bitter over the official government coverup. It even affected his appetite. According to the History Channel's *MUFON, Hangar 1* in 2014, the flabbergasted and traumatized Gleason "couldn't eat for three weeks" after the encounter.[35] He was apparently unable to cope well with bland, everyday reality after the exciting ET realities hidden at Homestead. The enforced silence was killing him. He wanted to tell the whole world.

Gleason evidently concluded to his fascinated spouse that the aliens were friendly, perhaps reasoning that he knew of no attack on America nor any other part of the world. They were probably "coming from a friendly place," Beverly quoted Jackie directly ten years after their memorable conversation. "We should communicate with them!" For Gleason, "we" probably meant the U.S. government space exploration programs. However, with his high-frequency radio sets in the upstairs spare bedroom, it is possible Jackie meant that *he and Beverly* should try to contact aliens too.

As mentioned in the previous chapter, Jackie's airbase encounter

PAUL BLAKE SMITH

with deceased visitors from beyond the stars confirmed something he had recently learned from an astronaut. The interaction occurred while "co-hosting a TV show," Beverly Gleason wrote in the 1983 *Enquirer* article. Gleason had taken that NASA employee aside and candidly admitted to him backstage that he believed in UFOs. They truly exist, the astronaut replied. He knew this for certain because he had "seen one with my own eyes during our mission" in space. But the United States government wanted all talk of aliens and their mysterious craft squelched, so he was "sworn to secrecy."

Beverly stated in her tabloid article that Jackie was thrilled to have his suspicions confirmed by such a serious, experienced man. She summed up: "Actually seeing the bodies of those aliens" at Homestead "was the final proof." This indicates the airbase visit happened sometime *after* the astronaut discussion. Therefore, Jackie must have been telling his wife about his own string of appearances in November 1972 as co-host of *The Mike Douglas Show*.[36] That daily talk show flew to Miami and set up shop to produce two weeks of programs just after the re-election of the president. The first show aired on November 13, 1972, the day after one of Nixon's flights from Homestead AFB back to Washington D.C., and the last show aired on November 24. Jackie made sure his favorite South Florida pals were guests, including the governor of the Sunshine State and the mayor of Miami Beach. Unfortunately, online records of the other guests don't list a U.S. astronaut, but the Douglas program appears to have been the only television show that Jackie Gleason ever *co*-hosted, and the online description of the guests who were on the late 1972 programs with Gleason may simply not be complete. Additionally, we know that NASA astronauts resided in South Florida, not far from Gleason's home, and would have been a natural inclusion on such a show.

Who exactly *was* this mysterious USAF pilot turned astronaut? Beverly described him as "one of the early American adventurers in space," apparently indicating he might not have been one of the recent moon mission astronauts. Once again, Leroy Gordon Cooper fits the description perfectly. During his sixth mission in space, executing 22 orbits around Earth, Cooper reported seeing a strange greenish-glowing object. It was on May 15, 1963—in the early years of NASA's programs—when then-Major Cooper saw this unexplained disc "with a faint red glow on one side," while making his final orbit of planet Earth in a NASA space capsule. Supposedly, 200 persons in a tracking station watched the UFO in their monitoring equipment as the craft approached Cooper's vehicle. It then turned and veered out into space. Cooper's comments on the UFO were reported by NBC television.[37] But when he and his team landed, NASA informed the media that they would not be permitted to ask questions on the matter.

Was this startling incident something he shared with Jackie Gleason behind the scenes of a TV show? Cooper had a full ten years to relate the story before the comic's February 19, 1973, encounter at Homestead since both men were based out of South Florida.

One other possibility is astronaut John "Jack" Swigert, Jr. (1931-1982), who appeared on the *Mike Douglas Show* earlier in November 1972. Although Gleason is not listed online as a fellow guest—he would be in just a week or so. Swigert died some eight months before Bev Gleason's article was published, perhaps spurring her to go ahead and tell the backstage tale. Still, by the summer of 1983, she could have used Swigert's name in the article but didn't.

In returning to late Monday night, February 19, 1973...we must understand now that Jackie Gleason's claims *all fit within a proper timeline*. His tale, filtered through Beverly, seems chronologically possible and believable, including the finer details and emotional reactions he had experienced. It all adds up. His account seems pretty solid.

After the publication of Beverly's riveting 1983 article, with its color front-page photo of an aging Jackie, more notoriety and controversy spread regarding the sensational claim, unchanged over the course of the decade. Once more, the entertainer would have easily been able to disprove and dismiss the story if he chose, but Gleason

PAUL BLAKE SMITH

tellingly remained silent. He didn't publicly slam his ex-wife as crazy, drunk, exaggerating, or delusional. He did not accuse Beverly of getting too creative or whipping up a story for money or attention. Keep in mind that, by August 1983, Jackie likely hadn't even *seen* Beverly in nearly a decade. He probably only kept in touch by way of his lawyer, Hugo Black, and via signed alimony checks in the mail. His movie career had taken off again, and Bev was just a faded memory.

We know that Jackie Gleason did see Beverly's startling *National Enquirer* article—as she had to have known he would. Predictably livid, he got on the phone and had a few choice words for his ex-wife all over again, just like after the September 1974 *Enquirer* story. Perhaps his personal attorney also telephoned Beverly and angrily reminded her of stipulations within the divorce paperwork, ones that were related to keeping quiet. Now it was Bev's turn to be rattled. She abruptly ditched her tell-all book idea altogether, and only a few stories about the aging superstar's private occult beliefs were bandied about in the press in the years to come, overshadowed by articles about his fading health.

As the hubbub died down, Beverly slipped back into the background once more, getting on with her post-Jackie life in her native Maryland.

In hindsight, just about everything that Jackie Gleason was accustomed to doing professionally ground to a halt, or nearly so, after his alleged Homestead encounter. These facts lend more credence to Bev's account: that it did happen and cut him to the quick. Here's a list of examples of how deeply affected Gleason's career was...

1. Jackie didn't act in a TV show until the fall, when he appeared in a single one-hour rehash of *The Honeymooners* on CBS, airing on November 11, 1973.[38] His familiar Ralph Kramden character required little effort, frankly, and was his only substantial project of the year.

2. Jackie didn't act in a motion picture for the remainder of the year. In fact, he wouldn't act in a movie until 1976, when filming his scenes for *Smokey and the Bandit*[39] and a rather strange flop of a picture called *Mr. Billion*,[40] both released in 1977.

3. Jackie only acted in two TV commercials that year—a pair of 30-second ads for the latest General Electric televisions that first aired in September 1973.

4. Jackie didn't make any cameo or guest appearances on anyone else's television show, minus his brief participation in a one-hour tribute to a fellow comedian that aired in October.

5. Jackie didn't appear on the stage—either through stand-up comedy or performing a role in a theatrical play—in all of 1973.

6. Jackie didn't produce a single or full-length record album in 1973, breaking his streak of creating one every single year since 1952. In fact, he would never again produce a record of new music or comedy.

7. Jackie didn't make any radio appearances in 1973, not even for an interview (apparently).

8. Jackie didn't give any magazine or newspaper interviews, either (apparently).

9. Jackie didn't write his memoirs; that's for sure. He evidently did not write any film scripts, TV sketches, nor music.

10. Jackie didn't play in anyone else's celebrity golf tournament for the rest of 1973, televised or not (apparently). He did, however, show up and play golf in his own pro-am that week in February. Home movie camera footage (now available online) shows him scooting around on the course in a cart, often with comedian Bob Hope.

The whole enticing story might have died out completely if it were not for the laudable investigatory powers of determined UFO researcher Kenny Young (1966-2005)[41], an author from Ohio who passed away at the age of 38 from leukemia. Before his untimely demise, he looked up the former Mrs. Gleason, still living in the Baltimore area—Easton, Maryland[42]—in the summer of 2003, and attempted once more to get the complete story on Jackie's supposed alien encounter. At the time, Beverly was not quite seventy years old and was remarkably quite unwilling to change or retract her *Enquirer* claims in any way. She also had almost nothing else to add to it. She did, however, help clear up something important.

Writing at length for presidentialufo.com afterward, Kenny described speaking to Beverly by telephone. She reasserted to him that she recalled her *first* printed interview on the unusual topic was with *Esquire* magazine and that it featured a photo of Jackie and a sub-headline about him on its cover. Again, this is not correct, but it is an understandable mistake. Gleason appeared on the cover of *several* magazines and newspapers in his time, but *Esquire* covers from 1973 to 1975 do not show Jackie whatsoever.

Beverly repeated to Kenny Young the same story she told in the *National Enquirer* articles, with one notable difference. She made mention of a key figure who previously had been left out of the Homestead tour. Someone important who was *there* alongside Jackie.

Who was it?

Answer: *President Nixon!*

In Bev's August 1983 *National Enquirer* article, she made no mention of Richard M. Nixon actually *being* at Homestead. She had only repeated Jackie's claim of arriving and being shown things "arranged by President Nixon."

An emotional Jackie, Beverly fully explained to Kenny in 2003, had come home late that night and claimed that he was *with* President Nixon at the local base. He claimed that it was Richard Milhous Nixon who had been his Homestead tour guide. In the *Enquirer* articles, the president's involvement was not mentioned or made clear.

This notion was reasonably believable to Beverly because, in those halcyon days, Mr. Nixon was "in contact quite a bit" with her then-husband. Bev had even met President Nixon once, while everyone was having a drink by a swimming pool. She postulated that the Florida airbase visit was likely arranged in advance by communicative and supportive aides on both sides, just as get-togethers between the famous duo had been in the past. However, she made it clear that Nixon was definitely *there*. Perhaps we can speculate reasonably that the president picked him up at Lauderhill in his helicopter—via the Inverrary course landing pad visited earlier—and they flew together to Homestead. Perhaps President Nixon showed the comedian around the large lab-like room as the "host" for the evening—an important detail that got lost in the retelling decades earlier.

The most likely candidate for coordinating the special airbase visit was Sydell Spear (1930-1993), Jackie's longtime, loyal secretary.[43] She received extra money from Gleason's revised will, changed by the ill entertainer the day before he died. Sydell was cheerful and discreet, experienced in keeping Gleason's secrets. In 1973, she lived in Hialeah and might well have taken and placed calls to any Nixon representative in arranging a piloted chopper to and from Homestead on that Monday night, all without knowing exactly what was waiting for her boss at the installation.

A second strong candidate to have acted as a go-between is Jackie's personal appellate attorney, Hugo Black, Jr.[44] He had been in South Florida for many years and knew solid, trustworthy locals to help arrange certain legal matters—but it is possible he had connections in the military or government as well. Hugo Black had met President Nixon at his father's D.C. funeral in late September 1971, after the just-retired Supreme Court Justice Hugo Black, Sr., died of a stroke. Hugo lived in Pinecrest, just 17 miles north of Homestead AFB, where he died at age 91. But that was still some 42 miles south of Gleason's beloved Lauderhill.

To her credit, even in 2003, Beverly McKittrick did not

embellish her account to make it sound more wild or self-aggrandizing. Thirty years had passed since the event, along with Gleason and Nixon themselves, but at last, this key part of the story was cleared up. Kenny Young simply wrote the facts, published online on July 9 and August 6, 2003, through Canadian UFO researcher Grant Cameron's aforementioned site. Grocery store tabloids had nothing to do with this update. The issue was now a bit clearer to a more open, modern audience, aided by the long reach of the world wide web.

In their conversation, Beverly also confirmed to Kenny that she had ditched the idea of a tell-all book in 1983 when Jackie's reaction to the second *National Enquirer* story was so alarmingly hostile. She admitted that she had never even gotten words down on paper. It seems likely she never will. We are the poorer for it, bereft of the entertaining showbiz and supernatural tales Bev could have aired.

Jackie Gleason remained mum about the Homestead visit—he took any account of his own to his grave. Again, at one point in the mid-'70s, Jackie Gleason did say in an interview that he had finally witnessed something exciting in the Florida sky. "These were "definitely not objects made on our planet. They weren't secret weapons but were solid craft.'" At least one of these daytime sightings occurred, evidently, while he was out walking on a beach, possibly on the soft white sand in front of the waterfront home he ditched by 1971 to move to Lauderhill's country club. That was about all he was willing to say in public.

In what Jackie did spill to Beverly, The Great One appears to have relayed the basic facts as candidly as he could recall them. However, is it possible there were *more* experiences that night that he withheld? There might well have been other important details he accidentally or deliberately left out to shorten his explanation or protect certain individuals involved. Many *more* questions and issues remain unanswered, and they probably always will be. For instance...

1. Where did the four dead aliens come from? What was their home planet, galaxy, or dimension? How did they get to Earth, and why?

2. Did the aliens crash-land a ship somewhere in America? If so, what are the details of that crash? What were they trying to accomplish when they died?

3. If the aliens had no visible injuries, *how* did they perish? Did anyone try to revive them before death? Were they peaceful? Did they have weapons or abducted humans with them when found?

4. Who brought the aliens to Homestead AFB, and when? Was it under Nixon's order to show them off to Gleason? Were they first housed at the "W-P Blue Lab"[45] near Dayton, Ohio?

5. Did Nixon or Gleason do or see anything *else* unusual or otherworldly at the base that night? Who left the military installation first? What aide was with the president that night? Did he have Secret Service protection the entire time?

6. Who, if anyone, was with Nixon and Gleason?

7. Were any military personnel living at the base exposed to the aliens that night? Was everyone gathered and sworn to secrecy that night, just to be sure?

8. Was there any discussion of President Nixon, or perhaps a future chief executive, revealing the ET finds to the nation? Why did the bodies have to be kept such a big secret?

9. Were the aliens really embalmed? Were they just preserved naturally because they had a different physical composition than humans? Were they cut open and given autopsies, either before or after the Nixon-Gleason visit? Was that what the special Homestead building was designed for?

10. Was anyone else allowed in to see the alien discoveries that night or at any other time? Are there any photos, films, or reports—any tangible artifacts—of the creatures that Gleason saw?

So much remains mysterious. So far, no one has come forward with their own corroborating story from that night nor submitted evidence or testimony anonymously.

As of 1986, Jackie became increasingly ill with liver and colon cancer, emphysema, and other serious, debilitating health problems, including heart disease, phlebitis, and diabetes. His comically rubbery body was finally collapsing on him. He bravely managed one last movie role in 1986 but spent a lot of his final two years in and out of South Florida doctor's offices, cancer clinics, and treatment centers. Unfortunately, Jackie doesn't seem to have dictated any sort of Homestead admission to be released postmortem. He was allegedly a Master Mason, accustomed to being sworn to secrecy, even to the end. Perhaps he was regretful that he had slipped up—just once—to his genuinely concerned wife.

Jackie was hospitalized in the spring of 1987, but he eventually insisted on going home to die. In late June, The Great Gleason was taken home by ambulance, led by Marilyn, determined to honor Jackie's wishes. He was gently placed in his own Glea Manor bed and received almost no visitors and very few phone calls (one that *was* patched through was from his TV wife, Audrey Meadows). At the end, he could barely speak. He was weak and medicated for the pain as his body deteriorated. A day before his demise, Jackie asked for his will to be changed by his other attorney, Brian Patchen. He was feeling more affection for his two daughters and his longtime secretary, who was like a daughter to him. He died in his Glea Manor bedroom as Inverrary club members golfed outside his windows on Wednesday, June 24, 1987. Again, there was evidently no deathbed confession. It was a sad, silent end for the gifted, garrulous Great Gleason.

Beverly McKittrick Gleason, living in Maryland, had no public comment on her ex's demise. Of course, neither did Richard Milhous Nixon, then living in New Jersey[46] as a grandfather and retired statesman, trying to rescue his tarnished reputation with a series of self-serving books.

Media obituaries concentrated solely on Jackie's impressive career in showbiz, especially *The Honeymooners*. There was little mention of the entertainer's fascination with the mysteries of the occult. Just after death, his body was kept in a closed casket for a public viewing in a North Miami funeral home. He was buried not long after in a large white vault in a private Miami cemetery, with only a small, invited circle of loved ones in attendance. When contacted some years later about the Homestead incident, Marilyn Taylor Gleason wrote back to a UFO researcher [47] rather enigmatically: "So sorry, we cannot be of any help to you." She didn't say she *knew* nothing, just that the family—"we"—chose not to offer any help. Marilyn died in 2019.

But was that truly the end of the remarkable matter?

---

1. Wikipedia contributors, "National Enquirer," *Wikipedia*.
2. Wikipedia contributors, "Lauderhill, Florida," *Wikipedia*.
3. Nixon presidential library, December 1972: Trivia: President Nixon once posed for photos in the White House with the publisher and CEO of the *National Enquirer*, Henry O. Dormann (1932-2018). Hours after that December 5, 1972, get-together, Nixon spoke on the phone to three Apollo 7 astronauts, long distance to Cape Kennedy in South Florida.
4. Photos and data available on *Zillow*, as of 2021.
5. Charles Feiglstok, "Away He Goes, or Does He? The Strange Jackie Gleason Caper," *People magazine*, March 24, 1975.
6. Stephanie Nolasco, "Gleason Embraced..."
7. For a review of Esquire issues of the 1970s, go to https://www.backissues.com/publications/Esquire-1970s
8. This author, unfortunately, could not find a copy to read.
9. John Franch, "The Secret Life of J. Allen Hynek," *The Skeptical Inquirer*, Jan/Feb 2013.
10. John Greenewald, "Jackie Gleason and the Pickled Aliens," *The Black Vault*, May 25, 2015.
11. "How Sweet It Ain't: The Jackie Gleasons Split," *People*, March 24, 1975.

12. Beverly Gleason, "Jackie Gleason Saw the Bodies of Space Aliens at Air Force Base," *The National Enquirer*, Number 556, August 16, 1983.
13. "Arthur Godfrey," *Washington Post*, May 13, 2002.
14. "Arthur Lincoln 'Rawhide' Godfrey," May 2003.
15. Stephen Bull, "Bebe Rebozo's Driving," *Nixon library*, February 13, 1973.
16. Wikipedia contributors, "Walter Tkach," *Wikipedia*.
17. Wikipedia contributors, "Ron Ziegler," *Wikipedia*.
18. "MAJ William Henry 'Bill' Shaw."
19. "David Rippetoe," *Tampa Bay Times*, updated 2005.
20. Craig Basse, "David Rippetoe, former deputy at MacDill command," October 18, 2005.
21. "Brig. Gen Alonzo J. Walter Jr.," *Military Hall of Honor*.
22. Daily Presidential Records, Nixon library.
23. Nick Redfern, "Are There Really Dead Aliens Stored Away in Military Facilities?" November 2021.
24. Carey and Schmitt did excellent research in their 2013 book *Inside the Real Area 51: The Secret History of Wright-Patterson*, by Weiser Books.
25. Paul Seaburn, "Connections between Wright-Patterson AFB, Ray Szymanski and hidden aliens," *Mysterious Universe*, September 2017.
26. Vicky Verma, "Are There Crashed UFOs & Dead Alien Bodies In So-Called Hangar 18 of Ohio Military Base?" *Hows and Whys*, December 2021.
27. Wikipedia contributors, "Terry Lee Gabreski (nee Walter)," *Wikpedia*.
28. Wikipedia contributors, "Papua New Guinea," *Wikipedia*.
29. *Earthfiles.com* subscriber content
30. "1955: The Hopkinsville Alien Invasion," *Think About It*, updated March 18, 2021.
31. Marcus Lowth, "The Bizarre and Forgotten Broad Haven School UFO Incident of 1977," *UFO Insight*, February 21, 2017.
32. "1954 French UFO Humanoid Encounters."
33. Wikipedia contributors, "Night Skies," *Wikipedia*.
34. Wikipedia contributors, "E.T., The Extra Terrestrial," *Wikipedia*.
35. Mitch Marcus director,"Presidential Encounters," *Hangar 1: The UFO Files*, 2014.
36. The Mike Douglas Show, November 1972.
37. "Major Gordon Cooper, USA Astronaut, and UFOs," *Unexplainable.net*, October 4, 2004.
38. Wikipedia contributors,"List of The Honeymooners Sketches," *Wikipedia*.
39. Wikipedia contributors, "Smokey and the Bandit," *Wikipedia*.
40. Wikipedia contributors,"Mr. Billion," *Wikipedia*.
41. Kenny Young Archives.
42. Wikipedia contributors, "Easton, MD," *Wikpedia*.
43. Mary Williams, "Sydell Spear, Devoted Employee of Jackie Gleason," *South Florida Sun Sentinel*, December 27, 1993.
44. Wikipedia contributors, "Hugo Black, Jr.," *Wikipedia*.
45. Anthony Braglia, "Opening the Door to 'The Blue Room' - Where UFO Debris is Hidden," *UFO Chronicles*, June 13, 2012.
46. Christopher Maag, "Bergen County Became Richard Nixon's Adopted Home," *The Daily Record*, August 10, 2014.
47. Various articles by Tim Beckley and Kenny Young on Jackie Gleason & Richard Nixon.

CHAPTER FOUR

NIXON AND GLEASON—AND EISENHOWER

"Volunteers from our armed forces have participated in diplomatic and cultural exchanges with ETs in the 1970s."

White House logs show that on the "morning after"—Tuesday, February 20, 1973—President Nixon was ready for breakfast at 8:19 a.m. He then chatted with government contacts in person and on the phone, and nothing seemingly out of the ordinary was going on. There is no record of his actions from 8:35 to 10:16, but that might have been time spent packing and getting ready to leave town. The president and his entourage walked out to the helipad and took Marine One to—naturally—Homestead Airbase.

Did anyone at the airbase recognize the arriving president from the night before? Whatever the case, records show that Nixon and his party boarded Air Force One at 10:35 a.m. and took off, back to business, first in South Carolina and then D.C. Upon arriving home at 3:00 p.m., the president oddly skipped the White House and went straight to his special office within the Executive Office Building next door. There, he met with some aides, then with top NSA adviser Dr.

Henry Kissinger at 4:15. Could this have been related to his recent secret meeting with Gleason?

The research findings of UFO investigator/writer Tony Brunt were first reported in 2011, after interviewing Mrs. Maria Wang, the Albuquerque-based widow of Air Force scientist Dr. Eric Wang, in 1984. In the '50s, Wang was a protégé of Henry Kissinger. Before his death in 1960, Dr. Wang was a key behind-the-scenes player as "an academic and consultant to various intelligence and military programs," reporting to Kissinger.[1] Maria remembered meeting Henry several times in the study of her family's home. She declared to Brunt that her husband had been helping the government secretly reverse-engineer alien spacecraft at Kirtland Airbase in New Mexico. This location, about one hundred miles south of Los Alamos National Laboratories, has long been rumored as a site for examining alien recoveries. "He is deeply involved in the flying saucer program," Maria said of Kissinger. "In fact, he was completely in charge of it at the time that Eric was still alive and involved with it." Dr. Wang was a Special Studies director at Wright-Patterson AFB during the Eisenhower years, from 1952 to 1956, until the project was moved to Sandia National Laboratories in Albuquerque.

In returning to President Nixon's February 20, 1973, schedule...after some closed-door discussions with Dr. Kissinger and dinner, he trooped upstairs to his White House residence at 8:21 p.m. It was the end of a long day—especially if Mr. Nixon had not gone to bed until close to midnight the night before.

Apparently, no one suspected a thing. Despite their close proximity at the hotel and golf course the day before, the media was apparently clueless. While Gleason's golf tournament continued that ensuing week, life at the White House went on without a hitch, with the president attending to public governing policy and private Watergate strategies. That went on for the rest of the month, if not the year. The ugly scandals that eventually engulfed his administration slowly mounted in 1973 and suffocated him in 1974. He gave up the fight and left office in August of that year and fled to his upscale California beachfront home.[2]

In hindsight, there might be two significant matters to highlight regarding the friendship between Nixon and Gleason during this time.

First, the twosome evidently never played golf together again. In fact, there seems to be no record of their meeting in person after February 1973, and Gleason didn't mention Nixon much, if at all, in his media interviews after that point. Was there something going on that caused the bitterness and breakup?

Secondly, Jackie's bold public offer to provide up to one million dollars to anyone with indisputable proof of ET visitation seemed to dry up. This author cannot find a record of Gleason discussing that tantalizing financial offer ever again.

Could it be that, once home at Glea Manor in the days after Homestead, Gleason wrote Nixon a check or series of checks to be dispensed by a trusted operative? Was there a grand total of one million dollars to help hush up Nixon's henchmen? Was that projected exchange the end of their friendship? This is purely speculative, of course, but the timing seems pretty precise here. Again, there is no smoking gun proof that Gleason ever paid Nixon a dime for the viewing of Homestead Airbase's amazing contents—but *so* many friendships are lost over the issue of giving or lending money, even in private. The various ways that donors slipped Nixon money were creative in those shady days.

But hold on there. What about the one-year anniversary of the February 1973 visit to Homestead? Was there any suspicious activity going on regarding Key Biscayne or Miami and the beleaguered U.S. president?

In a word: *yes.*

On Wednesday, February 13, 1974, President Nixon and his entourage flew from Washington to Homestead Airbase in the late afternoon. Within Nixon's White House records, two relevant pages have been removed and dubbed "restricted documents."[3] One was the passenger manifest listing who traveled aboard Air Force One with the president. This is reminiscent of the subterfuge a year earlier, but it gets worse...

The next day, February 14, Nixon toured a Miami hospital before meeting with the head of the FCC from 2:00 to 3:00 pm. And then...*nothing*. Suddenly the trail goes cold, and nothing is recorded for the rest of the day, which is *most* unusual. Yes, supportive documents were occasionally removed or obfuscated, but to leave the appointment log blank? Additionally, there is nothing logged for *the entire next day*. A note simply informs all: "The Office of the Presidential Papers and Archives did not receive any information on the president's activities for this day." What was going on in Florida?

The record of Saturday's schedule is also unprecedented in its enigmatic incompleteness. Nixon's actions on February 16, 1974, were barely mentioned. He spoke to two U.S. politicians on the phone from 10:46 to 10:56 a.m. That's it. The normally meticulous logging "just happened" to have stopped at this critical time.

On Sunday, President Nixon is only noted as having met with a lawyer from 2:00 to 2:17 p.m., and nothing else was put down in print at all.

Aides noted later in life that the Nixons rarely went to church, so their Sundays were quite open to any activity. However, if Richard Nixon was busy in the community on that particular Sunday, it went weirdly unrecorded. *The previous three and a half days are a complete mystery.* There were no domestic or foreign crises going on to attend to in private. That's why Nixon was able to fly to Florida for his break in the first place, right? Nor was there any shocking breaking news on the unfolding Watergate fiasco during this time frame.

This behavior, coming as it did almost exactly twenty years after the Eisenhower-ET incident of 1954 and one year after the Gleason affair, is obviously deeply suspicious. The logs were normally kept meticulously, but it appears Nixon ordered his secretary to not record certain actions and meetings during this time. It is also clear

PAUL BLAKE SMITH

that he made sure information was removed from what was published for the public years later.

Precise record-keeping finally resumed on Monday, February 18, 1974. The presidential daily diary only begins around 10:00 a.m., which is later than normal. On this day, documents show that Nixon spoke by telephone to his Secretary of State, then flew by helicopter to—you guessed it—Homestead Air Force Base.

The files show that Nixon then boarded Air Force One on the Homestead runway for a trip to Huntsville, Alabama, where some of the U.S. space programs are based. His specific destination was published in the presidential daily appointment log as the Redstone Arsenal, an Army Intelligence post adjacent to Huntsville.[4] The commander-in-chief arrived at 1:05 p.m. and was received by the Redstone base commander, among others. After attending to a Boy Scout event nearby, Nixon returned to the Arsenal again at 2:42 p.m. and entered the "Base Operations Building." While there, he met with some Republican dignitaries, but any other actions are unknown. He apparently departed around 3:00.

Why is this significant? In the 1989 secret Defense Intelligence Agency briefing documents that were leaked in 2017, a section of the report mentions that government extraterrestrial investigations were carried out by a covert research team called MAJESTIC, or MAJIC-12. "Scientific and technical research and analysis for MAJIC-12 is being conducted at several places around the country," the brief explained, adding, "Aeronautical research is being carried out by the Redstone Arsenal in Alabama." Was there data from any recent ET contact at Homestead that needed to be directly handed over by President Nixon (or an aide) to a MAJIC-12 representative at Redstone?

Note: President Eisenhower visited the Redstone Arsenal facilities in September 1960, when he dedicated the nearby Space Flight Center. Two years later, on September 10, 1962, ex-President Eisenhower met with President John Kennedy at the White House for a long stretch of time—from 12:30 to his eventual departure at 8:15

p.m. This time included many meetings, often with military personnel. Remarkably, the very next morning, JFK flew with some space program personnel directly to the Redstone Arsenal in northern Alabama![5] Vice President Lyndon Baines Johnson (1908-1973)[6] also arrived on a separate plane, bringing military officers with him. They were met by the base commander and toured the Redstone setup. By noon, JFK flew from Redstone's airfield to Cape Canaveral[7] in South Florida, meeting there with military, scientific, and astronaut personnel, including none other than Gordon Cooper.

By 3:00 p.m. on February 18, 1974, President Nixon visited his daughter in an Indianapolis hospital and then flew back to D.C. He returned to the White House by 7:23 p.m. What he did that evening is anyone's guess. Once again, *the Nixon library removed documents from the digitized file*, including notes taken on who was with the president as he flew out of Homestead and headed north that morning.

Meanwhile, just as Nixon was leaving South Florida, Jackie Gleason was busy hosting the first day of his week-long golf tournament at Inverrary. The tourney, of course, continued through February 19 and wrapped up on Saturday and Sunday, February 23 and 24, on CBS television.

On Tuesday, White House documents tell us that President Nixon simply attended some routine Oval Office meetings and an official reception in the evening, nothing too exciting. There is no record of Jackie Gleason being contacted. Nixon started the next day, February 20, 1974, at the White House, but then he walked to the nearby Executive Office Building, where his actions and visitors were not recorded for three hours. After this unusually long break—a mere nap?—it was noted that the chief executive met with his lawyer and then some presidential assistants associated with the military. He did not leave for the White House again until 6:10 p.m. Nixon spoke (for four minutes) with Florida Senator Ed Gurney[8] by a phone in the upstairs residence of the White House; both men were in grave legal and political peril at that time and wouldn't last the year in office.

What could President Nixon have been discussing in private that night? We can only speculate. *However*, according to a 2001 book,[9] "Seven UFOs, described as about the size of a small house, were sighted on February 19th, 1974, by more than twelve persons over Hattiesburg, Mississippi, that evening. Harold Arthur Stanton, an employee of WDAM-TV, said several persons in cars followed five orange and two blue objects as they 'hop-scotched to three open fields.'" Stanton (1945-2022) claimed the glowing flying objects darted toward the ground and then back up into the sky, in "some sort of formation," before disappearing. *Five* spaceships? Near Camp Shelby, which has an airfield? Perhaps much like the five UFOs landing exactly twenty years before at Edwards military airbase, flitting about similarly for then-President Eisenhower.

As 1974 moved along, it proved to be a strange year for both Nixon and UFO sightings. There were too many UFO reports to recount them all here. For the whole nation—especially the president—it was a bit of a bumpy ride.

On August 9, 1974, government business came to an abrupt end for Richard Nixon. He resigned office and left Washington D.C. for good, and Gerald R. Ford became America's 38th president. To Jackie Gleason's delight, the new president was a fellow Freemason. Ford was, in fact, a "33 degree Master Mason from Washington's Naval Lodge #4," according to masonic websites.[10] So, there existed another potential strong, private bond Gleason shared with a commander-in-chief. Less uptight than his predecessor, President Ford actually golfed eighteen holes with Jackie at Inverrary in February 1975. Jackie took pride in showing off his new Rolls Royce golf cart to the president. In 1966, then-Representative Ford had called for a worthy government investigation into a recent wave of UFO sightings in his home state of Michigan,[11] which included stories of round craft *landing* there. Project Blue Book famously dismissed it all as "swamp gas," which so disgusted now-famous

USAF science consultant and investigator Dr. J. Allen Hynek that he quit the team and took to researching UFOs on his own.

Less than two years later, Gerald Ford was no longer president, replaced by a Democrat who evidently had his own UFO sighting in January 1969. It took place at night, with others present, in Leary, Georgia. Other than that intriguing experience, Jackie Gleason had little in common with Jimmy Carter (1924-) [12] and disdained the new president's liberal policies. However, Jackie was undoubtedly interested in the UFO sighting report that Jimmy filled out in 1973 on the Leary event. [13] While campaigning for president in 1976, Carter told U.S. reporters: "One thing's for sure, I'll never make fun of people who say they've seen unidentified objects in the sky. If I become President, I'll make every piece of information this country has about UFO sightings available to the public and the scientists." [14] Then, once in office, President Carter strangely clammed up on the subject, evidently rattled by what he learned.

As of January 1981, Gleason's old Hollywood friend and fellow conservative Ronald Reagan reigned as president, taking over after Carter's defeat. Reagan was already quite intrigued by the subject of ET visitation. In the summer of 1974—the precise date is still unknown—then-Governor Reagan related a first-hand story to the Washington Bureau chief for the *Wall Street Journal*, Norman C. Miller [15]: "I was in a plane last week when I looked out the window and saw this white light. It was zigzagging around. I went up to the pilot and said, 'Have you seen anything like that before?' He was shocked and said, 'Nope.' And I said to him: 'Let's follow it!' We followed it for several minutes. It was a bright white light. We followed it to Bakersfield, and all of a sudden, to our utter amazement, it went straight up into the heavens." The pilot of Reagan's plane, Colonel William "Bill" Paynter, backed up Reagan's claim. He explained: "It appeared to be several hundred yards away. It was a fairly steady light until it began to accelerate, then it appeared to elongate. The light took off. It went up at a 45-degree angle, at a high rate of speed. Everyone on the plane was surprised. Governor Reagan

PAUL BLAKE SMITH

expressed amazement. I told the others I didn't know what it was. The UFO went from a normal cruise speed to a fantastic speed instantly."[1617] Knowing Jackie Gleason, he likely ferreted out every minute detail of this surprising encounter from Ronald Reagan and perhaps Bill Paytner as well. Reagan's daughter, Patti Ann Reagan Davis (1952-), has admitted that in private her father seemed "fascinated with stories about unidentified flying objects, and the possibility of life on other worlds"—and let's remember that he was at various times in touch with Nixon.

On Thursday, February 19, 1987—that familiar anniversary date again—White House records show that President Reagan called up Richard Nixon for a private phone chat. Later that day, he made calls to two other previous U.S. presidents. Coincidence? Just three months after Jackie Gleason's June 1987 death, President Reagan startled many by addressing the United Nations General Assembly by saying: "I occasionally think how quickly our differences worldwide would vanish if we were facing an alien threat from outside this world."[18] However, he did not mention his own UFO sightings.

In hindsight, Jackie Gleason's motives for keeping quiet for the rest of his life about his 1973 Homestead visit are clear. It is possible he was subtly threatened with, or at least carefully warned of, the unpleasant consequences of speaking out publicly. He surely did not need shadowy government agents following or harassing him or his family. He didn't need any tapping or taping of his phone calls or agents going through his mail. He didn't need an IRS audit or his past missteps being uncovered and leaked to the press. He knew it was *most* wise and advantageous to keep his yapper shut after his brief, initial stunned revelations to his then-wife on that emotional night. Jackie wanted to preserve his amicable relationship with Nixon and the FBI as well as his professional reputation. This would have been *especially* true if he retained hopes of learning or seeing more in the future.

Why did Nixon choose to meet with Gleason specifically on February 19, 1973, of all the times and dates of the year? After all,

Nixon flew to Homestead AFB and stayed in his Key Biscayne house a whopping *fifty-five times* during his presidency. He could have easily selected any one of these many other visits to bring his pal Gleason to the installation. And he could have arranged their visit to the base on one of the other evenings of his mid-February 1973 idyll in Florida. Without a doubt, though, it "just happened" to occur *on the precise nineteenth anniversary of President Eisenhower's airbase encounter with aliens.*

That's when—as the 1989 DIA report revealed—the U.S. president entered into a formal agreement with human-like space visitors, asking them to not show themselves, if at all possible, when flitting about our country and planet. In exchange, he allowed them to land at a remote Nevada desert airbase to complete their research unharmed. This agreement also included a provision that U.S. representatives would provide scientific data and objects for them to study if the ETs would reciprocate for us "item for item." [19] Also, during their 1954 meeting at Edwards Airbase, the advanced aliens set down near an airplane hangar and conversed with calm Mr. Eisenhower, who was surrounded by six bodyguards. But why specifically at that particular hangar? Was this one that held the remains of a crashed disc or bodies? Evidently, the friendly visitors asked Eisenhower to cease America's nuclear weapons testing, going on in the secretive "Operation Castle" detonation program in the Pacific.

As if to show serious extraterrestrial interest, a distinct "unidentified luminous object" passed over an American military ship monitoring testing at Bikini Atoll on April 7, 1954. [20] It was described further as "oval-shaped, bright orange, and silent." It had "buzzed the ship from bow to stern," according to unearthed documents released online by the federal government. When a UFO researcher highlighted this startling data, the section of digitized report pages in question was quickly removed from its government website. A second report was included, regarding a similar "cone-shaped" flying object also reported in April 1954, soaring over "an operational

PAUL BLAKE SMITH

site" for the South Pacific testing. Many UFO sightings were recorded in that April.[21]

Is it possible Nixon's 1973 airbase visit was about renewing Eisenhower's formal agreement with ETs? If so, his Homestead adventure was likely planned well in advance. He probably just invited Jackie Gleason along for the financial payoff and, perhaps, to gauge his reaction during and after an inspection of the cadavers.

By 1973, *did Gleason—with all his many connections who were aware of his obsession with space visitors—already know about the 1954 Eisenhower-ET Encounter?* Did he learn it from Nixon or Eisenhower himself? The five alien ships that landed at an Edwards Airbase hangar were said to have been three disc-shaped craft and two elongated ones—just like the "UFO house" and smaller buildings Jackie had custom-built on a hillside outside of New York City, which had been Dwight Eisenhower's stomping grounds some two years earlier. What is more, Jackie had his "Mother Ship" home custom-built *inside an airplane hangar!*[22] It was then trucked to the Westchester site and slotted together. Gleason's second wife, Beverly, never mentioned these details, but was she told *everything?* The Eisenhower-ET encounter at Edwards may have been something he kept secret from her since she was so generally disinterested in UFOs and ETs.

The Great Gleason and the popular Eisenhower almost *had* to have met. You can bet that when they did, Gleason would have quizzed the war-hero-turned-president about his favorite topic: aliens. When one ponders Dwight "Ike" Eisenhower and John "Jackie" Gleason, one finds an amazing number of things they had in common. Such as...

1. Ike covertly visited an Air Force base at night on February 19 (in 1954) to witness genuine extraterrestrials...and so did Jackie (in 1973).

2. Ike lived in New York City from 1949 to 1953 (as president of Columbia University)...and so did Jackie (as the biggest star at the Columbia Broadcasting System).
3. Ike smoked up to five packs of cigarettes a day for many years...and so did Jackie.
4. Ike was hospitalized with a serious heart attack (at age sixty-four)...and so was Jackie (at age 62).
5. Ike was obsessed with golf and played it as often as possible...and so did Jackie.
6. Ike was a conservative Republican who, as an older man, built up some wealth and moved to a country club's recently built golf course home with palm trees and a backyard swimming pool (in Palm Springs)....and so did Jackie (in Lauderhill).
7. Ike played golf at times with Richard Nixon and Bob Hope, and with popular pros Jack Nicklaus and Arnold Palmer...and so did Jackie.
8. Ike was a husband, father, grandfather, and a fine card player...and so was Jackie.
9. Ike achieved the very pinnacle of his professions (the military, a university, and the federal government)....and so did Jackie (via movies, television, and record albums).
10. Ike became a beloved legend, a world-renowned figure, a name still well-remembered to this day...and so did Jackie.

The best bet for an encounter between Jackie and Dwight—planned or unplanned—was likely during that four-year period in the early '50s when both lived in The Big Apple. Perhaps they met at a social event or out on a local golf course. It is easy to imagine Gleason writing checks to contribute to Eisenhower's presidential campaigns.

The Masters golf course in Augusta, Georgia, may have been another site where the two men could have "linked" up (pardon the pun). Both were obsessed with golf. News stories show Jackie attended the April 1975 Masters Tournament in Augusta.[23] An Augusta newspaper reported that Gleason brought a dozen "June Taylor Dancers" with him and attended after-hours events in town, including a pool tournament he eagerly entered (and won). Was the comedian already quite familiar with the famously lush, gorgeous course from visits during the '50s—just like Ike?

One showbiz personality, of sorts, that Jackie Gleason was particularly fond of was Mutual Radio broadcaster Frank Allyn Edwards[24] (1908-1967), a stocky former pro golfer who reported the news out of WWDC in the nation's capital. The two men would share UFO reports in private and over the airwaves late at night on New York City radio programs (some of which can be found online today).[25] Edwards had at least one source that filled him in on the top-secret Eisenhower-ET affair in 1954, and he reported it publicly on his show—which was coincidentally unplugged soon after. In 2022, dedicated researcher Richard Geldreich[26] revealed a two-page, type-written letter from August 1954 that the radioman received from Ed W. Hermann from esteemed MacGraw-Hill Publishing in New York. In it, Hermann reveals to Edwards: "Our *Aviation Week*[27] has been trying to get news out of Edwards Air Force Base, Muroc, California, regarding the report of 5 aeroforms having landed there in April [the second ET landing], and that they were investigated by high-level Government authorities, including Eisenhower on 'vacation' in Palm Springs [the first ET landing]. Report has it that materialization and dematerialization of the craft instantaneously have everyone baffled and concerned. We have contact with the 2nd man in command at Edwards AFB...but so far (4 weeks) nothing but utter silence to our wires." This was the very sort of data that radio star Edwards knew television star Gleason craved like candy.

We know that the rotund entertainer gobbled up every paranormal newsletter he could find. He subscribed to several in the '50s, so it is possible he was familiar with the *Lodge of Light Bulletin*, a monthly pamphlet produced by associates of San Diego's Borderland

Science Research Association.[28] This association is headed by Newton Meade Layne and Gerald Light, two aging students of the occult who are mentioned extensively in *President Eisenhower's Close Encounters*. Bulletin Number Two, from mid-April 1954, was unearthed in 2022 and mentions "...THE SAUCER PROJECT AT MUROC CALIFORNIA," and "Here is a memo from our BSRF Director [Layne]: "By all means, please include in your next Bulletin a statement about the wonderful doings up at Muroc. And tell our friends the truth once and for all. Tell them there ARE spaceships in the roped-off sections of this secret base. They have been there since before President Eisenhower took his strange vacation at Palm Springs, and we will all hear about it shortly in the papers if Ike has his way." In a 1958 newsletter, Meade Layne referred to all this again: "Many of our Associates will remember the MUROC INCIDENT, in April of 1954, which involved the (alleged) landing and/or detention of five or more types of 'aircraft' (since called UFOs) at Muroc Base, and the careful though fruitless study of these by our own technicians. Such is the pass—or impasse—to which public information has already come, that even today, if we could 'prove' every item [in Light's amazing letter], to print such proof would be risky and pointless." Layne added: "The matter of an alleged visit by President Eisenhower to the Muroc Base is clearly reported simply as personal inference and belief." He finished by again touching upon "the Muroc affair—concerning which I still get many inquiries."

Thus, we can repeatedly see how the TV icon was intrigued down to his baggy pants and seltzer bottle about top-secret presidential contact in 1954 that his sources assured him was true—without hard physical proof, like a photograph, piece of film, or leaked government report.

There's one more enticing possible link for Jackie Gleason in 1954, a solid government insider. He was a respected member of President Eisenhower's National Security Council, the type of secretive high-level power broker that would very likely be involved in any behind-the-scenes military/government communications

PAUL BLAKE SMITH

program with aliens. According to records, Sarrell Everett Gleason[29] (1905-1974) was—like Jackie—born in Brooklyn, New York. Everett in 1905, and Jackie in 1916. After a while, Everett's family moved to Evanston, Illinois, where he was raised. He was educated at Harvard, then taught there. From 1942 to 1946, he served as a lieutenant colonel in various intelligence matters, then as Intelligence Chief for the Office of Strategic Services, the forerunner of the CIA. He was eventually named Deputy Executive Secretary of the National Security Council.

White House logs show intelligence analyst S. Everett Gleason met with President Eisenhower in the Oval Office on February 10, 1954, then again on February 11. On February 12, the president left on a quick bird-hunting vacation to Georgia, then returned on Sunday. On Wednesday, the president met with Everett Gleason and his entire National Security Council, including Vice President Nixon and Air Force Secretary Nathan F. Twining[30] (1897-1982), another key figure likely in the know about the ET contact that would occur in a few days. Within a few hours of this high-level confab, the First Couple left Washington aboard Air Force One ("Columbine II") for Palm Springs.[31] Two nights into their visit, Eisenhower traveled under the cover of darkness to Edwards AFB and stood before a group of friendly, human-like extraterrestrials, discussing atomic testing, another issue of importance for the NSC.

Was Everett Gleason a blood relation to Jackie Gleason? That is not yet known, but it would make sense considering their common name and background. In theory, it is conceivable that sometime after the Eisenhower-ET summit in southern California, Everett could have slipped a few details in very strict confidence to his famous relative, who became so excited he started designing his "UFO house." Perhaps the purpose of that design was to entice his *own* extraterrestrial landing and encounter somehow.

Records show that Eisenhower met at the White House with Everett Gleason (and the NSC committee) again on February 26,

1954. Everett served for several more years in government, keeping a low profile before and after his retirement.

Thus, it seems likely Jackie Gleason learned at least *some* whispered aspects of the 1954 alien summit, although he may not have been able to badger the president himself. Jackie may well have heard the tale from other well-informed sources. It is speculation, yes, but Gleason sure seems like a consistent link between Eisenhower in 1954 and Nixon in 1973 (and perhaps again in 1974). He had reliable access to various insiders, thanks to his government, military, showbiz, and Freemasonry ties. He wanted *in*, and Richard Nixon eventually obliged.

When precisely Vice President Richard M. Nixon learned of Eisenhower's 1954 alien summit is anyone's guess. Was it via a briefing by Everett Gleason? It now seems certain he was informed at some point in the mid-to-late '50s and later patterned his own 1973 trip to Key Biscayne on Eisenhower's golf-vacation cover story.

Various clues point to a formal secret treaty having been agreed upon—at least in principle—in February 1954, with Eisenhower asking his reasonable off-world visitors to stay aloof, not land in populated areas, nor try to meet earthlings lest they touch off a panic. In exchange, the peaceful, curious aliens would be given a remote airbase in Nevada to conduct scientific research. That location is very likely the S-4 site mentioned in this book's Introduction. Did this stunning agreement need periodic updates, amendments, and renewals by succeeding U.S. presidents? It would certainly seem so. For instance, President John Kennedy flew to Palm Springs and met with retiree Dwight Eisenhower at least three times, according to his published schedule[32]. Why did they need to huddle in private like this, when they often communicated via telephone, written correspondence, and in person at Camp David? The subject of these private meetings must have been something classified and explosive. Rumors abound that Kennedy had his own airbase examination of alien evidence[33] while he was staying in Palm Springs, and JFK flew in and out of Homestead AFB a few times. Was *he*, in fact, the first president to order recovered alien bodies be moved to a lab there for presidential convenience?

In mid-February 1964, on the tenth anniversary of the Eisenhower-ET summit at Edwards, President Lyndon B. Johnson also dropped what he was doing in D.C. and flew 2,700 miles out to Palm Springs[34] to meet with an aging Eisenhower at his golf course home. LBJ repeated this mysterious journey in 1968, on the precise fifteenth anniversary of the Edwards AFB meeting, with Eisenhower becoming increasingly frail. Indeed, he would die of heart failure one year later after a few visits by new President Nixon to his D.C. hospital room.[35] "He was devoted to the common cause of humanity," Nixon noted in his statement to the nation that sad afternoon.

Notice that Presidents Kennedy and Johnson did *not* visit retiree Eisenhower at his Gettysburg, Pennsylvania, ranch home. That location was, of course, much closer to D.C.—a *much* shorter trip from either the White House or Camp David. Despite all the times they had spoken over the phone, exchanged letters, and had aides pass information between them, JFK and LBJ *had* to meet with Ike in Palm Springs. Furthermore, there are some unexplained gaps in the printed schedules of both men that may have allowed for possible otherworldly activities during those visits. Nixon also visited Eisenhower's golf course home in the '60s as a former vice president.

While "Ike" Eisenhower and "Dick" Nixon were two very different people, there seems to be a real, repeated method of operation here. Although separated by nineteen years, their military airbase visits are eerily similar. It cannot be considered coincidental that...

1. Ike arranged in advance a February "relaxing golf vacation" as an excuse for being in the area to covertly go see ETs in 1954—and so did Dick in 1973.
2. Ike chose February 19 to handle his intergalactic business —and so did Dick.

3. Ike sneaked out at night, probably with a trusted aide—and so did Dick.
4. Ike made sure the White House press was kept at a bit of a distance and distracted with a party at their hotel—and so did Dick (Well, *probably*).
5. Ike traveled several miles by air to an Air Force Base, arriving home by air, under the cover of darkness as the clock neared midnight—and so did Dick.
6. Ike saw genuine outer space aliens—and so did Dick (only *his* were dead—unless he stuck around later to meet some live ones).
7. Ike had armed bodyguards with him and a key eyewitness (who talked later) just outside that inner circle—and so did Dick.
8. Ike was taken back to his vacation home safely, with generally no one—not even his wife—the wiser—and so did Dick.
9. Ike got up the next morning and kept his set public schedule like nothing unusual happened—and so did Dick.
10. Ike remained completely mum on the topic for decades, even to his death—and so did Dick. *Not one word.*

In retrospect, it becomes clear that these similarities cannot be mere coincidence. It would seem the patient underling learned plenty from the master of subterfuge. Remember that Nixon said that the one thing which surprised him about Eisenhower was how sneaky the man could be, more so than what the public understood.

Bev Gleason's August 1983 *National Enquirer* article came ten months after an October 1982 *National Enquirer* article (by Dary Matera[36]) regarding Eisenhower's adventure at Edwards AFB.[37] Did Bev actually miss out on a much bigger story? We'll get to that notion shortly, but let's consider this claim first...

"The Council of Five" is (allegedly) a special group of representatives from five protective alien races who communicate paranormally to selected humans, purporting to give inside ET data. Its main writer, Dante Santori (1971-), once described a visiting extraterrestrial species called "Emerthers." Santori aired their (alleged) message to our world: "They met with President Eisenhower on three different occasions, and they also met with two high-ranking USSR leaders on three occasions, and they tried (they do not 'force' anything upon Humans) to meet with President Nixon, but he refused, claiming that it would be too dangerous as they could maybe read his mind and find out about delicate national security secrets concerning the relations with USSR."[38]

Admittedly, this seems like flimsy evidence to support the notion that the president was initially *going* to speak with friendly ETs but changed his mind. Yet it does sound par for Nixon's course. He was a schemer, maybe a little paranoid, and deeply involved with foreign affairs, especially attempted détentes with the Soviet Union during the Cold War. This was where his adept mind was at: trying to set one nation's government against another to bring them down while aiding America's interests—and his own. To that end, crafty Nixon may well have desired to meet aliens and broker a deal with them, just as he would try to do with North Vietnam, China, or Russia. In this alleged ET statement, however, it appears that he refused to get near them for reasons of national security.

Allegedly a special forces sergeant while in Europe, Santori went on to describe how he and a friend got their hands on a Russian spy notebook about alien visitation in 2008. It was called *KL-44*, and while it is not entirely clear, it seems to show that American information on recovered ET craft was being recorded as early as 1951, with updates and revisions as the decades went by. The controversial book was mostly a collection of Soviet Union intel on ET races and their ships. For those interested, Santori posted the book online in 2014.[39] It makes one ask: did the Russians have their own contact with landed, friendly space folk? Both the 1989 DIA document and the Russian spy notebook seem to indicate they *did*.

On December 7, 2012, Russian Prime Minister Dmitry Medvedev (1965-) was caught speaking about ETs on a live microphone after a press conference.[40] He was sparring with reporters, not realizing his words were being recorded. He stated: "...the president of the country is given a special 'top secret' folder. This folder, in its entirety, contains information about aliens who visited our planet. Along with this, you are given a report of the absolutely secret special service that exercises control over aliens in the territory of our country...I will not tell you how many of them are among us because it may cause panic." Obviously, this statement sounds like confirmation.

In 2011, a hacked computer file's amazing but brief video surfaced on the internet. An ET was featured, later given the name "Skinny Bob."[41] It was a thin, bulbous-headed, gray alien with huge black eyes, long arms and legs, and three long fingers and a thumb on each hand. The creepy images look amazingly realistic and might well be. The film is said to have been secretly taken by a KGB hidden camera when that elite spy unit was interrogating an otherworldly entity apparently recovered from a UFO crash in the Soviet Union in 1942. That was the backstory given to the grainy, black-and-white footage followed by an authentic KGB logo of that era. The alien is shown sitting and standing. He seemingly smiles *knowingly* for the camera at one point in the footage. His eyes blink, his head pulses somewhat, and his fingers move lightly. While some skeptics feel this video was somehow a computer-generated hoax, many believe the footage to be a real piece of leaked evidence. If true, this indicates the Russians had access to a crashed ship, ET corpses, and at least one live alien well before Eisenhower undertook his February 1954 encounter but one year *after* the April 1941 Cape Girardeau, Missouri, UFO crash recovery[42] (which featured three identical dead gray aliens, according to a key eyewitness). Had an elite section of the Soviet KGB been handling private, top-secret communications with stranded interplanetary beings since World War II?

Knowing that America's geopolitical enemies in the Soviet Union had an ongoing covert program with friendly ETs might have forced either Eisenhower or Nixon to act, to take a more active role in learning about alien races. Even if Dick didn't speak to a single "live one," his representatives could have handled that for him. Thus, appearing to sign or officially renew an alien-American treaty initiated by Eisenhower seems logical for Nixon, whether or not any sentient beings showed up to co-sign it that night. Is it possible he did so after Jackie Gleason departed?

One upshot of the Homestead AFB visit is that Gleason's emotional reaction afterward personified and justified President Eisenhower's concern in 1954 about the repercussions of allowing aliens to openly visit humans here. *Nixon may have felt that Jackie's psychological upheaval was a perfect example of why we, the human race, cannot handle the truth.* Imagine such a drama playing out within every single citizen around the globe. Societal and economic chaos would likely result if every human considered the traumatic truth with its full repercussions as poorly as the comedy actor. It might still be that way. Hence, secrecy continues to reign.

Dante Santori alleges that President Eisenhower and British Prime Minister Winston Churchill met several times in the '50s to exchange information on UFOs and ETs. The two leaders discussed how best to cover up the reality of the situation. The result was a special task force called SILK, Dante claimed. A third-party military general "of English descent that belonged to the military of Uruguay" was carefully selected to head the new SILK team, which consisted of "two USA and two English Secret Service agents" in the '50s. They were to investigate sightings—apparently overseas—without actually recording any of their findings. They could only give Dwight Eisenhower and Winston Churchill face-to-face oral briefings. Vice President Nixon was apparently not included at that time.[43] Meanwhile, in America, Project Blue Book's USAF investigation of UFOs was already underway, having begun in 1952. Apparently, Eisenhower desired UFO reports from Europe, and so did Churchill.

It is not known if Eisenhower ever returned to Edwards Airbase. As a southern Californian, Richard Nixon could have flown to Edwards without raising suspicion. As vice president, he officially visited the base on October 15, 1958; what he saw while touring the installation before delivering a speech to a small crowd is unknown. When leaving the presidency amid scandal, Nixon flew from Washington D.C. to El Toro Marine Airbase in Orange County, California, on August 9, 1974. Instead of spending a long stretch at San Clemente, however, Nixon visited the Palm Springs area, where he was infrequently seen over the next weeks. He was keeping a low profile and golfing in the area when his official pardon from new President Ford was announced one month later. Nixon had previously enjoyed the Thunderbird Country Club, and its website mentions: "President Eisenhower on two occasions brought his Vice President Richard Nixon to play golf at Thunderbird. He was also responsible for President Lyndon Johnson visiting Thunderbird and playing the course on a number of occasions."[44]

Before continuing, we must remember that at least a full year of top-secret radio communication was going on between American military intelligence's most trusted scientists and the orbiting aliens visiting our solar system. This was done in order to set up the initial Eisenhower-ET encounter in 1954. Some have stated that the program was code-named "Project Sigma." Richard Nixon in 1973, of course, had no Eisenhower to rely on. In getting back to his visit to Homestead, was there something *else* going on that night *beyond* Jackie Gleason, even beyond the inked Eisenhower-ET contact agreement needing re-approval?

Brace yourselves. From this point, there's going to be some stunning speculation as to what *could* have caused the great 1973 presidential Homestead visit. However, these conjectures are based on logic, facts, and a few statements within the leaked 1989 Defense Intelligence Agency government document, as we shall see. If true, it will blow your mind, but I do admit that proof is lacking.

Buckle up. Here we go...

First, let's ask this important question: *why didn't Nixon simply order the four dead aliens to be brought to a different site, such as to his Key Biscayne beach house?* Why choose an Air Force base, which required a chopper ride for the president and his guest? For instance, Richard *could* have utilized the nearly empty house next to his (516 Bay Lane) and had the ET corpses brought over, perhaps to be set out on a sofa. He could have simply ordered the bodies be brought in a covered military truck to his curb and parked near his beach house. He could have had Gleason driven or choppered from Lauderhill to the secure Biscayne Bay compound. The commander-in-chief could have stationed some extra guards, just to be sure, just like those at the remote Homestead lab. This would have made the trip a twenty-second stroll for Nixon. Much more convenient than a helicopter ride to and from the airbase. When Gleason arrived, he could have stepped up into the back of the parked vehicle and been given special access to view the cadavers with Nixon—if that's all that needed to happen that night.

Is it possible something occurred *after* Gleason left Homestead between 10:30 and 11:00 p.m.? Is there another reason Nixon was required to be *at* the military installation in the first place? Something important and perhaps shocking...

For this scenario, we must explore a stunning assertion that originated in the 1989 DIA briefing document, leaked in 2017 to a podcast host (*Midnight in the Desert* with Heather Wade[45]), labeled "Ultra Top Secret." A section of that blockbuster document told of the American government's covert involvement with communicative extraterrestrials from the '40s onward. Within its amazing details about the feds establishing a behind-the-scenes diplomatic friendship with some benign, informative aliens, there was a stunning assertion that caught the eye and boggled the mind.

The report's conclusion, excerpted here, details events that may have taken place in great secrecy:

"The ETs decided on a long-term program of carefully calculated and seemingly random contact...and this program was escalated to include eventual diplomatic contact with many of Earth's governments...In several cases, volunteers from our armed forces have participated in diplomatic and cultural exchanges in the 1970s and early 1980s, and have visited the EBE's home worlds."

Say what?! Could it be true that, in the groovy '70s, our government had diplomatic and cultural contact and "exchanges" with friendly extraterrestrials? Various off-world entities stepped out of their landed spaceships at one or more restricted U.S. airbases and talked to us at length, then some of our more adventurous military types—astronauts and pilots?—volunteered to get aboard their craft and *fly with the aliens back to their home planets*?!

WOW.

If this stunner is genuine, we must remember who the leader of the free world at that time was. For the first five years of that decade, it was, of course, Richard Nixon, who had the ultimate say in all diplomatic matters between the government and space as America's commander-in-chief. Thus, he was the one visiting aliens would have communicated with, either directly or indirectly (through intermediaries). Where would they have undertaken this staggering contact? At a remote, secure military installation, as Eisenhower established back in the '50s. Remember Eisenhower's agreement to "item for item swaps" mentioned earlier? Apparently, this modus operandi was taken to a new level under Nixon.

When Nixon visited Homestead in February 1973, and again in February 1974, he may have not only viewed alien corpses but also possibly communicated with our own diplomatic and military representatives on the anniversary of the original 1954 government pact—and then saw them off as they departed for other worlds. He may have even welcomed human-like alien visitors to our soil. Perhaps he did not engage in lengthy conversation because he feared the advanced entities were capable of reading his thoughts, and he desired to keep his thoughts on some topics, such as the Soviets, who might have been conducting their own such contact and exchanges, to himself.

This scenario could be the *real* reason why Nixon was "vacationing" in Florida to start with and was able to give Gleason a quick tour, then send him home. If true, it explains why official records revealing President Nixon's whereabouts and companions in South Florida on key dates were removed from his digitized daily logs and why it has been kept hushed ever since. It would also explain the statement in the 1989 briefing document: *diplomatic exchanges!* Truly "Ultra Top Secret" stuff!

The clandestine efforts on both sides of the unique, breathtaking visitation program had to have been a top priority since Nixon loved gaining the upper hand on his enemies: Russia, China, Vietnam, and even liberals. He was always looking for information to leverage to get a good deal for America—and himself. He loved statecraft most of all, and it is likely that would continue to be true even on a larger scale: with other *planets* and *ET races*. He certainly enjoyed the NASA space program and wanted to be thought of as a great peacemaker, so *all* of this was right up his alley.

Anyone selected to meet ETs and even travel with them would have been chosen from the most elite group of intelligence officers from each branch of the military. *This is just like those who were based out of high-tech Homestead AFB, near the Atlantic Ocean.* As mentioned previously, intelligence operations and complex communications were going on at Homestead, and the Army, Navy, Air Force, and likely Coast Guard were all present and participating at the expansive installation. Just the right people in just the right place. This information explains why Nixon would need to *go* there. He was not only viewing alien corpses—before they were transferred to their home planet?—but also handling "diplomatic and cultural exchanges."

And that is why the big-eared alien bodies were not merely trucked to Nixon's door in Key Biscayne for Jackie to view quickly and go home, satisfied. Much more was afoot, in theory.

Security was paramount, of course, and Homestead offered that, along with flat runways and the inky blackness of the nearby

Atlantic Ocean. There were no witnesses to see any arriving alien spaceships, some of which allegedly carried our own people. It was *perfect*.

Brave and adventurous Americans from our military journeyed to alien home worlds and came back to report what they had found, filling white-hot intelligence files. It staggers the mind and sounds more like a science fiction movie than reality. Each journey promised intelligence agents the chance to learn about the ET spaceships and get up to date on what planetary system they were visiting. Once there, they'd gather information on the intelligent lifeforms and their manner of existence. Their customs and cultures, their plants and animals (if they had any), their problems and resolutions, etc. And, presumably, these trusted diplomats would return eventually —in an hour? in a day? in a full year?—to a military installation like Homestead. Meanwhile, congenial aliens from that same race would be kept comfortable in a remote airbase building and give interviews to our own intelligence personnel, imparting information they felt acceptable for humanity to learn. Incredible if true!

Backing this up, at least in theory, is something known as "Project Serpo," a concept presented in paranormal show discussions and web pages since at least 2005.[46] Critics charge it as pure science fiction hogwash. Project Serpo[47] was an alleged "foreign exchange program" that President Kennedy—so fond of utilizing Homestead AFB during his administration—allegedly agreed to in the early '60s. An information leak in 2005 claimed that representatives of an extraterrestrial race of beings from a planet called Serpo—within the Zeta Reticuli star system,[48] visible on certain nights from Earth— contacted the U.S. government with a proposal. It regarded a plan to carry twelve American diplomats in one of their advanced space-ships to their world (more to study the humans than for us to study them). In exchange, the aliens would drop off one of their own to communicate in private; gift us with some groundbreaking technol-ogy; and allow advanced, secret communication with their society. In July 1965, about nineteen months after JFK's murder, the exchange took place, evidently with the approval of Nixon's predecessor President Johnson.

Theories about Project Serpo have been debated for over seventeen years, without gaining mainstream acceptance. The topic popped up in 2005 in an e-mailed confession from an alleged anonymous DIA source, supposedly representing others there. The journey was also described by MUFON investigator Len Kasten in his book, *Secret Journey to Planet Serpo*.[49] In his tome, Kasten claims that the 1947 UFO accident near Roswell, New Mexico, may have been the arrival of alien diplomats from Serpo in two different ships, which fatally collided on their way to a nearby desert base where they had planned a covert meeting with expectant military officials. When the 1965 swap occurred, Kasten hypothesized, the ET victims of the Roswell crash were taken back to Serpo along with the one dozen brave humans (seven of whom came back in 1978 with radiation poisoning, unfortunately). The otherworldly information they returned with was (allegedly) turned into a 3,000-page book, which was kept secret but supposedly leaked in 2005. Was all of this, in fact, merely creative embellishment in a fictional fantasy? Is it possible this evidence offers genuine insight at last?

Obviously, it would take far more evidence to fully believe such a fantastic scenario: genuine eyewitness accounts, government documents, and maybe some footage, photos, and actual files. But it is certainly electrifying to contemplate.

The 1989 Defense Intelligence Agency brief reported further: "There are now hundreds of complicated studies of the Extraterrestrial Biological Entities, their worlds, and their objectives."

Hundreds! What a fascinating and successful program it must have been, if true. It would have been an exciting and precious opportunity, needing to be protected at all costs. One would think that if Jackie Gleason was privy to his, he *might* have related it to Beverly, but he did not. He settled for describing four dead aliens at Homestead instead of living ones. He either kept part of the exchange a secret, or he missed out on the biggest story in human history.

If the DIA brief is accurate, there has been far more going on behind the scenes at select airbases since Eisenhower's bold contact in 1954, hidden behind an impressive veil of secrecy. President Richard Nixon would have been traveling to Homestead and Key Biscayne to privately oversee some details of this program in person. If it was truly going on, it was far more thrilling for Nixon to read about than mundane government files on everyday business and military matters. Such reading and pondering would have required quiet isolation, something the chief executive certainly engaged in when in South Florida.

Were American agents arriving home from space the night of February 19, 1973? Perhaps they were taking off with human-like aliens in the relative darkness of the Homestead runways for a month, or even a year, abroad? Rather like the ultimate Peace Corps volunteers. Was this why Nixon had to order some of his daily logs purged from mid-February 1973 and 1974? Is this why his fired CIA director was shredding his most sensitive files that early February 1973? Was he concealing evidence of totally top-secret ET contacts and intelligence missions that had to be monitored and recorded, approved by the highest leader in the land with the "Majestic diplomatic task group" handling the details, as mentioned in the 1989 report? This could be the reason why the list of those traveling with Nixon to and from Florida aboard Air Force One had to be lifted from his official records. Even the Marine One's passenger manifest about the brief flight to the Gleason golf tournament that day was scrubbed. Such names might tell us too much about who was with Nixon and Gleason at Homestead later that night.

According to retired USAF airman Charles James Hall[50]—who began to speak out on ETs in 2004—the American government has been hosting alien beings and facilitating exchanges at secure military facilities ever since the '50s. Hall alleges these visitors include some curious "Tall Whites," whom he supposedly witnessed in person in the Nevada desert.[51] While some of these particular ETs were not always friendly—able to prey on animals and even a few *human beings* with a "pencil-like device," Hall claimed—some interacted peacefully with military officials in Hall's presence. During the '60s, Hall allegedly overheard conversations between U.S. generals and aliens discussing exchange programs and interplanetary flights that were conducted on what they referred to as "space buses." The American brass longed to develop their own trustworthy interstellar travel vehicles so they would not have to rely on extraterrestrial "buses" to journey to habitable worlds (some of which were less than eight light-years away, Hall alleged). If all of this is true, could this be why President Nixon enthusiastically supported and funded the new "Space Shuttle" program in 1972?

Charles J. Hall further alleged that the Tall Whites gifted some of their technology to U.S. scientists. Hall recalled: "When you encounter the undisguised Tall Whites it's such a shock. You are not sure if you are looking at a ghost or an angel, or if you are dreaming." Hall possesses a master's degree in nuclear physics and comes across as a very intelligent and believable individual, and his startling account of "Tall Whites" was seemingly supported years later by a space program whistle-blower named Corey Goode.[52] The white aliens supposedly traveled to Earth from the Arcturus star system, about 100 light-years away, and preferred the hotter climates on Earth that were similar to their home world. It is unknown if they ever landed at Homestead AFB in steamy South Florida.[53]

If this human-ET exchange program was conducted between 1969-1974, it was undoubtedly *with* controlling Nixon's approval. The aforementioned 1989 DIA briefing may not have actually *named* Nixon, but it expressed the following allegation:

"Many volumes could be and have been written on the details of this ongoing contact process...Little threat to national security has occurred."

"*Ongoing*"? In 1989? Perhaps it simply meant "ongoing" from the Nixon era. Was it stopped—at least at Homestead AFB?—after the public exposure of the Nixon-Gleason affair in Beverly Gleason's 1983 tabloid article? Perhaps it restarted after Jackie's death in 1987? Or are those events merely coincidental? Recall that the document references "exchanges in the 1970s and early 1980s," which would have been under the direction of President Ronald Reagan.

Evidently, as of at least 1989, U.S. intel operatives and their higher-ups were learning and recording plenty. Presidents who dig deep enough into this field could have easily spent many hours reading the astonishing "Ultra Top Secret" transcripts and briefing reports on what life is like aboard an alien spaceship, planet, or dimension. It probably depended upon the trustworthiness of the chief executive, his degree of curiosity, and his level of "need to know" in this unique field. It likely also depended upon how long he was expected to last in office. Why bother to tell a failing, flailing president who might be gone in a year or two?

Was the whole diplomatic swap program even Richard Nixon's bold and cunning idea? To Nixon, information was king, even if he had to authorize it being stolen from his political enemies and perhaps even if it was being leveraged in return for some captured cosmic corpses. He also treasured diplomacy and foreign relations, so hosting ET "exchange students" was right up his alley.

Remember that President Nixon informed the world in a 1972 speech: "We are learning the imperatives of universal brotherhood and global ecology, learning to think and act as guardians of one tiny blue and green island in the trackless oceans of the universe." Was he, in fact, referring to the fledgling diplomatic exchange program and what we were learning from other races and worlds? Reputedly, such "foreigners" were aghast at how we have treated planet Earth, a fact they expressed during the 1954 Eisenhower encounter. Around the time of Nixon's speech, the controversial decision was made to cancel the rest of the Apollo moon landings, claiming there was no federal funding for them. It may have felt like a waste of money in 1972 when the U.S. government was privately conducting far more exciting (and less expensive) space missions with approved diplomats. Highly trained military intelligence personnel were traveling *with aliens* to other galaxies or dimensions and bringing back much more important data than mere moon rocks and dust. Perhaps this was done while "cloaked," as the expression goes, in advanced ET technology that was invisible to the human eye and possibly radar. American military programs have been developing cloaking technology ever since, coincidence or not.

Let's consider the claims of controversial Scottish citizen Gary McKinnon[54] (1966-). He earned a snootful of legal trouble in 2002 when he got caught hacking into American military computer systems and discovered—he says—files from NASA's secret extraterrestrial database. These included pictures of alien hardware and a list of "non-terrestrial officers," which sounds like an ongoing diplomatic contact program like Serpo. McKinnon uncovered data that "contained information about ship-to-ship material transfers."[55] One secret government file contained an image of a cigar-shaped craft floating above Earth's northern hemisphere. Unfortunately, McKinnon was unable to secure physical proof before he got caught, and he only retains his memories of what he witnessed. He was not able to provide specific dates of when the alleged secret contact began. Did he stumble into evidence of meetings Nixon approved and led in private?

According to White House aides, President Nixon was certainly a "control freak" who had to know everything going on in his administration. His attention would have been required from time to time at Homestead to make decisions about our personnel and theirs. He would need to review the people from other worlds and what they brought to Earth with them, with patient intel operatives and reliable scribes getting it all down for Nixon to read and ponder. This would need to be accomplished with no leaks and certainly no reporters anywhere near the well-guarded base.

Such an ongoing, highly classified program would also explain why there was a guarded, remote Aerospace Medical Research Laboratory on the Homestead base—for examining both humans *and* aliens arriving from or departing on long space journeys. Travelers would need to be tested for any sort of radiation or disease they picked up on another planet or spacecraft. Enforced isolation was ordered for mere NASA mission astronauts as soon as they splashed down in capsules in the nearby warm ocean; there's no telling how critical it was for other such U.S. personnel to be held in lonely lab conditions for study if they had traveled much further in the cosmos, even if their journey had taken only minutes or hours in advanced ET craft.

If we can ponder this amazing hypothesis a step even further, the "celestial diplomatic exchanges" late at night at Homestead combine to neatly answer a number of riddles about President Nixon. For instance, it may tell us why he just *had* to buy two houses in Key Biscayne in the first place (when he had one in California and could always stay with wealthy supporters *anywhere*, frankly). It gave him the excuse to be near Homestead airbase. It would explain his whopping fifty-plus trips to South Florida during his secretive tenure. A total of 157 days were spent at the "Florida White House," out of reach of the media and the public.

This possible scenario also explains why Richard M. Nixon was such a loner, even during his presidency, often lost in silent thought and unable to express his ruminations aloud. His mind was spinning in loftier spheres than those around him. He could not verbalize mind-blowing ET data and operations. It might also explain why even his loyal White House aides—kept at arm's length when in southern Florida—admitted that there was very little government business going on during the Key Biscayne vacations. Those assistants who weren't privy to the otherworldly landings and takeoffs were left with a lot of idle time in the Miami area, wondering why they were there so darn often. Military personnel at the base might not have known much, since some could have been given leave and others restricted to distant barracks, sleeping and blissfully unaware of the silent arrivals and departures occurring across the installation. Those who *did* know were warned, sworn, and rewarded not to talk

—ever. Although interplanetary information brought back was of great interest, it is probable that nearly none of it was applicable in modern America. It was over our heads. It is probable no great technical hardware was turned over by the ETs, lest the U.S. government attempt to weaponize it. Meanwhile, the Cold War continued, and the Vietnam War effort only slowly melted. Otherworldly races likely did not trust humanity with anything too tangible and replicable, lest it get twisted into machinery of violence. What else was learned was generally beyond the limited technology and mindset of the '70s.

All of that reading Nixon did in Key Biscayne, those highly classified files...perhaps now we know, at least partly, what absorbed him so in his downtime: sensitive, startling, celestial secrets. Perhaps he was distracted by the complexities of extraterrestrial existence. The way other worlds, other races, and other societies functioned in peace would have been enough to capture the imagination of any person privileged enough to read about it, particularly a leader like Nixon.

Again, we must recall that the commanders of the Homestead base, David Rippetoe and Alonzo Walter, had their own history seemingly in line with this type of alleged ET contact. Rippetoe was once chief of the "Space Division in the Office of the Deputy Chief of Staff, Operations," and Walters had been a "Plans Officer at the Aerospace Studies Institute." There is also a suspiciously large gap in the official history of the base provided by its online site. According to the base's webpage, the 31st wing group under the command of Rippetoe "became the host unit" at the facility in 1970, and yet there was no information to report to the public about the installation until 1981 (when the 31st "took on a new task, the training of F-4 air crews"). On top of all that, there were so many UFO sightings over or near the airbase in the years after 1973 that the Mutual UFO Network initiated an organized investigation of the Homestead area in January 2014. In their own words: "Many people have seen 'triangle craft' in the night sky...many, many people have seen 'dozens or so white lights moving in the night sky'...and many people have seen 'white orbs' floating erratically, then break into 3 or 4 smaller orbs...and many people—including Homestead AFB personnel—have seen 'saucers over the base.'"[56]

Tellingly, MUFON added to their 2014 Homestead-area reports: "Many people have actually seen flying saucers (approximately 30-50 feet across) ascend in the night sky." And, perhaps describing advanced ET cloaking ability, some were sighted "sitting temporarily 'invisible' on the land," then reappearing!

After interviewing a government scientist we'll call "Dr. E" in April 1990, UFO researcher Ron Madeley reported that President Nixon "had several special meetings" with ET contact program officials to monitor ongoing human-alien communications. "He got into all that damn mess. I answered some of his questions," Dr. E recalled of Nixon. In the early '70s, there were dozens of alien landings out west, in New Mexico and California, including Edwards AFB, Madeley's source claimed, and that "there were some [bodies] at Homestead. Actually, it was right behind Homestead. It's one of the most secure bases." This seems to confirm Jackie Gleason's memory of having been driven across the farthest part of the base, if not technically beyond the facility itself[57].

In going even one more step "out there" in theorizing, let's recall the many stories of "missing time" and "dimensional vortexes" off the coast of southern Florida. There are many tales of the "Bermuda Triangle"[58] that often include UFO sightings and abrupt weather changes. Were any of these incidents explained by a nearby alien arrival and departure "window" at Homestead Airbase? Perhaps charged-up ions and electromagnetic energies in the atmosphere, whipped up by advanced cosmic visitors, formed largely unseen travel portals or gateways for their occasional coming and going. We can speculate until the cows come home—or at least until the off-world diplomats do—but this amazing explanation is worth considering.

In theory, President Richard Milhous Nixon could have made

several unrecorded visits from his beach house to the base and back via helicopter without a wealthy supporter or aide at his side. Certainly, his own kin—so often not with him at Key Biscayne—would not have been made aware. It could have been considered strictly "off the record" presidential travel. If so, extraterrestrial awareness, file-reading, and even limited contact may have become no big deal to Nixon. After all, in no version of the Nixon-Gleason tale does the *president* react with shock or exhilaration at the sight of the dead aliens. Unlike Gleason, Nixon apparently took it all in quite calmly, almost stoic and nonchalant.

Unless something more concrete and supportive leaks out on this "ultimate exchange program" notion, it will likely always remain spine-tingling speculation that perhaps lends additional importance to the Nixon-Gleason saga, making it potentially far more exciting than a brief viewing of four little dead bodies.[59]

1. Jay Francis, "Dr. Kissinger's Key UFO Role Revealed," *UFO Digest*, July 27, 2011.
2. History.com Editors, "Nixon Resigns," *History.com*,, last updated August 5.
3. Presidential daily records, Nixon Library. February 1974.
4. Wikipedia contributors, "Redstone Arsenal," *Wikipedia*.
5. Staff. "Published in the Interest of Personnel at Redstone Arsenal, Al." *The Redstone Rocket*, September 14, 2022.
6. Wikipedia contributors, "Lyndon B. Johnson," *Wikpedia*.
7. Wikipedia contributors, "Cape Canaveral," *Wikipedia*.
8. Wikipedia contributors, "Ed Gurney," *Wikipedia*.
9. Curtis Sutherly, "UFO Mysteries: A Reporter Seeks the Truth," *Llewellyn Publications*, December 2001.
10. "Freemasons Honor Former President, Brother Gerald R. Ford Masonic Historic Event," *baumbach.com*, 2006.
11. Marcus Lowth, "Michigan, 1966 – The Swamp Gas Incidents," *UFO Insight*, September 2018.
12. Wikipedia contributors, "Jimmy Carter," *Wikipedia*.
13. History.com Editors, "Jimmy Carter Files Report On UFO Sighting," September 2021.
14. Bryce Zabel, "UFOs Hovered Over 1976 Election," September 8, 2020.
15. Wikipedia contributors, "Norman Miller," *Wikipedia*.
16. Grant Cameron, "Ronald Reagan's UFO Sightings," *Free Republic, freerepublic.com*, January 1, 2011.
17. Bill Paynter "Ancient Aliens," Season 15, Episode 12, aired April 18, 2020.

18. Steve Hammons, "Reagan's 1987 U.N. Speech on 'Alien Threat' Resonates Now," *Culture Ready*, July 29, 2015.
19. For more details, see *President Eisenhower's Close Encounters*.
20. Francis Ridge, "USS Curtis Carrying Nuclear Weapons Buzzed By UFO, April 7, 1954," *Water UFO*.
21. "1955: The Hopkinsville Alien Invasion,"
22. Lucy Wang, "Jackie Gleason's Spaceship-Like House Hits Market For #12M," *Dwell*, August 15, 2018.
23. Wesley Brown, "Gleason Showed Real Hustler Skills in Augusta," *The Augusta Chronicle*, July 12, 2014.
24. Wikipedia contributors, "Frank Edwards," *Wikipedia*.
25. Charles Lear, "UFOs on the Radio," *PodcastUFO.com*, March 15, 2020.
26. Richard Geldreich prefers to relay his UFO/ET information on his Twitter page: https://twitter.com/richgel999
27. "Aviation Week" is still in business today.
28. Now known simply as "Borderland Sciences," still around online at https://border-landsciences.org.
29. Wikipedia contributors, "S. Everett Gleason," *Wikipedia*.
30. Wikipedia contributors, "Nathan F. Twining," *Wikpedia*.
31. "President Eisenhower's daily appointment logs," *Eisenhowerlibrary*, February 1954.
32. Digitized at https://jfklibrary.libguides.com/jfkschedule
33. John Austin, "JFK Saw Evidence of Aliens and UFOs While He Was President, Former Pilot Says," *Express.com*, May 31, 2017.
34. LBJ Presidential Library, daily appointments finder.
35. Richard Nixon, "Statement on the Death of General Eisenhower," *Presidency.ucsb*, March 28, 1969.
36. Dary Matera, "Bio." *darymatera.com*.
37. "Eisenhower Met Space Aliens-The Story They Tried to Hide for 28 Years," *National Enquirer*, October 19, 1982.
38. Donna Hawthorn, "Starseed Origins."
39. Dante Santori and Gil Carlson, "The Book of Alien Races," *Primedia E-Launch LLC*, 2014.
40. Michael Salla, "Russian PM Not Joking – Extraterrestrials Live Among Us, According to MIB Documentary," *Exopolitics.org,,* January 2, 2013.
41. Full_Strength_Beer, "Skinny Bob- Alien," *Youtube,* 2011.
42. Paul B. Smith, "MO41, The Bombshell Before Roswell: 2020 Revised and Updated," *Argus Books*.
43. Santori book site, archived December 12, 2011.
44. "Club of Presidents,"*Thunderbird Country Club*."
45. Heather Wade hosted that show after original host Art Bell retired, and at times the podcast *The Kingdom of Nye*.
46. Gaia staffers, "Project SERPO and and the Zeta Reticuli Exchange Program," *Gaia.com*, November 26, 2019.
47. Project Serpo data, compiled at https://serpo.org
48. Wikipedia contributors, "Zeta Reticuli," *Wikipedia*.
49. Len Kasten, "Secret Journey to Planet Serpo: A True Story of Interplanetary Travel," *Bear & Company*, May 2013.

50. "Charles Hall and the Tall White ETs."
51. "10 Shocking Secrets of the Tall White Aliens, Revealed by Charles Hall," *alienufos-ightnings.com.*
52. Corey Goode, *The Cosmic Insider.*
53. For more, see ancientcode.com or exopolitics.org, among other sites.
54. Wikipedia contributors, "Gary McKinnon," *Wikipedia.*
55. See *fourthkind.com*, or *newcarsz.com*, and many other sites on this.
56. Mark, "MUFON goes to Florida city / Homestead, FL, 1-15-2014" January 15, 2014.
57. *Earthfiles.com* data summarizing the work of UFO investigators Leonard Stringfield and Ron Madeley, subscriber content, 2005 and 2010
58. Wikipedia contributors, "Bermuda Triangle," *Wikipedia.*
59. Could there have been more to what met the human eye going on in the skies at night in the vicinity of Homestead Airbase? Maybe. Let's recall how poorly homo sapiens see at night, and that infrared, or "night vision" technology was not widespread or as advanced in the early 1970s as in today's world, and certainly not available to civilians then. The human eye can only see between 430-770 Terahertz, while human ears can only hear 20Hz-20Kilohertz; this range makes up only a FRACTION of the total light and sound frequency going on around us. In other words, there is potentially far more going on that the human race cannot perceive, even in quiet daylight hours.

CHAPTER FIVE

OTHER VERSIONS; OTHER VOICES

"In the building was a circular craft that was secured to the floor with cables. The craft was still hovering above the floor."

As we speculate on the possibilities of the true nature of the 1973 Homestead Airbase inspection, additional questions arise. *Did Jackie Gleason tell fellow conservative comedian Bob Hope about the four alien cadavers?* And did it influence Bob Hope[1] to create his own "UFO house" just like Gleason's?

Or even more wildly: *did Bob Hope also go along to Homestead to see it all for himself?*

Let's be clear: there's no indisputable hard evidence that Bob Hope saw what Jackie saw or even learned of it a bit later. Hope never spoke publicly about metaphysical matters, perhaps wisely. He had a respected place in showbiz to protect and a friendship with President Nixon (and other conservative U.S. leaders) to preserve. However, there are some amazing facts and circumstantial evidence that could inform us on this point...

As usual, Bob Hope was Jackie Gleason's golf tournament partner that key week in 1973. They were old showbiz buddies who even starred together in a (flop) 1969 movie, *How to Commit Marriage*. The two performers enjoyed talking showbiz, golf, and conservative politics. Both were friends of President Nixon, Vice President Agnew[2], and the successor to both, Gerald Ford.[3] They both enjoyed singing, dancing, and acting in TV skits. Jackie and Bob even put on "drag" to perform as competitive "women"—undercover cops, actually—on Hope's 1974 TV comedy special. Obviously, for two men separated by a continent, they were close.

According to *Modern Palm Springs*,[4] at one point in early 1973, Hope conferred with his commissioned architect, John Lautner (1911-1994), who then created plans for a specially requested house design. *Despite already owning a few homes*, Bob was suddenly filled with enthusiasm for a unique look he wanted for his latest house, built overlooking the California desert. He gave Lautner a list of specific desires, and the architect returned weeks later with a model. As palmspringslife.com[5] put it: "In 1973 when Bob Hope first saw a model of the Palm Springs home modernist architect John Lautner conceptualized for him and his wife Dolores, the Hollywood legend walked around the pool table it sat on, inspecting the model's futuristic domed roof with a hole that opens to the sky, and cracked, 'Well, at least when they come down from Mars, they'll know where to go.'"

It took a good deal of time and money to create, but the resulting remarkable rounded residence is still popularly referred to as "Bob Hope's UFO House." Bob personally oversaw the eye-catching motif (along with his wife) and settled on an even more spaceship-like design than what we see today. However, the original structure caught fire and burned nearly to the ground in mid-1973. Resulting photos of the charred framework reveal it really looked like a typical flying saucer. It was eventually completed in 1978, and Hope quipped it was like "living inside an airplane hangar."

Incredibly, just like Jackie Gleason's custom-designed "UFO house" built on the edge of a bluff in New York, Bob Hope's custom-designed "UFO house" was built on the edge of a bluff in California. And, just like Jackie's property in Peekskill, Bob's new estate in Palm

Springs featured smaller, rounded utility structures—like a guest house and maintenance shed—set around the larger "mothership." Most of these surrounding buildings had shiny, round, silver metal roofs, so they all resembled a fleet of alien craft that landed in the desert when seen from the air. The comparisons are astounding and cannot be coincidental.

Oddly, architect Lautner eventually dropped out of the spaceship home project because Hope "interfered" too often in the creation of the place after the fire.[6] Thus, the legendary funnyman was responsible for its stunning appearance. As abcnews.com reported: "The home, which resembles a spaceship, was put on the market ten years after Hope's death in 2003...It's a 23,000-square-foot estate featuring tons of open space with floor-to-ceiling windows that offer amazing views of Palm Springs. The largely curved structure also allows for stargazing through the home's circular ceiling windows."[7] Perched on the highest peak of a ridge near Indian Point, the hillside estate is still a local tourist attraction. It was carefully restored in 2019 and recalls Gleason's "Round Rock Hill" estate in New York in every way.

Just like Gleason, Hope found his new desert digs to be too over-the-top and huge for anything but busy parties. Perhaps it felt more like a country club's cavernous clubhouse or a sleek train terminal than a home. The novelty of living in an enormous, expensive spaceship house overlooking the community below wore off fast. Bob and his family continued to spend most of their time between Toluca Lake, near L.A., and two *other* houses in Palm Springs.

What could have inspired Bob Hope's desert UFO house in the early spring of 1973? Certainly, Bob Hope never spoke about extraterrestrials beyond joking about them in a comedy monologue. Being so close to Gleason, Hope must have heard about "little men from space" and their rounded spaceships many times. Hope had spent time golfing and socializing with both President Eisenhower and Nixon. Who knows what these powerful, high-profile men revealed to each other in private, especially over drinks that loosened their tongues? Bob's first links encounter with Eisenhower occurred just three months into his first term; the pair golfed two consecutive days with a former Air Force Secretary in D.C. and later again in Palm Springs, where the retired commander-in-chief turned up to observe (but not play) at Hope's popular celebrity pro-am. That's where, in 1975, Hope lured reclusive Nixon out of his San Clemente retirement for a party and perhaps golf, according to a biographer.[8] During this meeting, Nixon likely got a look at Hope's "UFO house," under gradual reconstruction nearby.

Let's recall that just before he left D.C. for Florida, President Nixon placed two calls to Bob Hope, one of which connected according to White House logs. In those days, Hope openly spoke up for Nixon in public and donated money to Nixon's presidential campaigns as well, and Nixon returned the warm friendship. During the aforementioned phone call—in transcripts available online—Nixon recollected to Hope how the two played golf in a private foursome at Toluca Lake's course in January 1970. Yes, Richard Nixon enjoyed playing alongside celebrities—just with no gallery, TV audience, or media watching. It was less embarrassing that way. And how did he arrive that day? The president came by helicopter, with Marine One literally landing on Hope's lawn, very similar to Gleason's set-up in Florida a few years later.[9]

Jackie and Bob loved to play for money and had a bet going, as usual, during the 1973 Inverrary tournament. Video clips show Gleason and Hope buzzing around in a golf cart together that week, trading turns at the wheel.[10] They loved to swap showbiz stories, the latest gossip, old jokes, and a few drinks. Hope was not a Freemason, like Gleason, at least according to various masonic online sites. Still, the two comedy legends got along famously. When Jackie sank a putt to win their friendly wager that following Wednesday, Bob donated $25,000 to the Dwight Eisenhower Memorial Hospital of Palm Springs, California.

February 19 was a special night for Bob Hope—at least in theory. In 1973, it was his thirty-ninth wedding anniversary. The Hopes did not always celebrate together, due to his globetrotting work schedule. President Nixon was fond of both Hopes and always wished them well. What to give Bob as a present? Perhaps something really special that a man of great wealth couldn't acquire anywhere else?

On the night of February 19, 1973, Leslie Townes "Bob" Hope would have been relaxing after his afternoon golf and evening dinner —possibly with his wife—at a local hotel suite, likely with nothing of great substance to do. Perhaps he was even Jackie's Glea Manor house guest. Hope certainly needed to be in the Lauderhill vicinity for the next two days of the pro-am and was always at the beck and call of both Gleason and Nixon. It seems very possible the two comedy superstars were *both* at Glea Manor when they took their usual golf cart to the Inverrary course helipad, feeling giddy with conspiratorial secrecy and privilege. Was this deliberately left out of Jackie's recollection to his wife that night? Is it possible Jackie mentioned Bob to Bev, but *she* cut that part of the exciting story out because she did not wish to upset Hope? Beverly Gleason's 2003 interview with Kenny Young didn't mention Hope, either, but Bob was still alive during that final look at her memories of the event; the centenarian legend died shortly after Young's interview with Bev was published online.

Although Bob Hope did not publicly express much interest in the subject of life beyond Earth, he did narrate a 1960 television documentary on the peaceful life America enjoyed from 1945 to 1950, called *Not So Long Ago*.[11] In it, Hope discussed the summer of 1947's UFO sightings, described as "bright shiny things" and "flying saucers" that whisked across our national skies. Presumably, a star of Bob's stature would not agree to lend his voice to such topics if he did not want to.

Did Bob Hope see the ET evidence at Homestead for himself? Did Nixon want to display this for *both* of his wealthy, trusted golf buddies? Was Hope so excited and inspired in response that he set about designing his own Gleason-like "UFO house" in Palm Springs? That's purely speculative, of course, but it would make sense in such a scenario. Why treat one superstar to the experience of a lifetime and stiff the other? They might talk later and compare notes, leaving one of them hurt. In theory, Nixon could have brought Hope in for a tour after Gleason left. Either way, it is safe to assume that both were sworn to absolute secrecy about what they saw.

Both beloved entertainers had *millions* they could have contributed to Nixon's desperately needed legal defense fund for his arrested burglars. Nixon felt he needed that cash to protect his own reputation, and it is likely both of the showbiz figures would have agreed.

All it would have taken for Bob Hope was a quick phone call or two to finalize a trip to Homestead that night. Without his wife or kids around at his hotel suite afterward, perhaps a rattled Bob Hope didn't have anyone to blab the top-secret story to. He kept his mouth shut about it for good. Yes, this is conjecture, but it fits.

A few weeks after Nixon's Homestead AFB visit, Bob Hope was in Washington D.C. and dropped by to visit the president. Their meeting on Friday, March 8, 1973, in the (bugged) Executive Office Building also featured presidential aide John D. Ehrlichman (1925-1999), who was on the February Miami trip with Nixon.[12] They met there again a week later.[13] These encounters were captured by the bugging system, and some of the tapes can be heard online today but reveal nothing of any cosmic consequence. However, the audio of the conversation features a loud, oppressive ringing noise that begins suddenly and continues for several seconds as Hope brings up a topic one can't quite make out. The tape was likely checked and censored before the recording's release online. Do we really expect the Nixon Presidential Library to leave classified otherworldly information on tape for all to hear? It seems likely Bob had no idea the president had his EOB office bugged. One wonders again if Nixon put the bite on soft-touch Hope to contribute to his Watergate "hush fund" since Hope was remarkably well-off due to his many show business salaries, residuals, and real estate investments. Gleason was likely invited to D.C. by Nixon too, but Jackie was largely homebound due to his refusal to fly.

Apparently, Bob Hope left nothing behind after his 2003 death regarding his mid-February 1973 time in South Florida, such as a signed confession, diary, or videotaped message. If he did, his family squelched it. He was a good man who had gone on so many government-sponsored USO tours to entertain American troops that he likely considered it his patriotic duty to remain silent about any sensitive government secrets he learned over the ten decades of his remarkable life.

Speaking of special round "UFO houses," there was another one built within a year of the 1973 incident near Homestead, Florida! According to the abandonfl.com story, a rather shady-sounding local character engaged a Miami architect to construct a pair of unique, disc-shaped homes in the Homestead area in 1974. Locals called the concrete structures the "Alien Houses" or "UFO Homes."[14] Supposedly, the two were financed by a drug dealer who wanted reliable homes that could survive the high-velocity hurricanes that often threaten the peninsula. The buildings did so over the decades but were eventually abandoned anyway, their remaining shells vandalized and sprayed with graffiti. Finally, the pair of saucer-shaped structures were razed in 2013. Were they influenced by local rumors of the Nixon-Gleason encounter? Was their design a tribute to the many UFO sightings in the area?

The possible addition of Bob Hope to the Nixon-Gleason affair will always tantalize, but it is unlikely to be confirmed now, fifty years later, with nearly everyone involved long since deceased and the case stagnated. But not for lack of trying...

A former Pentagon employee still living in the Washington D.C. area read Beverly's 1983 *Enquirer* article and was determined to uncover every possible detail. Any scrap of evidence was explored to prove it true. Just like Jackie Gleason, this man had collected every UFO/ET book and periodical he could get his hands on. He knew the subject well enough to recognize the story of the century when he heard it.

Larry William Bryant[15] (1938-2020) was a respected Pentagon employee and civil service career man who headed a small organization of Americans seeking the truth in extraterrestrial matters.[16] He once attempted to sue the United States government to reveal the facts about alien visitation. He eventually mailed a Freedom of Information request to the managing office at Homestead Air Force Base in a valiant attempt to pry open the installation's secrets. Bryant was quickly informed that the airbase office did not possess any record of a special visit on February 19, 1973. It is no surprise that they would not record such a highly classified incident in the first place, and it is even less likely they would give that data to a citizen or UFO group who simply asked politely.

Undeterred, Larry Bryant then tried to contact Jackie Gleason for an interview but received no response.[17]

Not giving up, intrepid Mr. Bryant created some advertisements to be printed in the Homestead base newspaper, requesting further information on the alien artifacts supposedly housed there. Predictably, he was rebuffed once again. The Homestead AFB public affairs officer denounced the ad and "forbade its publication." The military installation would not print any sort of UFO/ET inquiry in *their* paper. At the same time, Larry wrote Jackie Gleason to provide him with a draft affidavit. He asked Jackie to execute the affidavit so it could be used as part of a growing collection of evidence needed for taking the government to court to force the release of all information on alien crash retrievals. As reported in greyfalcon.us: "Though I never did hear from Gleason," recalled Larry Bryant, "I did learn that he had been contacted by a third party in the film industry. At this confrontation, Gleason chose to neither confirm nor deny the story, saying that he would prefer not to discuss it all. The way I see it, Gleason easily could have set the record straight in reply to my proposal or in an explanation to the inquisitive film-industry representative. If the story was a fabrication or misinterpretation on the part of his wife, he now had every opportunity to say so. That he chose not to merely deepened the mystery."[18]

Bryant then tried to subpoena Gleason. Strike three. Jackie just wasn't talking—not even to one of the more respected researchers in the field, someone who could even access certain parts of the Pentagon. Stone walls had been effectively placed around the story. "Loose lips sink ships" was an old wartime motto that might have prevailed in the latter half of the twentieth century. The powers that be simply weren't ready for full disclosure during persistent Larry's lifetime.

Larry W. Bryant passed away in October 2020. His obituary—penned by his daughter—reveals he retired from the Pentagon as a Writer/Editor for the Chief of Public Affairs at the age of fifty-five in June 1994. He had directed the Washington D.C. office of CAUS, and Larry published articles, essays, commentaries, and litigation related to UFOs for over forty years. He also authored *UFOs and the White House*. He had submitted countless written requests through The Freedom of Information Act to gain UFO/ET data. Larry wrote columns and articles for several UFO magazines, some published by news outlets. He fondly referred to his beloved UFO books and magazine collection as "his children," sounding very much like Jackie Gleason. He did what he could on a limited budget, but it wasn't enough to sway The Great One, sadly.

It is clear that Jackie Gleason seems to have clammed up about this topic for the rest of his days. Keeping that in mind...

There are actually *four* different versions "out there" of the Nixon-Gleason airbase encounter. All of these stories are circulating with the sources claiming the entertainer exclusively divulged all to them alone. Unfortunately, these claims are rife with creative embellishments—to put it charitably—details that don't match Beverly Gleason's account or even simple known facts.

Here's a thumbnail sketch of each of the four versions:

Narrative #1—unfortunately the most widely reported on the internet—contains many errors, such as claiming Gleason confessed the saga in 1986 while living in his UFO house in New York, which we know Jackie sold to CBS in 1964. The Great One spent most of 1986 ill in Florida, minus a quick trip to Chicago to film some movie scenes. This source alleged that Gleason recalled he and Nixon golfed together "all day," when we know the president dropped by for only twenty minutes on the opening day of the pro-am and didn't golf at all. Later, "around midnight," Nixon supposedly showed up alone in a car outside Glea Manor and drove the comic over fifty miles in the dark of night—not likely! Beverly said Jackie *got home* at 11:30 p.m., and the Secret Service would *never* have allowed Nixon to take a car out alone. To do so, he would have needed to somehow slip past the guards stationed at two street entry posts at his Key Biscayne compound. Plus, he'd never have found his way on his own through the winding streets and highways of Miami/Fort Lauderdale in the dark. Such a car trip would have been *thirty-seven miles* north to Gleason's house, then *fifty-seven more miles* south to Homestead. It was further claimed that the aging superstar remembered that he and Nixon passed through a *series* of laboratories with "six or eight" mangled ET bodies inside "glass-topped metal freezers" of sorts, while Beverly said Jackie merely referred to stepping into a single large room to view only four bodies laying out on four tables. There are still other problems with this story, but we'll move on.

Narrative #2 claims Gleason flew to Tampa at Nixon's request in 1971 in order to view an entire crashed ET ship plus alien bodies at an airbase there, which just happened to be not far from the source's home. The storyteller—who has been accused of fraud and been in trouble with the law—never mentioned Homestead AFB or Nixon being present for the encounter. {Source: ufoinsight.com.}

Narrative #3 seems to glom on to the first fable but with some small but noticeable extra touches, like adding in the Holloman Airbase UFO film footage claim (see next chapter), from well-known UFO legends. This third shaky story features Jackie Gleason during the unhealthy year before his death, driving all the way from his Lauderhill home to a north Miami highway rest area specially to relate the tale to the stranger—who claims he once encountered a nine-foot-tall alien—in a secretive undercover public meeting.[19] The two men couldn't just talk on the phone, meet at Gleason's house, at the Inverrary clubhouse, or even out on the course. That apparently would have been too convenient. However, we know that Jackie never drove anywhere, and he *loved* his chauffeured limo, making the tale still more unbelievable.

Narrative #4 features a UFO researcher's wife claiming she once talked to a famous TV actor who played golf with Gleason in 1979 and heard him spill some details on his tour of Homestead with Nixon. According to this account, Gleason admitted he saw four dead ET bodies but also a captured silver spaceship that resembled a large recreational vehicle. The researcher's spouse apparently only revealed this vivid memory out of the blue in the tumultuous year 2020. Why the nearly forty years of silence until then? Plus, why would Jackie confide in his actor friend in 1979 when the comic wouldn't go public with it? {Source: many sites, including nationalufocenter.com.}

All four narratives originated with hardcore UFO/ET fanatics, eager for attention and headlines and, doubtlessly, quite familiar with Beverly Gleason's *Enquirer* articles and 2003 online interview. They all ignored the fact that Gleason angrily chewed out his ex-wife twice for her tabloid revelations, repeatedly ducked answering earnest Larry Bryant's entreaties, and continually refused to issue a public comment on the event. Stony silence was clearly Gleason's firm overall policy. So why would he break his oath of secrecy and spill his guts to complete strangers? It seems unlikely he would choose to confide in these UFO buffs, who could then be expected to eagerly tell the whole world their incredible scoop, thus stirring up the press all over again—*the very last thing he wanted.*

These four far-fetched tales lack credibility and believability as well as any sort of supportive evidence that they occurred.

If only we could find a source with a fresh angle on the story without having a UFO or paranormal background and nothing to be gained from such claims. Sadly, these problems occur yet again with another source who has claimed alleged access to knowledge about the Nixon-Gleason affair...

K. T. Frankovich (1947-2020), a self-styled psychic/wildlife researcher/poet/film writer who penned a 1999 autobiography on her supernatural experiences in Florida (*Where Heavens Meet*), once resided not too far from Homestead AFB, in Dade County. K.T. said she was the daughter of a U.S. Navy commander and knew of the 1973 Nixon-Gleason alien encounter. How? Probably by reading Beverly Gleason's story going viral, frankly. However, she alleged: "Jackie Gleason was an avid fan of psychic phenomena and UFOs, and so was President Nixon, whom I spent many conversations with discussing my psychic abilities."[20] {Source: educate-yourself.org.}

Psychic phenomena? *Many* conversations? With the isolated, socially awkward, and very conservative *Richard Nixon*? The notion seems unlikely, to say the least.

Frankovich further claimed that President Nixon told her he was also intrigued by visiting space people. "I knew he had a deep-seated fascination with UFOs, as more than once I was privy to be present during conversations he had with Bebe Rebozo on the subject." To her credit, the late author admitted she never met Jackie Gleason, "although I knew he lived on the beach just outside of Miami, which was not too far from me."

She further alleged that in May 1992, she personally witnessed an otherworldly entity while out walking her dogs in an abandoned citrus orchard near SW 152 Street, a few miles from Homestead. Her apartment was situated just ten yards from the edge of the thick trees. Neighbors had supposedly warned her previously that "strange things" had been happening in the old orchard and to stay out of that dangerous area, but they wouldn't say what was going on that was so scary.

Frankovich said she looked up during her stroll amid the trees and suddenly locked eyes with a small, gray extraterrestrial wearing a kind of t-shirt and shorts and staring right at her. The alien had two hands, each with five fingers and one thumb, and "odd-looking clothes, made out of a weird metallic-looking substance."[21]

Shocked and frightened, K.T. turned and ran away with her dogs. A few days later, she encountered "two strangers, identifying themselves as U.S. federal agents, who persistently tried their hardest to obtain information from me. How they even knew about my encounters is beyond me." The duo was seated in a black sedan that slowed down outside her apartment to address her. They allegedly flipped open ID badges to back up their claim of being government operatives. They gave her a business card which featured "a raised emblem of the White House, done in solid gold. It was very impressive looking." The two kept hovering around K.T.'s apartment for months, supposedly, checking up on her and creating an intimidating presence.

There's no proof to back up this saga at all. It might have simply been made up, but it does seem at least *possible* that Frankovich ran into a visiting alien who wandered off from Homestead AFB and then reported its encounter with her to the military intelligence agents handling the "diplomatic exchange program." At least, that's one theory.

Not too long afterward, K.T. said, she was relaxing at home, watching television at 11:15 p.m. when "a brilliant green fluorescence" began to "seep through the corners" of her apartment living room, from the ceiling to the floor. It was the stunning start to another alien encounter. Once again, a six-fingered gray entity appeared before her, apparently, out of thin air. She believed it to be the same ET from the nearby orchard, and this time it brought along a friend, a similar but smaller gray alien who also emerged from the greenish fog. After staring at each other wordlessly, the two ETs eventually headed outside *through* a mesh screen window—quite a neat trick—and ran off, seemingly turning the tables on her.

Frankovich wrote in her autobiography that she did not "find any secretive activity involved with the Homestead Air Force Base to be shocking...The reason I have no problem believing the base is directly linked to cover-ups is due to what I witnessed in the lime grove. Homestead Air Force Base was just minutes away from the lime grove. Why would these strange-looking beings be in the lime grove to begin with? Where did they come from?"[22]

By August 24, 1992, the entire area, including Frankovich's apartment, was wrecked by Hurricane Andrew. She allegedly suffered multiple injuries as the 220 m.p.h. winds drove objects through her walls and windows. In effect, she never fully recovered and lost everything she owned. She moved away, eventually landing in Eustis, Florida—which was promptly damaged by *three* different hurricanes in the late summer of 2004. She continued to experience great poverty and health problems, including cancer and eventual loss of eyesight. Yet she supposedly continued to experience a few UFO sightings, some of which she claimed were also witnessed by neighbors. UFO researchers and radio show hosts who knew her had to plead with followers to help raise funds to support K.T. in her last years.

At the time of the Nixon-Gleason affair, K. T. Frankovich was twenty-six. Her name doesn't appear within Nixon's meticulous White House logs, even during his activities while visiting Key Biscayne. Yet K.T.'s online bio reads: "Her honorary poetry performances include audiences such as the former President Richard Nixon and the First Lady." *Former?* Nixon certainly didn't vacation in South Florida after his 1974 resignation, and it is tough to picture him sitting through *any* poetry reading. Yet the biography adds: "K.T. Frankovich specialized in major motion pictures, true documentary films, and television," but her only showbiz media database mention is that she wrote for a short 1975 documentary film called *Cries*— that's it. She was forty-one years old when she supposedly saw those gray aliens, but she produced no supportive witnesses or documents, no photograph or video footage, not even that unusual White House business card. An online reviewer wrote of her book, released December 30, 1999: "As a survivor of Hurricane Andrew and still a resident of Miami, Florida, I have to say that most of her accounts about the hurricane are completely false...In the two chapters I read, this lady seemed to know just everyone and anyone important. Yet, with all her 'connections,' she remained poor with no one to help her. It all seems odd."[23] More importantly, he added: "About the aliens at Homestead Airbase, she has gone overboard."

Frankovich's ET saga is inconclusive at best and creative at worst. However, a far greater embellishment was employed in another book about the Nixon-Gleason episode...

Self-published in 2014 by Justin Tully, *Jackie Gleason UFO 1973* is not a helpful nonfiction analysis of the Nixon-Gleason incident; it is a fictionalized drama and not a well-written one at that, according to online reviews. The book received almost no attention or sales, and its few readers turned into online critics who slammed it. The title turned out to have been a "dramatized short story," not really a full-length book and not a big help in getting to the truth of what happened at Homestead.

Me-TV, of all sources, also delved into the now-famous encounter at Homestead with an online article created for social media on June 21, 2019. The piece's subtitle may say it all: "It's a story that sounds too wacky to be true...but could it be too wild to have been made up?" The online article even quoted a recent tweet on the topic by curious *Star Trek* actor William Shatner. It also mentioned how Snopes.com noted: "The claim cannot be definitively proved false."

A most intriguing comment was posted in mid-2021 in response to the two-year-old Me-TV story, posted by a "Frank Noone" who said: "Gleason did ask Nixon if he could see UFO evidence. Nixon arranged for Gleason to be escorted to a building in Florida that could be seen from a highway. In the building was a circular craft that was secured to the floor with cables. The craft was still hovering above the floor!" These are some unusual details not heard before: the airbase building the president and performer toured was visible from a nearby highway? Yet there was a whole alien spaceship fit into it at some point, right in front of traffic and eyewitnesses? And it had to be tied down as it floated "above the floor" of its hangar? One wonders who Frank Noone is and where he got his unique but entertaining information since Beverly Gleason never reported Jackie describing a captured alien vehicle at Homestead.

Many websites have discussed the basics of the Nixon-Gleason affair, too many to recount here. Even *Wikipedia*, the online encyclopedia, has a brief description. "According to writer Larry Holcombe, Gleason's known interest in UFOs allegedly prompted President Richard Nixon to share some information with him and to disclose some UFO data publicly." Holcombe's popular book *The Presidents and UFOs*—released in 2015—offers quick summaries of the various versions of the Nixon-Gleason affair, but, in the end, the author had the guts to admit the truth about the "alternate accounts," those four creative narratives listed in this chapter. "I think it's highly unlikely that the president had a few martinis, jumped into his car, picked up Gleason, and drove past bewildered guards at what would be one of the most secure areas on the planet." And he's right; it's absurd. Yet Holcombe adds the initial Bev Gleason story "cannot be dismissed." That's right, too, partly because it originally came straight from the comic's mouth with no great embellishing or self-aggrandizement by Beverly, and because Jackie had numerous opportunities to deny the tale and refused. "Considering what we know there most likely are some, perhaps *many* factual elements, within her story," Holcombe summed up.

Grant Cameron, a respected UFO researcher/author from Canada, has written about another unusual but genuinely fascinating—and not well-known—UFO incident from Nixon's presidency. Cameron's presidentialufo.com startling story originated in *UFOs: The American Scene*, a 1976 book by author Michael Hervey. "The event in question apparently took place in January, but of what year?" Cameron asked in his special webpage on the Nixon-era claim.

Cameron—*ufocasebook.com*—summarized matters this way:

Mrs. Sherry Eckhardt in Oklahoma City was talking on the phone to her mother. During their conversation they heard a voice saying, 'This is Norad Tinker UNG Two. Red Alert.' Mrs. Eckhardt contacted her husband who listened in on the phone. He reported that there were conversations between Air Force Bases in Texas, New Mexico, California, and the North American Air Defense Command head-quarters in Cheyenne Mountain, Colorado. Assuming someone was playing around, Mr. Eckhardt hung up the phone. Mrs. Eckhardt phoned her mother again only to find out that the strange conversa-tion was still taking place. The Eckhardts and the mother all reported that the subject of the conversations seemed to be the serious tracking of *two sets of UFOs; one group was approaching Houston and the other Los Angeles*. The conversation reported a jet scrambling being ordered, and a reminder that this was not a test, but a serious *Red Alert*. The Eckharts [sic] were witnessing a genuine emergency. The voice on the other end then stated, 'Hold the line for the President.' Moments later a voice sounding very much like Presi-dent Nixon came on the phone and stated: 'This is probably the most unusual phone call I'll ever make.' [24]

What was said after that is a mystery; it is possible the Eckhardt family realized this was highly classified information and quickly hung up, not wanting to get into trouble. Perhaps military personnel on the other end of the line overheard the Eckhardts talking to each other and discontinued the call. Online information[25] tells us: "Okla-homa City Air Force Station (NORAD-ID: Z-52) is a closed Cold War United States Air Force air defense and communications-electronics headquarters and radar station. It was located 10 miles east-south-east of Oklahoma City, Oklahoma, just to the southeast of Tinker Air Force Base. It ceased to be a separate Air Force installation on October 1, 1983, when it merged with Tinker."

The Eckhardts evidently spread the word about the phone connection incident. Grant Cameron continued: "When contacted later, the Nixon White House denied that he had been involved, stating the president had been in seclusion working on his State of the Union address...The department of Defense and NORAD also issued denials. Holloman Air Force Base, where the scrambled jets originated from refused to say anything."

If President Nixon was not at the White House when the phone-line mix-up occurred, just where exactly was he "in seclusion?" Can we track his whereabouts today using his official records and learn more?

The alleged event must have taken place in the month of January between the years 1970-1974 (Nixon didn't give the 1969 SOTU speech; LBJ did). It's interesting to note that Nixon's 1973 SOTU speech took place just seventeen days before the Gleason airbase encounter, delivered to congress on February 2, 1973. However, nothing in the president's daily logs indicates he left the White House to go into any sort of seclusion in the week or two before that speech. A check of these same digitized presidential records shows that early 1970, 1971, and 1972 also do not meet the listed qualifications for this unique story.

However, *there is a perfect match for late January 1974*: just weeks before the twentieth anniversary of the original Eisenhower-ET encounter of 1954 and eleven months after the Nixon-Gleason affair. Did something cosmically monumental occur, covered up for almost fifty years?

President Nixon was away from the White House in the final week of the first month of his last year in office. He was holed up at Camp David[26], likely working on his SOTU delivery with his top speechwriter. The important stem-winder was scheduled for Wednesday, January 30, 1974. The chief executive was currently bogged down in the Arab Oil Embargo[27], an economic slump, and the ugly Watergate crisis. The contents of his impending televised address were critical to persuade the public that life in America was better—or was *going* to be—under his charge. There was little else going on in America at the time. Even the NFL season was cleared away that chilly winter month, with Nixon's acquaintance Don Shula's Miami Dolphins winning the Super Bowl in Houston, Texas, just as they did the year before in Los Angeles—ironically, the two

PAUL BLAKE SMITH

major U.S. cities specifically named in this UFO squadron allegation.

Let's consider how this saga could conceivably have come together. On Saturday, January 26, 1974, pilots in the Santa Ana, California, area noticed—and later reported—five foreign objects encircling their plane in flight.[28] That would have been thirty-two miles southeast of Los Angeles. Meanwhile, in Europe that night, a V-formation of luminous objects—perhaps up to *fifteen* of them—were observed by the crew of an airliner over the skies of Lisbon, Portugal.[29] If there were any UFO sightings in the Gulf of Mexico or over the Texas landscape near Houston, such reports have not surfaced. On that specific date, however, appointment records have been lifted from Mr. Nixon's online presidential library archives! Just *gone*. Researchers are left with nothing to dig into.

The presidential daily records that remain verify Nixon's presence at the White House on Thursday, January 24, 1974, then he and the First Lady flew to Camp David, Maryland. "ITEM REMOVED FROM FOLDER" is noted in Nixon's White House logs for Friday and Saturday. It is simply stated that "The Office of Presidential Papers and Archives did not receive any information on the President's activities for this day." So, where was Nixon on Saturday, January 26, 1974—the day of these UFO sightings? Presumably, he was still at Camp David, for his records resume there on Sunday—yet the only activity mentioned *that* day was a single telephone call at 4:38 p.m., when Nixon spoke for one minute to his administrative head of Veteran's Affairs. Then, the next day, only two quick phone calls with Dr. Henry Kissinger were noted in the official accounts.

Was there an international, if not *interplanetary*, crisis going on the public was never informed of? The only gathering at the time that would have initially mattered to Richard Nixon was the very first CPAC convention—Conservative Political Action Committee— going on in Washington, D.C. At that press-scrutinized event, California Governor Ronald Reagan, his eyes on the presidency, gave the keynote speech. Nixon's entire reputation and legacy were at stake during that time, yet he did not attend.[30] Perhaps now we may know why. Obviously, if the Eckhardt claim is valid, he was preoccupied with something far more immediate and urgent.

We can accept as fact that Nixon was working during this period on his State of the Union speech because the logs show he brought Mr. Raymond K. Price, Jr.[31] (1930-2019), a trusted aide, with him to Camp David. On the evening of January 29, records show Nixon returned to the White House after consulting with Price, Kissinger, and a military aide on an unknown topic. The president calmly delivered his big annual speech to congress and TV cameras the following evening. No great celestial revelations were relayed. Life went on without a cosmic hitch.

Thus, we know that if President Nixon placed a top-priority call from Camp David to his military leadership to handle the incoming reports of alien craft approaching two major American cities—the UFOs being possibly mistaken for Russian or Chinese jets at first—he was indeed in seclusion and in the middle of his SOTU speech preparation, perfectly fitting this narrative. This otherworldly incident would have caused security personnel to remove two full days of records from his digitized files. Perhaps it even explains why two other days were restricted in reports back then. Moreover, Camp David in rural Maryland is a remote site, away from the White House, which might have caused less-than-stellar telephone communications, resulting in the phone-line mix-up overheard by the Eckhardts in Oklahoma. It all adds up nicely.

Did this January 1974 secrecy have anything to do with continuing censorship of the president's daily records when he returned to Jackie Gleason's neck of the woods in the third week of February? Obviously, more facts and less speculation are needed here, but this is quite the intriguing, though under-investigated, subject. What ET material does the government have stashed away? Is it being reverse-engineered? Two apparent insiders have offered an identical opinion, at least as far as one large corporation is concerned...

Benjamin Robert Rich[32] (1925-1995) was a highly educated

American aerodynamics expert and flight technology engineer, often regarded as the "Father of Stealth Technology." He was the second Director of Lockheed Martin's secretive research and its often-classified development program, called "Skunk Works," from 1975 to 1991. Allegedly, Rich explained to a source in the early '90s that the U.S. government had been quietly storing and examining some covertly retrieved crashed alien spaceships as well as some gifted, intact ET craft. According to this source, Rich claimed that President Richard Nixon ordered a purge of all government data regarding this crashed UFO reverse-engineering program.[33] Additionally, Nixon pushed for the recovered ET technology to be placed in the hands of some wealthy private corporation's board of directors. Evidently, Nixon felt that such large companies—who contributed heavily to Nixon's 1968 and 1972 presidential campaigns and expected something in return—should be allowed access in order to reverse engineer and reimagine ET technology to advance American innovation.

Also, Ben's son Michael Rich went on to serve as the President and Chief Executive Officer of the RAND Corporation, where Nixon's famous National Security Adviser, Henry Kissinger, was once a consultant[34] and later a guest lecturer.

Donald Phillips, an aerodynamics engineer and CIA contractor at Lockheed's Skunk Works, once stated[35]: "These UFOs were huge and they would just come to a stop [in the sky] and do a 60-degree, 45-degree, 10-degree turn, and then immediately reverse this action." In December 2000, Phillips stated on camera that the United States had possession of a recovered alien spacecraft. Allegedly, he had read a secret government file claiming that Nixon's former boss and later adviser, President Eisenhower, made initial face-to-face contact with friendly extraterrestrials in 1954 at Edwards Airbase. That military installation is located thirty-eight miles from the current Skunk Works headquarters in Palmdale, California. It would seem a likely conclusion, therefore, that Mr. Phillips at least knew, if not once worked with, the late Benjamin Rich. Judging from both men's age and career paths, this meeting took place at least partly during the Nixon administration.

Former Nevada Senator Harry M. Reid[36] (1939-2021), once the U.S. Senate Majority Leader, was quoted as saying that defense contractor Lockheed Martin—a substantial player in Nevada's corporate community—may have possessed recovered alien technology. "I was told for decades that Lockheed had some of these retrieved materials," Reid informed *The New Yorker*.[37]

James Goodall, a journalist who befriended Ben Rich, claimed that he spoke to him over the phone about ten days before Mr. Rich's 1995 death. "Jim," Ben supposedly told him, "We have things in the desert that are fifty years beyond what you can comprehend."[38]

According to an article published in the May 2010 issue of the *MUFON UFO Journal* by Tom Keller, Ben Rich had already revealed his shocking otherworldly information sometime before his death in January 1995. Keller was an aerospace engineer who once worked as a computer systems analyst for NASA's Jet Propulsion Laboratories.[39] In a statement, somewhat condensed here, Rich supposedly said: "We already have the means to travel among the stars...We now have the technology to take ET home. No, it won't take someone's lifetime to do it...There are two types of UFOs—the ones we build and ones 'they' build. We learned from both crash retrievals and actual hand-me-downs. The government knew this and until 1969 took an active hand in the administration of that information. After a 1969 Nixon 'purge,' administration [of captured ET technology] was handled by an international board of directors in the private sector."

In July 1986, after Testor Corporation model-kit designer John Andrews wrote to Ben Rich asking what he thought about the possible existence of either man-made or extraterrestrial spaceships, Rich responded: "I'm a believer in both categories. I feel everything is possible. In both categories, there are a lot of kooks and charlatans—be cautious."[40]

When it comes to some of the dubious UFO community sources

involving themselves in retelling the Nixon-Gleason encounter, this seems like a most appropriate description.

1. Wikipedia contributors, "Bob Hope," *Wikipedia*.
2. Wikipedia contributors, "Spiro Agnew," *Wikipedia*.
3. Wikipedia contributors, "Gerald Ford," *Wikipedia*.
4. "Bob Hope House, John Lautner's Modernist Masterpiece," *Modern Palm Springs*.
5. Nicolette Wenzell, "Explore Palm Springs: Bob Hope House," *Palm Springs Life*, July 22, 2013.
6. "Bob Hope's UFO House in Palm Springs, CA (Listed for $25 Million)," *Home Stratosphere*, July 6, 2020.
7. Joi-Marie McKenzie, "Bob Hope's UFO House Has Sold For $13 Million," *ABC News*, December 1, 2016.
8. "Bob Hope Says Nixon Seems In Need of Rest," *New York Times*, February 24, 1975.
9. Ann Brenoff, "Bob Hope's House In Toluca Lake, Calif, Had Enough Room For Nixon to Land a Helicopter," *Huffington Post*, September 24, 2013.
10. Jeff Shain, "Flashback: Jackie Gleason's Inverrary Classic," *Pro Golf Weekly*, February 22, 2016.
11. Harry S Truman Presidential Library record of the documentary.
12. Nixon presidential library 1973, 9.
13. Nixon presidential library 1973, 3.
14. "Homestead UFO House," *Abandoned Florida*, July 3, 2013.
15. "Condon, Gretchen," *Altmeyer Funeral Home*, October 2020.
16. "Citizens Against UFO Secrecy," at 3518 Martha Custis Drive, Alexandria, VA 22302.
17. Editors of Publications International, "Jackie Gleason Sees a UFO," *How Stuff Works*.
18. "Tim Beckley," greyfalcon.us.
19. Details of which can be found in many sites, including *inquisitr.com*.
20. K. T. Frankovich , *Educate Yourself*, 2005.
21. K. T. Frankovich , *Where Heavens Meet* (Oakville: Language of Souls Publications, 1999).
22. K.T. Frankovich , "The Lime Grove Encounters," *Soul Guidance*.
23. Miamiteacher, *Amazon.com*, Review, September 11, 2004.
24. "UFOs and American Presidents," *UFO Casebook*, June 17, 2011.
25. Wikipedia contributors, "Oklahoma City Air Force Station," *Wikipedia*.
26. Nixon.gov, presidential daily schedule for January 1974.
27. "Arab Oil Embargo," *Brittanica.com*.
28. "1974: January UFO & Alien Sightings," *Think About It*.
29. "The 1974 UFO Chronology," *NICAP*.
30. Jeff Parrott, "Ronald Reagan Spoke at the First CPAC Gathering in 1974. Here's What He Said," *Deseret.com*.
31. Wikipedia contributors, "Ray Price," *Wikipedia*.
32. Wikipedia contributors, "Ben Rich," *Wikipedia*.
33. Gaia staff, "Ben Rich, Lockheed-Martin, and UFOs," *Gaia.com*, December 3, 2019.
34. Wikipedia contributors, "Henry Kissinger," *Wikipedia*.

35. Richard Markosian, "Aliens at Dugway Proving Ground: Spaceships Taking Off From "The New Area 51"?" *Utah Stories*, April 18, 2018.
36. Wikipedia contributors, "Harry Reid," *Wikipedia*.
37. Brett Bachman, "Former Senator Harry Reid: I Was Told Lockheed-Martin Had UFO Crash Fragments," *Salon.com*, May 1, 2021.
38. Arium Walla, "Second Director of Lockheed Skunk Works Shocking Comments About UFO Technology," *bibliotecaleyades.net,* June 23, 2015.
39. "Extraterrestrials UFOs Are Real," *UFOresearchnetwork.com,* September 2, 2010.
40. "Ben Rich, Area 51, & Taking ET Home," October 14, 2014.

CHAPTER SIX

THE EMENEGGER ET EXPERIENCE

"In an unprecedented move, the Air Force, Army, and Navy gave their full backing to a UFO-themed production—so too did NASA."

It is an internet legend now, but an alleged impromptu extraterrestrial landing event from May 1971 may have resulted in some sustained airbase communication with Air Force officials in New Mexico. When these events were related to two Hollywood movie producers in the spring of 1973, it may have signaled a new government plan for carefully guided public disclosure, possibly inspired by the covert Nixon-Gleason Homestead affair two months earlier.

Robert E. Emenegger (1933-) was born in Richard Nixon's home-town of Whittier, California.[1] He is now a retired TV and film producer and advertising executive and, by all accounts, a kind and talented man. Back in his college days at the University of California Los Angeles, he became friends with Harry Robins Haldeman[2] (1926-1993), a UCLA fraternity brother who went on to find employment under Richard Nixon, most notably as his heavily relied upon White House Chief of Staff.

By the late '60s, Robert Emenegger had dabbled in showbiz projects, producing informative advertising and documentary films for large corporations and, significantly, the U.S. Department of Defense.[3] He even spent several years working for the United States Information Agency. He was not your average L.A. film producer, swimming in starlets and cocktail parties under the looming HOLLY-WOOD sign. Emenegger was well-connected with government officials in Washington, D.C.

Perhaps, then, it should be no surprise that Robert Emenegger was contacted by new President-elect Richard Nixon in December 1968. Nixon was seeking Emenegger's "active participation and assistance" in finding "exceptional individuals" worthy of jobs in his incoming administration. In this letter, Nixon referred to Robert Emenegger as "a leader" and "in a position to know and recommend...the best minds in America." Was it H. R. "Bob" Haldeman who recommended Nixon contact his old college chum Emenegger in late 1968? Haldeman had been associated with Nixon since at least the 1960 presidential campaign.

Supposedly, by "early 1973,"[4] as Emenegger begins his story in taped interviews, he and Allan Sandler, his production partner, were casting about for ideas for their next documentary. Emenegger said that, at one point in their relationship, he discovered that his co-executive "had very strange connections" for a producer and "did things for the CIA, and maybe even the FBI."[5] The duo was contacted by members of President Nixon's staff—specifically *whom* has never been stated—about creating a film exploring some interesting science projects that American military minds were working on. Comfortably re-elected, Nixon apparently wanted to pump up his profile as an ally of the scientific community after recently promoting an exciting new concept: a space station orbiting the earth, manned by astronauts and personnel arriving via a reusable shuttle program. These two pricey projects would replace the outdated Apollo missions to the moon of the past decade.

By the first months of 1973, second-term Nixon wanted to be

associated with great science and space projects—but precisely *why*, again? Let's take a look at one logical theory...

The truth may well be that "control freak" Richard Nixon was already thinking along the lines of another term as president—to campaign in 1976 despite having served two terms already as the law limited. *He didn't care to relinquish power.* In some candid Nixon biographies, it has been noted that he was privately bandying about the notion of attempting to repeal the constitutional law on a two-term limit for U.S. chief executives and running again to retain his "Imperial Presidency," as it was dubbed. This would explain his strong desire to cling to power during his developing Watergate scandals. Perhaps he was hoping the scandals would be explained away or forgiven and that a countermovement would push, instead, for misunderstood and unfairly slandered Nixon to be deemed worthy as a third-term candidate. He even had "The Spirit of '76" painted on the side of Air Force One. In the summer of 1973, Republicans partial to Nixon announced to the press that they wanted their president to be elected to a third term and organized a group called "The Committee to Repeal the Twenty-Second Amendment." Nixon not only knew of this but was rumored to be the main source behind the effort. On Oval Office tapes, for example, Nixon can be heard worrying about Democratic Senator Ted Kennedy (1932-2009) and "ruining him in time for '76."[6] That should not have been his concern after the November 1972 election victory if the legal two-term limit was observed.

A major dilemma for Nixon in 1973 was the improbability of the Democrat-controlled Congress cooperating with legislation to repeal the two-term limit. Getting Republican congressional candidates to sweep to victory in a successful November 1974 election, to seize control of both houses of Congress, became a critical goal of the Nixon team. Once in charge, conservatives would clear the way with bold legislation in 1975 that would allow Nixon his prized third term[7]—perhaps even a fourth. Hence, it was more important than ever in February 1973 for "Tricky Dick" to silence Watergate burglary participants and keep raking in campaign contributions. He and his inner circle *had* to overcome the growing storm of criticism and investigations in Washington. How could he swing public support for the entire grand scheme?

Perhaps a special documentary on national television—promoting Nixon's fascinating science programs as a splendid, exciting vision for America's future—might help set the table. Publicly promoting popular NASA space missions, described as possible under his insightful leadership, would cement his image as progressive and indispensable in the eyes of voters and historians. If such a film went a step further and included government admissions of current ET contact, perhaps including brief landing and communication footage, that would *really* capture the public's imagination. When the subsequent controversy exploded, Nixon could then calmly step forward and openly confirm the rumors, saying he was engaged in delicate U.S.-ET negotiations that were destined to take several more years to complete. He could argue that he alone was needed in the White House to manage ongoing, complex alien contact and lead new scientific programs, like the space station. He could even admit that some of this extraterrestrial communication was first established when he was Eisenhower's vice president during secret meetings at U.S. airbases in 1954 and 1955. Twenty years later, it was reaching an important crescendo under his cautious but clever stewardship, and America needed his expert handling of the situation to continue without interruption.

And presto! Congress would be greatly pressured by the public to repeal the ban on a third term. A groundswell of support would build into a tidal wave. Nixon could surf it for four, or even *eight*, more years as president.

All of this was possibly on the mind of Nixon when he met with Gleason (and Bob Hope?) at Homestead in 1973. The late-night airbase tour may have even been a first step in the process. Gauging their reactions, having big-name celebrities in his corner when UFO disclosure *and* a third term was to be announced in the next years, and reaping financial windfalls to afford pricey silence from his jailed henchmen...this was Nixon at his craftiest.

It's not really a far-fetched notion. President Franklin Roosevelt[8] managed to convince the voting public that he was indispensable and worthy of not one but *two* more terms, after having already served a pair. This depended upon swaying the country's voting populace that it needed FDR's invaluable stewardship to keep us out of the ongoing European war—like no other candidate could?—and then later to *win* World War II. "Don't change horses in the middle of the creek," as the old political axiom goes. And, after all, several U.S. senators, bureaucrats, and FBI Director Hoover had been in power for *decades*, so why not Nixon in the '70s? By the spring of 1973, America's chief executive was only sixty and appeared healthy and vigorous, with a picturesque First Family that maintained a public air of dignity and morality. First, he had to crush the Watergate scandal (which would, in turn, crush him).

Nixon also kept his eyes on another grand prize: a most lauded place in history books. Obviously, any ET contact revelation would be an electrifying blockbuster with global shockwaves. Who wouldn't want to take credit for it?

To accomplish all of this, Nixon first needed that crucial Hollywood documentary to be released in 1974 or early 1975, either on television or in theaters. It would start the ball rolling with convincing images of genuine UFOs and perhaps even of an ET landing on American soil, *during* his presidency. Again, Nixon's goal here was to get the initial word out and thus brace the public for more announcements and information sometime before the 1976 campaign season. The public needed time to adjust to the news, and Congress needed time to repeal that pesky amendment. Again, this could also explain why Nixon kept on raising "campaign funds" *after* his 1972 re-election.

To emphasize again, this is only a theory of what could have been floating around in the scheming president's mind in early 1973, but it is based upon facts and logical speculation.

Now, let's get back on point...

There were three advanced scientific research projects the federal government had been working on that producers Robert Emenegger and Allan Sandler were offered in the early spring of 1973, but none had any ostensible connection to UFOs. They were allowed onto American military installations—including Wright-Patterson AFB—to view exhibitions that included trained dogs, trained porpoises, and cool lasers. Then...an invitation was offered in May 1973 to learn more about a fourth project by traveling from Los Angeles to Norton Air Force Base,[9] located about seventy miles east, outside San Bernardino, California. Once there, they'd speak to the top man from the Air Force Office of Special Investigations, and he would send them to the source who controlled some fascinating film they needed to augment the science documentary. All Air Force footage went to Norton in those days for safekeeping.

Not much is known about Paul Shartle, an Air Force officer who was the head of the Norton Airbase audio-visual department in 1973. He was a former head of security, well-prepared to oversee the storage of top-secret film that had been locked up by the U.S. Air Force.

After some discussion with this Air Force representative, the subject of UFOs was finally brought up to the movie duo. Emenegger recalled decades later being previously skeptical of such other-worldly matters. There's no telling what Sandler felt. Shartle had run only an electrifying *idea* past the production partners as a kind of hypothetical: "What would you say if I had footage of an alien craft landing at Holloman Air Force base? Would that make for a good documentary movie?" At first, Shartle seemed to edge around whether he actually *possessed* such amazing film, as if dangling the proverbial carrot on a stick. Emenegger and Sandler went for it, eagerly asking for more info.

A UFO landing? Genuine extraterrestrials? On the runway of an airbase in New Mexico? When did *that* happen?

"A few years ago," Robert Emenegger recalled hearing in

response while interviewed on camera decades later for paranor-maltv.com.[10] More specifically, he recalled that the filmed UFO/ET encounter happened one fine morning—6:00 a.m.—in May 1971, supposedly. The specific day was not discussed. But it was more than a landing event, the producers discovered to their delight. There was Air Force *interaction* on the ground with the visitors.

The alleged interaction occurred during Nixon's third year in office and was conveniently captured by an Air Force camera crew who were in the vicinity recording "acceleration rates" of our latest jet planes at the desert base, which is ringed by distant mountains. It was truly an alien vehicle, Emenegger was assured; it was circular, silent, and nothing man-made. It came down out of the sky silently that May 1971 and settled flat on a Holloman base runway for some reason. Maybe ETs wanted to show off for the cameras? Was it all a mistake as to the prearranged time and place for setting down? Or perhaps the alien ship was having mechanical problems and simply made an *emergency* impromptu touch-down?

Obviously, the footage proposal raised a whole series of ques-tions, likely none of which the Air Force wanted to answer. But Paul Shartle had broken the ice and made the offer: would Emenegger and Sandler like to assess—and even *possess*—the exciting footage? Would they place it within their new science documentary for Presi-dent Nixon?

Enthused by the notion, the two filmmakers accepted, assured they would receive the classified footage as soon as official military and government clearances allowed them to have it. They went back to Hollywood and changed the course of their documentary. Instead of just a little science film for television, they'd make a full-length major motion picture *exclusively* on alien contact. They could feature images of UFOs as they were described in past centuries and sight-ings in recent years. The thrilling footage of the Holloman incident would be the dramatic highlight of their bold new film. But there was one person Emenegger wanted to consult with before getting carried away at the prospect of such a historic advent: his old buddy Bob Haldeman.

By late April 1973, H. R. Haldeman had suffered a severe reversal of fortunes. President Nixon had recently fired him. Out of work and in expensive legal peril for authorizing criminal conduct *and* participating in the cover-up of the Watergate fiasco, Bob had been thrown overboard by his old White House boss and was currently back in Los Angeles, at least from time to time.[11] Did he know anything about a May 1971 extraterrestrial landing at Holloman Air Force Base?

According to Emenegger, ex-aide Haldeman was vague on the 1971 ET allegation, saying evasively that he'd only heard rumors of it and was unsure if President Nixon knew about it or not. Was Haldeman being purposely coy, or even outright *lying*, regarding something that was likely classified as top secret? Despite being already exiled, Haldeman still needed to observe security codes or face recriminations if he talked about sensitive subjects. He was in enough legal trouble as it was. Perhaps he could also leverage some secrets learned during his White House tenure, potentially pressuring Nixon since the ex-Chief of Staff knew plenty and *might* just spill some shocking stories if he received no financial aid or help to reduce or dismiss the charges against him. Thus, Bob had genuine reasons for his hazy reply to Emenegger. It should be emphasized that Haldeman, a Christian Scientist, did not deny or dismiss the claim.

Let's return to May 1971 and the Holloman footage allegedly taken then. Is there any sign of an alien landing in New Mexico lurking within President Nixon's White House digitized records?

A check of those presidential logs, unfortunately, shows no great flurry of calls to or from Holloman Airbase that month in 1971. Certainly, there were no presidential visits to New Mexico or even Oval Office meetings with USAF or New Mexico-based government officials. However, there is one *possible* red flag.[12]

If this landing episode truly occurred at 6:00 a.m. Mountain Time in May, that would be 8:00 a.m. Eastern Time at the White

PAUL BLAKE SMITH

House. On Friday, May 7, 1973, the official logs show that after a six-minute breakfast that early morning, Richard Nixon visited the Lincoln sitting room, which was not normally one of his haunts. This was a White House site that—one would think—had no bugs, no recording devices that could capture conversations on sensitive security matters. Once seated comfortably there at 8:37, Nixon spoke on the phone—in theory without being overheard by anyone—to an aide who provided updates of some kind *three* different times over the course of the next hour: Bob Haldeman, who had been on the February Key Biscayne trip.

What was going on here? What topic required a bug-free phone (presumably) in the executive mansion instead of Nixon's wired EOB office or West Wing Oval Office, where he almost always headed after his morning meal?

When Nixon and Haldeman conversed, it was always about the most important government matters—never small talk. In the spring of 1971, all of the scandals that drove Nixon from power when exposed were not even dreamed of yet.

At close to 10:00 a.m. that May 7, Nixon, his wife, and a couple of aides had to depart for a prearranged opening of a "Salute to Agriculture" going on in Washington. By 10:40, the president returned and settled in at his Oval Office desk to attend to regular business matters. This included a half-hour meeting with Haldeman. So, obviously, something substantial enough to require updates and briefings was going on. *Quite remarkably, this half-hour face-to-face confab was repeated three more times that day* in addition to Nixon huddling with a brigadier general. Then it was time to host a planned White House dinner for the "Salute to Agriculture" crowd.

This intermittent plotting could have been about *any* matter, but it was logically some high-level stuff involving, as it did, the busy Chief of Staff. The unspecified issue at hand that day obviously needed regular discussion, updating, and strategizing. Was it related to issues of the ongoing cosmic situation at the New Mexico military site?

That's about as close as we might get to a possible matching date for any alien contact at Holloman in that month and year. President Nixon resumed his regular schedule in the days to come, and nothing unusual seemingly occurred in the days and weeks after, no more half-hour Haldeman huddles three or four times a day.

To historians and Nixon biographers—people in the know—Bob Haldeman was a man privy to many secrets, which is only natural as he was incredibly close and loyal to the president. He even perjured himself to protect his beleaguered, beloved chief executive. Haldeman handled almost every matter for Nixon, right down to the amount of toilet paper available for the president's use at Camp David.[13] It was a private conversation between Nixon and Haldeman a year later (June 20, 1972) that led to something eventually called "The 18 and a Half Minute Gap." That was the infamous audiotape from the Oval Office, recorded when Nixon and Haldeman talked candidly about the implications of what the newly arrested presidential aide Charles W. Colson[14] (1931-2012) might be able to tell the FBI, the police, or the press about the Nixon presidency. What juicy secrets of crude, criminal, or classified conduct did Colson know? Someone—likely Nixon himself, who was clumsy with mechanical devices—deliberately erased the tape in five different sections, resulting in over eighteen minutes of silence for investigators to ponder. What precisely was discussed on the tape? Mr. Haldeman wrote in his memoirs only that he and the president worried aloud on various sensitive matters Colson was aware of. The question now arises: *could it have been about the May 1971 alien landing at Holloman Airbase?* That would have been something Charles Colson might have learned and worth the potential "obstruction of justice" charge Nixon risked to blatantly cover it up. Still, this is purely speculative.

Was historic ET-human contact really undertaken—planned or unplanned—on Friday, May 7, 1971, in New Mexico? Were the footage and the landing it depicted legitimate? To this day, it remains uncertain.

Some versions of the Emenegger tale have inexplicably dated the alleged Holloman UFO landing as April 25, 1964, when Lyndon B. Johnson was president. On that specific Saturday, LBJ was entertaining Harry S Truman—two political enemies of Nixon—at the White House.[15] If so, just why would the Nixon people want a documentary made of an event from nearly a decade earlier, during the liberal Johnson administration? What good would that do for Nixon and his team? If it had happened in 1971, however, scheming Nixon could have logically taken credit someday by saying, "Look who landed during my administration and chose to make contact while *I* was in charge." Some other interpretations of the Holloman airbase incident have insisted that April 1964 truly featured an ET landing but that the May 1971 affair was a *continuation* of that ongoing contact program.

Some UFO researchers claim there was 600 feet of 16 mm footage of the New Mexico incident. There are other claims that it was about 800 feet,[16] or even 3,200 feet, in total. Paul Shartle apparently told Emenegger that three different Air Force cameramen, stationed in three diverse areas around the Holloman base, captured the startling images while hardly anyone else was around in those early sunrise hours. They were only intending to make a short military briefing film about the latest jets taking off with exciting new acceleration rates. The footage that the crew ended up with featured the event of a lifetime.

The aliens supposedly did more than just land for a few seconds. According to Paul Shartle—who described the footage—the visitors settled their craft, opened a doorway, and lowered a ramp. After a pause, the ETs stepped out. They walked around the ship as well—possibly assessing damage and making repairs. At one point, they were approached by curious base officials. Afterward, they ended up sticking around for a day or two, communicating peacefully with them. If all of this is true, then this fantastic event would have been of great government and military concern and quickly classified as "ultra-top-secret." President Nixon surely would have been notified within an hour or two of such historic contact.

As the year progressed, a Pentagon spokesman informed the two L.A. filmmakers that "the Secretary of the Air Force gave us the order to cooperate."[17] That order would have been issued by newly appointed John L. McLucas[18] (1920-2002), an extremely bright and capable individual who attended three different universities and served in the Navy, the Air Force, and later as head of the FAA under President Ford. *Wikipedia* tells about John's immediate past: "From 1969 through 1973, McLucas also served as director of the National Reconnaissance Office, working directly for the secretary of defense with support from the CIA...McLucas was an associate fellow of the American Institute of Aeronautics and Astronautics, in 1971," which would have been when the interplanetary spacecraft set down at Holloman—if it did.

Secretary McLucas was graced with two distinguished honors in 1973. He became the very first winner of the Bronze Palm Award and the U.S. Air Force Award for Exceptional Service. On May 24, 1973, McLucas and Bob Hope were among the honored guests at a White House dinner for POWs. The next day, Nixon flew to Homestead AFB and Key Biscayne, and, once again, the list of passengers for this Air Force One flight was strangely deleted from White House logs.

As one UFO website summed up of Emenegger and Sandler's government approval during that time: "In an unprecedented move, the Air Force, Army, and Navy gave their full backing to a UFO-themed production—so too did NASA...The roots of the project likely lead back to Langley, Virginia, and to the CIA." Emenegger explained he received his briefing at Norton Airbase inside a CIA "clean room, so there was no way anyone could eavesdrop on us." As Robbie Graham of mysteriousuniverse.org mentioned, "Emenegger told me that a 'CIA courier' named Richard Beske shadowed him and his crew throughout his documentary's entire production process. Beske was 'always hanging around us,' Emenegger said." Sandler is also alleged to have had some CIA connections in his past, as had the approving Air Force Secretary McLucas. If they were not exploring a truthful UFO tale, why all the CIA "spooks" hovering about?

{According to mysteriousuniverse.org, Richard Beske "later became a member of a steering committee for Veterans Intelligence Officers For Sanity" in 2003 to help protest the use of false intel in foreign affairs.}

Apparently, word of Emenegger's top-secret film project got out. A 1974 *National Tattler* article reported that the Defense Department was "already collaborating" with a film company, said to have been "Allan Sandler Productions of Los Angeles, on a major movie about UFOs."[19]

In interviews decades later, Robert Emenegger claimed to have been shown some other exciting footage. One example was described as top-secret footage shot on an unspecified date at Vandenberg Air Force Base. It showed two UFOs "playfully running behind" a fired missile. "It was clear now that Nixon had his own UFO interest and had directed his staff to get involved in some form of UFO disclosure," the retired Emenegger theorized in hindsight.

Furthermore, Emenegger recalled that UFO information from the yellowing old files of the closed Project Blue Book became accessible around this time. The new movie promised to be a major, unprecedented government disclosure project, throwing the curtain back on a previously taboo topic that was now of interest to the entire planet.

All of this—if true—means that very shortly after Nixon showed Gleason the goods at Homestead AFB, the president felt the time was right to introduce the public to the same revelation. Nixon was preparing for government disclosure, but he wanted it done slowly, within a documentary that he could take credit for or disavow if the need arose. If it was a well-reviewed success, the president could step in, take credit, and explain some of his actions in the potential media controversy. If the movie was somehow discredited or slammed by critics and audiences alike, he could try a different approach. The Nixon team must have known what was in production by mid-1973 and sent down the word to military personnel to quietly cooperate with the film crew because Emenegger and Sandler found some surprisingly open doors and accommodating government sites.

During this time, the ugly clown car of the Watergate scandal popped up, and a parade of dirty secrets spilled out for all to see and hear. Various devious and illegal schemes designed to undermine Nixon's potential Democratic Party opponents and vocal critics were exposed and repeatedly aired in the courts, congress, and media. The public slowly turned on Machiavellian Richard Milhouse Nixon. The American people realized they had been hoodwinked about what was going on behind the scenes of his administration, the prosecution of the Vietnam War, and federal programs over the past decade. Great cynicism, disdain, and disbelief in governmental authority resulted, and the effects of this distrust linger to this day.

At some point in rocky 1974, President Nixon made the decision to pull the plug on public disclosure but still allowed Emenegger and Sandler's film to go forward. Was this decision influenced by the mysterious UFO incident of January 1974 (see the previous chapter) or perhaps events at Homestead that February? Certainly, censorship of the president's daily records are clues to the secretive nature of his actions during that time. However, the Nixon administration—and that CIA observer lurking about—made no immediate attempt to shut down or sabotage the film's production. However, there would no longer be official government footage handed over and no grand, shocking official revelations. Great hopes for world-changing success, fame, and fortune died. Emenegger and Sandler were both furious and deflated—yet the duo kept going.

If President Richard Nixon truly desired official disclosure, why didn't he just arrange a big speech about alien visitation on national television, perhaps from the United Nations or Oval Office? In that way, he could personalize it and slant the resulting media hyperbole toward crediting his great leadership. Why allow the truth to get out first through a theatrical film? Nixon was evidently letting documentarians handle some of the riveting subject, which seems a bit odd. However, the finished film might have been intended as a mere first step, a lead-in to a grand national speech, broadcast, if possible, to the entire planet.

Was Holloman AFB *really* a site of alien-human contact?

Let's review a claim from an online UFO forum called thelivingmoon.com.[20] It featured a June 2005 post regarding a revelation given to the forum poster (a military man) by "an old retired NCO" (Non-Commissioned Officer). The older man said he and a partner once "drove past the back side of a old hangar" at Holloman AFB and quickly "looked in and saw a parked disk. By the time they drove back around to the other side of the hanger, two black sedans came tearing up to them and stopped his truck. The occupants threatened them with everything in the book if they ever said anything about it. So he didn't, until he told me. His age at the time would indicate that he was there in the mid-'60s."

Was the forum poster's figuring of time accurate? If so, it would indicate that an ET ship came down in the years *before* the May 1971 landing, although it is possible the NCO might have been an actual eyewitness of the same craft in Emenegger's missing film. That ET airship was said to have been taken to a nearby hangar.

Then there's information first presented by the late UFO researcher Art Campbell[21] and relayed in this author's 2020 book, *President Eisenhower's Close Encounters*. That's the tale of Dwight Eisenhower ducking out of a February 1955 quail hunt in Georgia to fly to Holloman AFB and meet with friendly aliens. On February 11, 1955, Eisenhower is rumored to have walked out of Air Force One on a Holloman runway and met with beings who had recently landed in a small, round spaceship while another circular ship hovered above watchfully. This meeting lasted only a few minutes before the ETs departed, and the president went inside to ask assembled base personnel to remain silent about his visit. The affair evidently did not involve any gifted or crashed extraterrestrial craft, however. It did establish Holloman AFB's runways as a safe site for ET landings and certified that another landing—planned or unplanned—would not come as a complete shock to base officials in 1971.

Robert Emenegger revealed years later that a few members of his film's technical crew were allowed to fly to Holloman Airbase and record footage of military jet planes landing—more on that subject coming up—and inspect two different base buildings (#383 and #1382). They were informed that calm, productive meetings were held between Air Force officials and the humanoid ETs in those structures during the May 1971 event. Was any of this face-to-face contact filmed? If so, where is it? What was said? What insights did they learn?

Again, the celluloid proof was supposedly held for safekeeping in a vault at Norton Airbase (which was located seventy-eight miles from Nixon's San Clemente home[22]). On October 14, 1988, in a syndicated television special called *UFOs: Government Cover-up Live!*[23], Paul Shartle appeared on camera alongside Emenegger at last and discussed what was recorded in that special New Mexico footage. Paul Shartle alleged that he had seen it "several times."

First, the film showed "three disc-shaped craft" that appeared over the arid desert base. One spaceship set down, oscillating at times, perhaps in destabilized peril. The other two seemed to take off or at least move out of range of the cameras that were set up. The one round metallic spacecraft sat there silently on the runway for a moment before "a sliding door opened, a ramp was extended, and out came three aliens." Naturally, Shartle remembered this part of the shocking images well: "They were human-sized. They had an odd, gray complexion and a pronounced nose." The trio sported "tight-fitting jumpsuits," he recalled, and were obviously no threat. This description sounds similar to the beings that stepped out of one of five ships that landed at a California desert airbase to meet in peace with President Eisenhower in February 1954. That interaction was also filmed and viewed years later by Hollywood producer Jaimie H. Shandera (1943-)[24], according to a military source.

Shartle said that Air Force officials based out of Holloman offices rushed out to greet the curious aliens, who were bravely standing their ground by their apparently damaged ship, looking around in the warmth of the morning sunshine. The uniformed USAF represen-

PAUL BLAKE SMITH

tatives were doubtlessly stunned by the scene playing out before them on the distant runway. *Cosmic contact was really happening!*

Linda Moulton Howe has reported on Earthfiles.com that Robert Emenegger once told her it was his understanding that Holloman officials later referred to the oval-shaped craft with thin metal legs as "The Bathtub."[25] According to Robert's sources, the alien crew members exhibited a "blue-white" skin color. They sported a kind of "silver leotard" for clothing and had an unusual "raised lobe" on the backs of their heads. There is, then, a clear disconnect between different sources and their descriptions of the impromptu visitors.

Supposedly, in the footage, Air Force officials watched the trio of kindly ETs—each about 5'2" in height—walk across the runway toward them. They had human-like arms and legs and, presumably, fingers and toes. The three entities appeared to have been serious "professional types," perhaps pilot-scientists, doctors, or botanists. They displayed no violent intent.

These descriptions are all completely at odds with Bev Gleason's account of Jackie's four alien cadavers at Homestead, so we can rule out a direct connection between the two species and cases.

One of the three aliens apparently clutched a kind of "translator" object: a high-tech rod encircled with a spiral. All the ETs had on a thin "headdress," which came down around their ears, over their foreheads, and just above their two eyes. These "skull caps" might have been for communicating thoughts or emotions or were necessary for flight within their advanced ship. Perhaps they were used to interacting telepathically with the shipboard computer system. Perhaps they were just considered fashionable.

Their faces featured distinctive, hooked noses that were larger than the average human nose and bent downward, with two nostrils. It is safe to assume that the ETs could breathe air similar to Earth's atmosphere. The beings also featured two eyes with vertical pupils, resembling those of a cat. "Their mouths were thin and slit-like, with no chins," Shartle explained. This might have explained why they needed the communications headgear, since they were not accustomed to or capable of speaking aloud. {Some data provided here by ufocasebook.com.}

Then the footage ended, Emenegger learned.

When Paul Shartle asked one Air Force official at Norton AFB about the mind-blowing celluloid, the response was that it was merely "theatrical footage" purchased by the military in order to be shown someday to privileged personnel as part of a "training film." Yet Shartle stated in the 1988 TV special— hosted by respected M*A*S*H actor Mike Farrell— that the celluloid imagery seemed to be "too real," *not* faked by a Hollywood production company or the U.S. military. It would have taken a sizable budget to produce the odd-looking, costumed aliens and their realistic-looking spaceship. Why would they spend so much time and money on something with no apparent purpose?

Also of note: there was no official record of the footage in Shartle's files when he checked. This was most unusual, he said. It was Shartle's job to record all USAF film purchases. Why wasn't this alleged "purchased theatrical film" included in the audio-visual filing system? Where were the receipts or records?

It became Shartle's opinion that the "purchased theatrical film" was a government or military cover story to keep the images from being leaked in a potential major news story. They had to come up with something to prevent unwanted disclosure.

Why did the alien ship land at around 6:00 a.m.? During the TV special, Shartle claimed that one of the crafts "appeared to be in trouble because it oscillated as it came all the way down to the ground." It eventually settled successfully on the runway "on three pods." Shartle made a wavy hand gesture as he explained the tale, simulating the shakily landing craft as it neared the ground, its pilots evidently trying to avoid a devastating crash on the runway. This makes it seem like a mere mechanical problem caused a sudden, unplanned landing and, later, airbase contact. The ETs were stranded, at the mercy of the United States Air Force[26], until they made repairs. It was all accidental and unintended.

Emenegger said he was told that one of the Holloman officials informed the 1971 extraterrestrial visitors that the U.S. government had been monitoring signals from an alien group in space, odd sounds with which they were unfamiliar. Did their unexpected alien counterparts know anything about this communication? The ETs allegedly replied negatively.

Kudos and congratulations must be relayed to Paul Shartle for risking plenty in telling all. What happened to him after the controversial 1988 syndicated broadcast? Not much seems to be available on the mystery man, but an online search returns an obituary[27]: "Paul Robert Shartle, June 30, 1922—September 19, 2001—of Redlands, California."[28] Even though he died in Cincinnati, Ohio, a San Bernardino post office box address is given, and, of course, that city is situated near Norton AFB.[29] The obituary also featured a quick mention of Shartle's connection to the "U.S. Army," but there is no U.S. Air Force service listed. Oddly, no further military information was relayed at all.

During the spring and summer of 1973, Robert Emenegger was naturally excited by the prospect of obtaining this unique, grand prize, but he admits he was never actually *shown* the impressive Holloman film. He kept waiting, patient but occupied as he pieced together the rest of his UFO documentary. He spent part of his time recruiting celebrities, such as high-profile Hollywood actors Rod Serling (1924-1975), Burgess Meredith (1907-1997), and Jose Ferrer (1912-1992), to participate. The footage that Emenegger was going to receive from the military would be the final scene, a perfect way to cap off the movie. It would really open some eyes and help attract theater audiences. Maybe Nixon and his people would take credit for the fantastic footage around the time of the movie's premiere. Great publicity! Nixon's official disclosure *and* the film would then be the talk of the nation, if not the world, and bring a fortune in box-office receipts in return. The great release was scheduled for August 1974.

Instead, it was Nixon who got released—on August 9, 1974.

To make a long story short, Emenegger claimed that, on the very day the Holloman alien footage was supposed to be turned over to him, he was denied instead at the last *minute*. He was informed that the official government approval was rescinded. The rug had been pulled out from under him. A Pentagon colonel informed him that the timing just wasn't right anymore. Nixon's Watergate mess was picking up steam by that point, saturating the media and causing the president's poll ratings to plummet. Revealing the Holloman footage would probably not help the flailing president and could even potentially *harm* him since the entire alien visitation issue had clearly been withheld from the public for years and hushed up by the Nixon administration. The public would be furious to find out *another* big cover-up had been going on, and they may also be curious to learn more, possibly opening more cans of worms. Nixon had enough scandals on his hands at the time. He didn't need one more.

Initially feeling snubbed, disappointed, and angry, Robert Emenegger said he was gently encouraged by his government contact to simply mention in the finished film the Holloman incident as a *possibility*, a scene from America's past "or perhaps from the future." Emenegger had a professional graphic artist draw some scenes of the alleged runway encounter and used that in the documentary instead. Emenegger and Sandler also utilized some of their own earlier footage showing an Air Force jet landing on a Holloman runway. Shown at a long distance, the jet and its landing lights created a small, glowing dot in the brief film segment. It was rather fuzzy, but it looked a bit like a UFO and would have to do instead of the real deal. They had no choice. Nixon had stiffed them.

As the spring of 1974 passed, Emenegger and Sandler wrapped up the documentary and dubbed it *UFOs: Past, Present, and Future*,[30] by Sandler Institutional Films. It was copied for theatrical release across the country. The team had also readied an accompanying book, which came out in paperback with the same title, to help promote the film. The Holloman event was described in three pages and placed in the "Future" section, along with the artist's illustrations of the event (still available on the internet today). The depic-

PAUL BLAKE SMITH

tion claimed to have been "based on eyewitness descriptions," which must have been rather confusing to readers at the time since it was supposed to happen in the future.

The written scenario specified the New Mexico airbase was first alerted just after 5:30 a.m. by personnel in the control tower, warning that an unidentified object was approaching the base, according to radar screens. Tower technicians attempted to contact the aerial vehicle and ask them to identify themselves. The colonel at the base ordered a red alert when there was no response, and the UFO proved to be three different airships getting closer. Two specific airbases were telephoned to see if they knew anything about the incoming flights: Wright-Patterson in Ohio and Edwards in California—two familiar sites for UFOs, as we've seen.

Robert Emenegger added in later years[31] that two intercept jets were scrambled to take a closer look. One camera crew was at work, already filming jets from within a helicopter hovering over the runways. Another crew was recording from the ground. That's how the footage of three circular UFOs approaching in the early morning sky was captured. "One object broke away and began descending," Emenegger recalled in an interview with Linda Moulton Howe on Earthfiles.com. It seemed to hover just ten feet off the ground at one point, "yawing" for about a minute before settling safely. The base commander and some other personnel had arrived on the scene by that time. There were greetings when some ETs exited the airship, and communication was first established there, then moved indoors, within an office in the "King 1 area." Later the meeting was moved "to the end of Mars Street, to the west area building, #930."

We can see the book explored explicit details at length, but the 1974 documentary consolidated the events more succinctly. In this climactic scene, Rod Serling narrated over the footage: "Let us look at an incident that might happen in the future, or perhaps could have happened already. The premise is that contact is made by extraterrestrial beings with representatives of the United States Air Force at Holloman Air Force Base in the deserts of New Mexico..."

Emenegger's finished documentary did reasonably well with critics and the public, but it wasn't nearly the attention-getting, historic blockbuster he had originally hoped. Today it is credited as the inspiration for famous motion picture director and producer Steven Spielberg[32] (1936-) and his 1977 semi-fictional classic drama, *Close Encounters of the Third Kind.*[33] Emenegger even gave a copy of his film to the budding director, but Spielberg had his own UFO film plans, even since high school, so credit for major inspiration is likely overblown.

Emenegger and Sandler's documentary made its debut in American theaters on July 31, 1974, just ten days before Nixon resigned from office. It made its American television debut on NBC on May 9, 1975, about four years after the alleged Holloman event. The film was nominated for a Golden Globe award but lost (in a January 1976 ceremony). It was re-edited and re-released in 1979, featuring additional content and a new title: *UFOs: It Has Begun.*

When the documentary was released in theaters, we can make some guesses about who rushed to watch it. Jackie Gleason: definitely. Bob Hope: maybe. And Richard Nixon: probably not.

In 1985, during the Ronald Reagan administration, yet another offer of the historic UFO footage was allegedly made to Robert Emenegger. A retired colonel from the Air Force Public Relations Office, then living in Florida, indicated to Robert that the time was right at last. The government might be willing to release that key May 1971 footage from New Mexico. The two met to discuss the latest proposal concerning the landing footage. Sadly, it proved a false hope yet again. The footage was ultimately pulled away from theatrical use once more. The situation was becoming more frustrating than Lucy repeatedly yanking the football away before Charlie Brown could kick it.

Or did Emenegger actually get clever revenge this time?

According to an anonymous online source called "Entertainment Lawyer"—not exactly a trusted source of hard facts—writing on the contemporary website Crazy Days and Nights[34] in the 2010s, Robert

PAUL BLAKE SMITH

Emenegger cleverly set up the visiting USAF colonel. The show business "Enty Lawyer" who posts so-called "Blind Items" about Hollywood people without naming names—but their subjects are usually easy to figure out—described the scenario this way: Emenegger agreed to meet with the Air Force retiree—Paul Shartle?—in his own home, but he set up a hidden camera without telling his guest. The aging serviceman brought his UFO landing film and displayed it on a screen via a movie projector for Robert to salivate over, *not realizing it was being filmed itself*! Supposedly, Emenegger recorded a pretty good reproduction of the priceless treasure.

What supposedly happened next is just as wild. According to "Enty" within crazydaysandnights.net: Emenegger contacted Steven Spielberg and showed him the copy of the footage. Spielberg was so impressed he decided to use it in his latest major motion picture production, a sure-fire way to publicize it around the world. "Enty Lawyer" described how this plan got quashed: "The government finds out about the [illicitly copied] footage and cuts a deal with the director. They will give him access to things he can use in all his films whether it is money or technology or ideas the government is working on. He can see the prototypes and incorporate them into his movies. It is why he has always focused on science and the future and aliens and the paranormal in addition to family fare. Apparently as part of the deal, he does have a copy of that footage. A clear copy."

If the online blind item is accurate—still a big if—it means both Robert Emenegger and Steven Spielberg possess a duplicate copy of the decades-old extraterrestrial touch-down at Holloman Airbase and perhaps even some footage of the alien trio that emerged from the craft. It is obviously not something either man would discuss after being confronted by government representatives and, in Spielberg's case, cutting a secret deal to keep it secret. We must also take note that if this 1985 saga is genuine, it would have taken place sometime after conservative President Ronald Reagan—who was privately fascinated by UFOs[35]—was safely re-elected (in November 1984), much like the UFO film proposal initiated in early 1973 took place sometime after conservative President Richard Nixon was safely re-elected (in November 1972). Both conservative leaders were on solid ground, politically, from any kind of repercussions that disclosure might bring.

It must be emphasized that while the "Enty Lawyer" twist in the tale is certainly enticing, it is completely unproven, uncredited, and neither Emenegger nor Spielberg is talking. It could well be that Emenegger *still* has not actually viewed the Holloman film. Even if there was an illicitly recorded copy by Emenegger, it was *not* utilized in the 1988 television special that both he and his USAF friend Paul Shartle appeared in, so the rumored Enty story may well be considered dubious.

Now, let's recall Steven Spielberg's *Close Encounters* finale. It features twelve people at a remote airbase, approved by the USAF as volunteers to step aboard a landed alien spacecraft and travel back with little "Grays" to their home planet. Is it a coincidence that this is just like the "diplomatic exchange" program of the '70s mentioned earlier? It was as if Spielberg— influenced by knowledgeable Air Force science advisor J. Allen Hynek—merged the Eisenhower and Nixon airbase ET encounters into one "fictional" motion picture. In a 1977 media interview, Spielberg edged close to discussing presidential contact with ETs: "I wouldn't put it past this government that a 'Cosmic Watergate' has been underway for the last 25 years. Eventually they might want to tell us something about what they've discovered over the decades."[36]

Robert Emenegger went on to publicly discuss the Holloman footage in appearances such as the aforementioned 1988 TV special, other ET documentary productions, book interviews, and UFO conventions. But is he telling the *whole* story? The full truth might be even more thrilling than a fictional movie drama.

Linda Moulton Howe did some very fine research on this saga, writing about it in her often-disturbing book *An Alien Harvest*,[37] originally issued in 1989. She reports: "In the summer of 1983, Connecticut police officer Larry Fawcett and I were dinner guests in

PAUL BLAKE SMITH

Los Angeles at the home of Bob and Margaret Emenegger. Larry headed Citizens Against UFO Secrecy (CAUS)." The group had a fruitful discussion of the old Nixon days. At one point, Robert "got up from the table and walked to a file cabinet, asking Larry and me to join him. Emenegger pulled out a file and showed us a typed letter addressed to Robert from President Nixon with the embossed White House seal at the top and Nixon's handwritten signature at the bottom. Emenegger pointed out the typed words 'Thank you for your discretion on this sensitive matter.'" Robert told Linda and Larry that the "sensitive matter" was the Holloman UFO/ET encounter footage. He claimed that the alien landing really did happen but was effectively kept from the world by Nixon and, apparently, the presidents that served after him. Today, the evidence for the 1971 affair may still be buried in a USAF storage facility or CIA vault.

In the end, was this letter Nixon's apology for keeping the once-promised footage locked up, thus wrecking the UFO motion picture Emenegger and his partner worked so hard on for over a year?

Today, not a shred of tangible evidence has ever publicly surfaced that friendly aliens once made an emergency landing at Holloman and spoke at length to Air Force officials. Like the Nixon-Gleason encounter, it is a remarkably enticing but frustrating legend. However, researcher Grant Cameron has claimed in a History Channel program[38] that he has a well-connected friend who has "talked to two ex-presidents, and they both confirmed that they had been shown the Holloman Air Force Base film."

But at least Emenegger and Sandler's finished theatrical film had an impact. It can still be accessed online today, although it doesn't seem to hold up well compared to more contemporary documentaries on the subject. However, something about the subject matter struck a chord with Robert Emenegger, who went on to produce several low-budget Hollywood movies featuring an alien or outer space theme.[39]

For some reason, just before his alleged 1985 encounter in New

Mexico with the Air Force colonel and his footage, Emenegger retired from show business. He remains so today.

Back in the summer of 1974, Robert Emenegger's theater-released ET/UFO motion picture may well have corralled the imagination of another celebrity greatly interested in the subject, living in America while fighting Richard Nixon for the right to stay...

---

1. Wikipedia contributors, "Whittier, California," *Wikipedia.*
2. Wikipedia contributors, "H.R.Haldeman," *Wikipedia.*
3. U.S. Department of Defense in Washington D.C.
4. Drew Costigan, "The Holloman AFB Film – Fact or Fiction?" *Youtube* video, 2018.
5. R. Graham, "When the Government Gave Hollywood Footage of a "Real" Alien Landing," *Mysteriousuniverse.org,* January 2019.
6. Chris Matthews, "How Kennedy Brought Down Nixon," *The Daily Beast,* July 14, 2017.
7. Compilation of articles, including excerpt from writer Frank Thomas, who quotes plotting Nixon as saying "If he (Kennedy) runs (in 1976) I'll kick his ass," "Four More Years–The Presidency of Richard Nixon,"
8. Wikipedia contributors, "Franklin D. Roosevelt," *Wikipedia.*
9. "1971 Emenegger/Sandler UFO Landing Film," *Think About It,* last updated March 14, 2021.
10. This site and video have apparently been deleted, as of mid-2022.
11. Natalia Megas, "45 Years After Watergate, H.R. Haldeman's Wife Finally Speaks," *The Daily Beast,* May 2017.
12. *Nixon.gov,* May 1971 daily schedule.
13. Chris Whipple, "How H.R. Haldeman Became the Model for Ruthless White House Chiefs of Staff," *History.net,* July 19, 2017.
14. Wikipedia contributors, "Charles Colson," *Wikipedia.*
15. LBJ Library, Johnson Daily Diary Collection.
16. Grant Cameron, "Disney, UFOs, and Disclosure," *presidentialufo.com,* July 11, 2002.
17. Robbie Graham, "When the Government Gave Hollywood Footage of a 'Real' Alien Landing," *mysteriousuniverse.org,* January 2019.
18. Wikipedia contributors, "John L. McLucas," *Wikipedia.*
19. Forum postings on "UFO Disclosure" over the years, mentioning *National Tattler* claim of Emenegger/Sandler film, within *AboveTopSecret.com,* Spring of 2020.
20. "Evidence! Holloman AFB Story True?" *Pegasus Research Consortium.*
21. Art Campbell, "Eisenhower's Incredible Journey," *UFOcrashbook.com.*
22. Wikipedia contributors, "La Casa Pacifica," *Wikipedia.*
23. Tom Owens, "1988-10-14: UFO Coverup? Live! With Mike Farrell," *Youtube* video, July 28, 2019.
24. "Jamie Shandera," *NOUFORS.*
25. Linda Moulton Howe, *earthfiles.com* subscriber content.
26. Wikipedia contributors, "United States Air Force," *Wikipedia.*

27. "Paul R. Shartle obituary," *Ancient Faces*.

28. Paul Shartle's wife Geraldine also died in 2001, gravesite at https://www.finda-grave.com/memorial/58084092/paul-robert-shartle

29. "Paul Shartle obituary," *Tributes*.

30. Jaded Truth, "UFO's (It Has Begun) Past, Present, and Future Documentary," *Youtube* video, September 30, 2017.

31. Drew Costigan, "The Holloman AFB UFO: Fact or Fiction?" *Youtube* video, April 2018.

32. Wikipedia contributors, "Steven Spielberg," *Wikipedia*.

33. Wikipedia contributors, "Close Encounters of the Third Kind," *Wikipedia*.

34. "Today's Blind Items: Government Cooperation," *Crazy Days and Nights*, November 26, 2018.

35. Christopher Welch, "What Did President Reagan Know About UFOs?" *Vigeeks*, March 20, 2020.

36. Huyen Dang, "Spielberg, Close Encounters, and Conspiracy Theories," *todaypress-world.com*, September 8, 2022.

37. Linda Moulton Howe, *An Alien Harvest, Special Limited Edition*, (Littleton, CO: Linda Moulton Howe Productions, January 1, 1989).

38. *Ancient Aliens*, "Aliens and the Presidents," 2020, described in *Internet Media Database*.

39. Robert Emenegger, list of film credits.

CHAPTER SEVEN

JOHN LENNON, NIXON, GLEASON, AND UFOS

"What the Nixon is this?!"

"Look out for the little green men, they may come through your window tonight," superstar musician John Lennon repeatedly told his personal assistant May Pang[1] (1950-) while recording a solo album in mid-1973. Lennon had become restless and bored with his wife of four years, conceptual artist Yoko Ono (1933-), so she encouraged him to take a mistress.[2] This plan backfired when a torrid Lennon-Pang affair ignited and lasted nearly two years after he moved out of his penthouse suite at New York City's Dakota Apartments. "Like a UFO you came to me," he sang on "Out the Blue" from the new album, which he credited to "John Lennon and the Plastic UFOno Band."[3] It turns out the final years of the Nixon administration, during which he repeatedly threatened Lennon with deportation, coincided with Lennon openly exploring his interest in alien visitation. Like Jackie Gleason, Lennon collected and read UFO books and magazines during this period[4] (May Pang still has them to this day). He subscribed to the British magazine *Flying Saucer Review* and *Analog* as, no doubt, The Great Gleason did as well. To be clear: there is no evidence John Lennon ever met either Nixon or Gleason. However, there are some eerie parallels and common themes between the men and their experiences.

As it turns out, John Lennon had shown a great fascination with extraterrestrial visitation at least as far back as the mid-'50s. As a teenager, he sketched various subjects, including alien beings, which he "sent to a long-term Liverpudlian friend who he bonded with over space while performing with The Quarrymen," according to a March 2019 British newspaper report.[5] That report goes on to detail a Los Angeles auction house selling the formerly obscure drawings to the highest bidder, including some ET and sci-fi magazines Lennon sent to his Liverpool chum. The owner of the auction site was quoted as saying: "'It's an interesting story and certainly not surprising given John Lennon's fascination with UFOs, space, and aliens."

It should come as no surprise, then, that a decade after this teenage interest, John and fellow Beatles guitarist George Harrison[6] (1943-2001) traveled with their spouses from London to Sussex, England, to meet with a supposed psychic for the purpose of a séance and contacting outer space beings! As relayed later in books by their ex-wives, Cynthia Powell Lennon (1939-2015) and Patti Boyd Harrison (1944-), the excursion to the large suburban Sussex "spa home" took place in late August 1967, just after the mysterious death of Beatles manager Brian Epstein. The two musicians and their wives had hoped to make contact with the spirit of the late businessman, who had died unexpectedly of a drug overdose. To further entice the two famous musicians, the psychic assured them that some friendly "Venusians" would be arriving under the cover of darkness to land their "V6 spaceship" on the grounds of the psychic's country estate. The four hip young adults patiently waited and waited for...*nothing*. No ETs or spacecraft materialized.[7]

As the two Beatles watched, the clairvoyant and her husband then tried to establish communication with some "Venusians" via a large, old-style radio, searching up and down the dial and listening intently for any special ET signals from space. This avid interest in

PAUL BLAKE SMITH

amateur radio setups sounds much like author George H. Williamson and, perhaps, even Jackie Gleason himself.

After a while, the radio endeavor also proved embarrassingly fruitless, so the psychic went into a trance and relayed messages from the astral plane in the booming voice of a powerful Native American spirit. Some of these relayed statements regarded Cynthia. When John got home, he scribbled a UFO, a typical disc-like craft, on a piece of paper and wrote "Cyn" below it (images available online today[8]). In a roundabout way, the evening in Sussex was actually a success: the two entertained couples laughed themselves silly all the way home and shared the amusing memories for weeks thereafter. But it must be noted that this interaction came at a rather strange time in that very part of England. Many UFO sightings *had* been reported in the summer and fall of 1967, some even making the papers. This publicity was likely a huge factor in convincing the newspaper-reading Lennon to attend the séance in the first place.

Ironically, it was only about a year later that Jackie Gleason first romanced his future wife, Miami country club secretary Beverly McKittrick, in the rural English countryside near London. The duo had a two-year courtship. Shortly after Gleason was finally divorced from his long-estranged first wife in 1970, he married Bev, and the honeymooners resided in a Wentworth Surrey rental house. John Lennon lived in his Surrey home, southeast of London, from 1964 to 1968, then moved out and divorced his first wife as well. Meanwhile, Gleason recorded Lennon-McCartney songs—"Here, There, and Everywhere" in 1968[9] and "Yesterday" in 1969[10]—for his latest instrumental albums. Whether Jackie ever met any of the Beatles remains unknown.

By late 1969, newlyweds John Lennon and Yoko Ono were plotting a huge outdoor rock concert in Toronto, Canada, for July 1970. "The John Lennon Peace Festival" drew immediate fan and media interest. John had promised promoters to perform, with or without his fellow Beatles, along with other rock stars. Two men from a California commune got involved in planning the festival with the

Lennons in the final week of the year while visiting the couple in Denmark. One of the two newcomers was pilot and "Celestial Synapse" festival organizer Donald James Hamrick[11] (1935-2011). He described himself as a "scientist/UFO evangelist," while some sources have since seriously claimed he was associated with the CIA. The odd physicist/minister and possible spy jazzed up the Toronto concert plans by promising the appearance of alien visitors in their spacecraft overhead—and even a landing at the festival site. Hamrick boasted he had once been on board an extraterrestrial craft, meeting with amicable aliens. He then bizarrely promised that the Lennons would be able to fly to the musical event in a "psychic car," fueled on good vibes, and land safely backstage.

Meanwhile, Don Hamrick's associate "said he was going to put some spells on everybody, just really crazy," Lennon recalled in a 1971 interview[12]. "And we were getting worried by then, it was getting out of hand." Likely remembering the Sussex UFO séance con-job of 1967, Lennon reluctantly but firmly canceled the planned music event—partly in a dispute over the admission price—and flew back to London. In the early weeks of 1970, John and Yoko privately laughed off their odd UFO-obsessed festival contacts. They reminded the couple of John's Greek electrical engineer friend, Yannis "Magic Alex" Alexis Mardas[13] (1942-2017), who had promised the previous year to build the Lennons "a flying saucer" that was going to be made from the V12 engines that he claimed he would lift directly from George and John's high-end automobiles. Lennon, like Jackie Gleason, at least *tried* various paranormal sources, but it is clear he found many fakes and hucksters. Still, he pressed on.

As the early '70s passed, John and Yoko moved to America and joined the protest movement against President Nixon and his Vietnam War policies. By February 19, 1973, the Lennons moved from their simple Bank Street loft in Greenwich Village to the upscale Dakota Apartments[14] in Manhattan (apartments #71, #72, and #9— used for storage). Oddly, Ono began the first full day of her forties, February 19, 1973, amid divorce rumors, as noted by a *Time* magazine issued on that now-familiar date[15]. John did indeed split from Yoko Ono and left social activism behind as well, with the exception of a quick flight to Washington D.C. in late June 1973 to personally attend congressional Watergate hearings[16] (while President Nixon was in San Clemente).

Lennon was still fighting the administration in immigration hearings, however, and hadn't helped himself much by recently placing a doctored photo of President Nixon, naked and dancing with the Communist leader of China, on the cover of his 1972 double album (which bombed). Nixon and Lennon were diametric opposites and despised each other. Just after he took office in January 1969, in fact, President Nixon swiftly ordered the FBI to begin a dossier on Lennon, who wasn't even *thinking* of moving to America at the time. By late 1971, however, Lennon had immigrated. Soon after, Nixon's White House audiotapes reveal a conversation where he worries aloud to aides that "This guy [Lennon] could swing the election."[17] Hence, kicking Lennon out of the country and away from young American voters before the fall of 1972 became an obsession for Nixon. He and his administration kept at it for the next few years.

John Lennon's so-called "Lost Weekend"—the mocking misnomer for his binge of boozy, bachelor-like freedom from the summer of 1973 to early 1975—took him from the U.S. East Coast to the West Coast and then back again. In this time frame, while reading his UFO magazines and books, John penned the line "... as if it came from outer space" in a new ditty.[18] He started work on a new album in Los Angeles, where he and May also linked up with singer Harry Edward Nilsson III[19] (1941-1994). They recorded an album together in March and April 1974. One of Nilsson's penned tunes—not used in the final release—was titled "The Flying Saucer Song."[20] It was produced by Lennon and featured a tipsy man at a bar relaying his sighting of a "strange light" in the sky to a stranger while a surly bartender blurts out annoying, disinterested statements. "Late last night, such a life...I looked off to the right and watched a ball of fire across the night sky," Harry Nilsson sang repeatedly in a kind of chorus. He also mentioned a friend in the recording who told him about "investigating this weird light," dubbed "a flying saucer." The messy "song" was rightly shelved, but the Nilsson album was released in America on August 19, 1974, just days *before* something amazingly similar occurred.

Settled back in New York City, Lennon attended a party where Secretary of State Henry Kissinger, of all people, listened to John discuss his immigration legal battles and decided to help. He called Nixon's Department of Justice to ask for assistance in fighting Lennon's deportation orders[21], according to biographer Ray Coleman[22].

On the East side of New York City on at 9:00 p.m. on Friday, August 23, 1974, the temperature had dropped to a cooler 72 degrees, and John Lennon sat nude on his bed, squeaky clean from a shower, with a bath towel nearby.[23] In the nearby bathroom, his girlfriend May Pang was also nude, just finishing her own shower. Both were sober. John got up and walked across his penthouse bedroom. He glanced out a window and saw something that caught his eye. His first reaction, he said later, was to think, "What the Nixon is this?!"

As recounted in many a UFO website, Lennon hurried out onto the terraced roof of his East Side apartment building, seventeen stories up on 52nd Street, for a better look. "This block where we lived," Pang recalled, "[there were] some highfalutin people. We're talking about Kissinger, you're talking up the block was John Mitchell," President Nixon's former Attorney General, once determined to throw Lennon out of the country. Always quick-witted, Lennon would surprise and amuse his friends with funny, often spot-on impersonations, and one of his favorites, according to a friend, was Kissinger. Now John used his own voice to call frantically for May to come out and see a passing object that was "so close you could have thrown a brick at it."[24] May heard the urgency in John's voice and came rushing out onto the terrace, both stark naked.

What precisely was visible in the sky nearby? Both Lennon and Pang later swore, without ever changing their story, that they saw a circular, wingless, metallic aerial craft floating silently by at a snail's pace. An unidentified flying object, for sure. It was a "flattened cone" in the twilight. Both recalled that the UFO "moved sideways," stunning them. This was decades before drones and rounded, remote-control hobby aircraft populated the skies. It was certainly no balloon or kite, the pair recollected. It was about "the size of a Lear jet...About twenty feet in diameter," John once estimated.

The couple gawked at the edge of the roof, clutching its protective wall, which came up to their waists (at least no humans could see them). The floating vehicle gave out "heat waves" from its bottom, Pang recalled to the media in 2012. It was "black or gray in the middle," John remembered in an interview the next day, with many white lights ("like light bulbs") flashing on and off ("*blink-blink-blink!*") around the entire rim, plus a small red light on top.[25]

May eagerly rushed back inside and grabbed a Polaroid camera, then stepped back outside to snap some images. The pictures didn't turn out because the film was overexposed. She also tried a 35-millimeter camera, snapping images hastily, but they also didn't turn out despite being developed by their professional photographer friend.

The silent "flying saucer," as John often described it, floated quietly along in the sky, then "turned right at the United Nations, and then left, and down the river," Lennon told a camera crew the next day as he pointed out the directions. "I watched this thing for a good, solid ten to fifteen minutes," May Pang remembered in a 2012 interview, recalling how warm and humid that day had been previously. She said the ship took a long time coming down and, at one point, seemed to "hover over this one building." Toward the end of its journey up the East River, May described it as slowly climbing and then speeding straight up and finally out of sight. She claimed it flew from the New York City skyline in the direction of New Jersey, which had its share of unusual UFO reports that summer.[26]

After she witnessed the passing spaceship, Pang dashed inside to retrieve a telescope, and the twosome took turns viewing the distant craft in detail as it moved along. Finally, "it went straight up." An amused Lennon wondered aloud afterward if the aliens on board noticed his and Pang's complete nudity while out on the terrace, "screaming" with excitement. "I shouted after it, 'Wait for me!'" John said, but decades later, May Pang denied that he called out to it. Perhaps, in John's mind, he *thought* such a thing.

May Pang also stated that their apartment building was rather dark and empty-looking at the time, with residents probably out and about on a Friday night or off on weekend trips, so the duo worried they might have been the only ones to view the UFO.

When the UFO was gone for good, they finally went inside and put on some clothes. They placed excited phone calls to friends[27] to relate the details of what they had just experienced: something truly out of this world! "I can't believe it, I've seen a flying saucer!" John proudly repeated over and over, in a daze, for the remainder of the night, reminiscent of Jackie Gleason's astounded emotional reaction to the Homestead evidence the year before. Since the airship flew out of view near the towering United Nations building by the East River, John speculated the alien crew was possibly undertaking research on the international representatives there, biographer Ray Coleman reported.

The next day, Saturday, August 24, John enthusiastically urged a photographer friend to call local radio stations, a newspaper office, and the nearest police station to ask if the shiny, metallic disc had been seen by others. The cops replied to "keep calm" and that a few other people had also phoned about the extraordinary sight. John called a radio station to give a brief but candid on-air report of what happened. "We couldn't stop talking about it" for days, May remembered. John and May excitedly dialed up some more friends and even called a TV station to invite over that camera crew, to which they gave an amiable interview on the rooftop (available on *YouTube* today). Lennon also posed for still photos, pointing toward the sky where the odd airship had been, "below the height of the buildings," referring to some towering apartments nearby.[28] "I wish they had

PAUL BLAKE SMITH

taken us both away," he told May with genuine disappointment. Years later, she submitted a drawing John made of the craft[29] to *UFO Universe* magazine, repeating the initial facts they had reported without embellishment. A second, fraudulent drawing popped up and was denied as authentic Lennon artwork by Pang.[30]

It is clear the incident had a deep impact on John, and he imparted it to others around him with such great excitement that it influenced their own lives as well.

Music for John's next album, *Walls and Bridges*,[31] was recorded in July and August 1974 in New York. John wrote: "On the 23 Aug. 1974 at 9 o'clock I saw a U.F.O."—and this was printed on the album's liner notes. Privately, he also sketched a circular UFO on a yellow mailing envelope that May Pang kept for decades. He drew a spaceship on white paper, a disc floating above a cityscape with people below, and that illustration sold decades later for $16,000! Decades after the episode, Pang startled some by recalling that Lennon said he felt he might have even been "abducted" by extraterrestrials while still a child, growing up in the Liverpool suburb of Woolton. "He felt that experience was responsible for making him feel different from other people for the rest of his life." Pang alleged that Lennon also once told her: "If the masses started to accept UFOs, it would profoundly affect their attitudes toward life, politics, everything. It would threaten the status quo. Whenever people come to realize that there are larger considerations than their own petty little lives, they are ripe to make radical changes on a personal level, which would eventually lead to a political revolution in society as a whole."[32]

John Lennon and May Pang's vivid description seems to match Jackie Gleason's UFO sighting on the beach in South Florida. In fact, there are plenty of circumstances in common between the unlikely pairing of Jackie Gleason (a heavyset, conservative comic actor) and John Lennon (a thin, liberal rock musician). Let's take a look...

1. Jackie had a great interest in the occult, consulted psychics associated with UFOs, and encountered obvious frauds—and so did John.
2. Jackie collected and read UFO and paranormal magazines —and so did John. Both men, at one point, wanted nothing more in life than to hole up in their Manhattan apartments and read their otherworldly materials.
3. Jackie developed a great interest in reading about UFOs before his own personal sighting—and so did John.
4. Jackie moved out on his first wife, divorced her, and was remarried to his second wife when he finally saw a UFO —and so was John.
5. Jackie owned two homes and was outside one of them (Miami Beach) when he saw a UFO—and so did John (two NYC apartment homes, seeing the UFO from his second flat).
6. Risking ridicule, Jackie later went public in describing what he saw in the daytime sky instead of keeping it private—and so did John.
7. Jackie had a former "special lady" (ex-wife Beverly) go public in 1983 when writing about his encounter with otherworldly visitors—and so did John (his ex-girlfriend May wrote her autobiography, *Loving John*, which was released in 1983 and included a report of their close encounter).
8. Jackie felt privileged and was unable to stop talking about his sustained UFO sighting for days afterward— and so was John.
9. Jackie was probably sober when he witnessed his two UFOs—and so was John. Both had a reputation for past excessive drinking that might have caused others to disbelieve them at first, but it was eventually felt both were being earnest.

10. Jackie loved Richard Nixon, but John Lennon hated him. Both were probably surprised when Nixon resigned and didn't think of him much afterward. Both Jackie and John likely paid money to see Robert Emenegger's 1974 film, *UFOs: Past, Present, and Future.* In fact, it had been in theaters for about three weeks when Lennon experienced his UFO sighting. Had he and May Pang viewed it just days before their encounter?

As unlikely as it may have seemed at first, Gleason and Lennon had quite a lot in common, passions and experiences they shared despite their opposing political views, nationalities, ages, and showbiz interests. It is not known if Jackie had a companion and second eyewitness with him when he viewed a UFO while walking a beach in Miami, but John certainly did. May Pang was considered the "stable one" among their mutual friends. She didn't drink or take drugs. No one has ever been able to discredit her story from August 1974.

Just after his 1974 sighting, John began a friendship with rock star David Bowie[33], who was also privately bewitched by the subject of otherworldly visitation. Like Lennon, Bowie claimed to have experienced a UFO sighting—or a *group* of them, he said of one occasion —with his girlfriend by his side.[34] No doubt this similarity bonded the two music superstars even closer. As a young man in 1968, Bowie worked for a British UFO magazine, quite possibly even one Lennon read. Bowie mentioned to the noted rock journalist Lester Bangs[35] (1948-1982) of *Creem* magazine that he even had "a metal pin in his body"—an alien abduction *implant?* In 1974, the gender-bending English superstar added to Bangs: "About six years ago. I made sightings six, seven times a night for about a year when I was in the observatory. We had regular cruises [of spaceships] that came over. We knew the 6:15 was coming in and would meet up with another one. And they would be stationary for about half an hour, and then after verifying what they'd been doing that day, they'd shoot off."

{Source: paranormalpopculture.com.} This story leaves us little doubt why Bowie would eagerly rent Jackie Gleason's UFO house in Peekskill years later. It makes one wonder if Bowie ever took John Lennon to see the place, since both had apartments in New York City.

Weirdly enough, Bowie created his "Ziggy Stardust"[36] stage character, a landed alien with a message for Earthlings, during February 1972 in England and performed it in concert for over a year with The Spiders From Mars as his backup band. He did two separate shows as the friendly ET just outside Philadelphia on February 19, 1973. Just a few months later, he left his extraterrestrial alter ego behind for good —never to return to that role.

One of David Bowie's most famous songs, *Starman*, was created from news reports of an October 1954 mass UFO sighting in Italy.[37] Even more wildly, as mysteriousuniverse.org tells us: "In her book about life with her husband at the time, Angela Bowie claims they were driving in 1974 on a concert tour near Detroit and witnessed a UFO...a UFO that was later reported to have crashed in the area with four aliens on board, possibly after engaging with US Air Force jets. There have been rumors of such a crash around that time, including bodies being taken to a base and a TV crew being fired for reporting it."[38] Records show that Bowie and his rock band toured the country that summer, performing a gig in Toledo, Ohio, on Thursday, June 20, 1974, and then another two days later in Detroit.[39] Another concert there was canceled that Sunday (for some reason), so it was back to Ohio on Monday, June 24, for a show in Dayton, home of the legendary Wright-Patterson Airbase. Bowie's alleged UFO sighting took place just before or just after Bowie's Saturday, June 22, 1974, concert—a full two months before John's New York City sighting.

President Nixon, meanwhile, was at Camp David in Maryland on that Friday, June 21, 1974,[40] and strangely enough, his entire day's schedule was not recorded. His daily diary states: "Did not receive any information on the President's activities for this day." Only two quick phone calls were recorded in the log for the next day. What kind of secretive activity was Nixon up to? UFO crash recovery direc-tives? Sunday records show a fairly routine day and ordinary calls for the president, but they included a five-minute, long-distance chat with an obscure congressman from Ohio, based about seventy miles north of Dayton. In the fall of 1974, David Bowie asserted in a published interview: "There's one [UFO crash] that you people probably haven't even heard of here, 'cause the U.S. government threw a blanket over it. It's all over Canada, though...[it] happened about three, four weeks ago in Akron, Ohio. Same sort of thing that Professor Carr is saying happened at Wright-Patterson Air Force Base. There was a decompression accident and they have a ship and four bodies: three feet tall, Caucasian, although weathered all over to make up for it. Same organic stuff, lungs and such, but different, bigger brains."[41] It would seem Bowie had an inside source or two to hear rumors with such details. One would think that Bowie and Lennon discussed this matter in the course of their friendship.

Did John convince his fellow former Beatle Ringo Starr[42] (1940-) about the existence of UFOs that summer of 1974? To backtrack to that month of June, John and May met with Ringo (then separated from his wife) in Los Angeles to record a pair of Lennon songs for the drummer's new solo album, *Goodnight Vienna*[43]. Months later, Ringo's finished album's cover art would feature a parody of the classic movie *The Day the Earth Stood Still*,[44] with Starr's image superimposed on the alien who stood before a landed spaceship in the film. This was even the theme of a special TV commercial made in L.A., showing a (cardboard) "flying saucer" landing on a Hollywood street with Lennon handling the promo's voice-over. Dressed in a one-piece flight suit, Ringo climbed into the "spaceship," which then "lifted off," heading straight up toward the Capitol Records building. Another scene shows the "disc" as it "flew" over L.A. (actually lugged on a cable by an unseen helicopter).[45] Did John influence Ringo to produce such an extraterrestrial video?

Around the same time, two British TV figures concocted a situational comedy featuring Ringo; the plot would involve Starr portraying a chauffeur who encounters "a flying saucer landed, bearing a robot." The sitcom notion never got beyond the planning stages. However, Ringo flew to Tokyo in October 1976 and filmed a TV commercial of—what else?—a flying saucer landing in a city park, with Starr popping out of it to say hello.

Did John also influence fellow Beatle Paul McCartney[46] (1942-) that summer? John and May—and Ringo—hung out with Paul in Los Angeles in mid-1974. Paul was about to begin work on his next album, which was eventually titled *Venus and Mars*.[47] Only decades later did McCartney reveal its title track was referencing John Lennon and his interest in astrology and outer space! Paul's opening song featured the lyrics, "Red lights, green lights, strawberry wine... a good friend of mine, studies the stars...Venus and Mars are all right tonight." Later in the album, Paul sang about waiting for a space-ship, "Starship 21RZNA-9." Since the rock music was recorded from November 1974 through February 1975, it seems likely McCartney, like Starr, was impacted by Lennon's UFO sighting story. The fourth Beatle, George Harrison, was busy recording in England and out of reach.

"He was fascinated by the subject but certainly not obsessed with it," Pang is quoted as saying of Lennon's interest in UFOs and ETs, which naturally accelerated during late August 1974. Frederic Seaman (1952-), another former aide to the Beatles, confirmed this within his controversial 1992 book *The Last Days of John Lennon*. John loved reading and discussing the metaphysical topics of his day, such as the mysterious "Bermuda Triangle" over the Atlantic Ocean. That's where UFOs had supposedly been sighted while planes, ships, and people had allegedly disappeared without a trace. It was a locale Lennon would nearly die in when, in the summer of 1980, he sailed to Bermuda amid a violent storm for several hours.

In March 1979, the Lennons flew with assistant Seaman (hired the previous month) to Palm Beach, Florida. In the kitchen of the oceanfront estate, Fred wrote later, he was startled to hear his boss speaking matter-of-factly about UFOs and aliens. John then read aloud an article from the *National Enquirer* to his teenage son Julian[48]

PAUL BLAKE SMITH

(1963-). That specific story was about a woman who had been abducted by aliens, experimented upon, and implanted with an unknown device. John rambled on to his family about ETs and speculated on whether they existed on earth in a different molecular form than humans, an effort to keep humanity in the dark about their presence. John speculated that perhaps some aliens in unidentified flying objects were actually human beings, time-traveling in advanced airships back to observe the past. One night, Lennon chatted with Seaman alone as they sat by the backyard swimming pool near the sea. Lennon craned his neck upwards, spotting something in the star-filled sky. He was sure he was eyeing an otherworldly craft as a light seemed to move about, high above them. John said it reminded him of his August 1974 sighting in New York's East Side, which he supposed might have been part of a fleet of extraterrestrial ships hiding out in rural, upstate New York. Additionally, he theorized in Palm Beach, visiting ETs in their advanced spaceships might have been draining too much power from Con-Ed and caused the famous July 1977 blackout in New York City.[49]

It is already well known that at least some of the things Seamen wrote about in 1992 may have been exaggerations or even outright lies. In September 2002, he issued the following statement: "I wish to offer this public apology to Yoko Ono. I did wrong by you and indeed am guilty of violating your trust. After more than twenty years, it is time for me to ask for your forgiveness for my actions...I wrote things about you and your family in my book and various tabloids that were factually inaccurate." So, the Lennon UFO revelations in Fred Seamen's book *may* not be trustworthy.

Speaking of what else may not be trustworthy: sixteen years after John Lennon's tragic murder, a strange, unsupported allegation was put forward by Uri Geller[50] (1946-), a so-called psychic who had become friends with Lennon, Pang, and Ono in 1974. The famous Israeli magician and illusionist—disputed as a fraud[51] by some skeptics[52]—wrote for a British newspaper "that Lennon believed in life on other planets and also that this planet was being visited by an ET presence." What is more, Geller asserted in 1996 that back in mid-1975, he had accompanied John to a coffee shop at New York City's Sherry Netherlands Hotel, where he learned something quite shocking. Geller dubiously claimed Lennon told him that some "six months earlier," he saw a bright shining light around the edges of his bedroom door at the Dakota apartment building near Central Park. That night he wasn't dreaming, drunk, or drugged; he swore. John got up and opened the door, curious about what was going on in the next room. He supposedly came face to face with four bug-like alien beings! Space "beetles"?[53]

One version of Geller's wild claim alleged that the beings never touched John but prodded him forward "by willpower," while another version stated two of the aliens took John by the hand and gently pulled him forward, and the other two gently pushed his legs from behind. They led him down a strange tunnel of light where he was shown images that made up a movie of his life. Lennon supposedly blacked out, then woke up later atop his bed covers with a smooth, gold-metallic "egg" in his hands. John supposedly said of Yoko, "I told one other person, and she didn't believe me. She laughed it off, and then she said I must have been high," which he denied.

His story finished, John Lennon allegedly reached into his pocket and gave Uri Geller his unmarked, golden "ET egg" right there in the hotel restaurant. "This is too weird for me, you keep it," John supposedly told Uri, adding, "If it's my ticket to another planet, I don't want to go there." Geller held onto the object and posed for pictures with it around the turn of the century. Geller's golden "egg," as it turns out, was actually identical to a stage performer's prop found in most magician shops, and Geller's other claims were eventually picked apart by May Pang in 2015.[54] The story, true or not, became a vehicle in which to publicize the premiere issue of Geller's personal magazine. Surely John Ono Lennon, so routinely open and candid with friends and the media, would have been raving about such a wild story to anyone he could get to listen. He would have taken pictures of the egg and even posed with it. Yet no one ever came forward to support this dubious claim, and supposedly Geller "just happened" to keep it to himself all those years until it was convenient to present something to promote his new periodical.

During his late '70s self-isolation, Lennon—in the penthouse at 1 West 72 Street—got a new neighbor, of sorts, in an old enemy. *Richard Nixon.* The ex-president began the process of selling his beachfront home in San Clemente in mid-1979 to move to New York City, which he and his wife completed in February 1980. The stalwart *New York Times* broke the news that Tricky Dick had put down a deposit on a nine-room penthouse at 19 East 72 Street, but the Nixons eventually settled on 142 East 65th Street. Nixon and Lennon were directly opposite in the physical sense now, separated by the green space of Central Park and a few blocks beyond.

It was six months afterward, following John Lennon's return from Bermuda in mid-1980, that Lennon's muse returned, and he began writing songs and recording again. One of these catchy new tunes for an upcoming album was titled *Nobody Told Me*[55] and featured the lyric: "There's UFOs over New York, and I ain't too surprised."

It was as if John was starting his career and his home life over. He had faced up to his own demons and survived intact. Until one named Mark David Chapman[56] (1955-) showed up on his doorstep, first in October 1980, then again in early December. The mentally unbalanced fan kept a handgun nestled in his coat pocket as he stalked Lennon outside the Dakota building. To kill time during the week, Chapman had been to see David Bowie in a stage play, one that Lennon had two tickets for, planning to attend on December 9. The night before that, however, the deeply unstable Chapman opened fire on John Lennon on the sidewalk by his dwelling just before 11:00 p.m.[57] On such a very still night, it is possible Richard Nixon heard the echoing gunshots. If he had kept his Manhattan apartment and was in town, Jackie Gleason might also have heard the noise and wondered what was going on.

As John Lennon lay on the pavement with four bullet wounds (a fifth shot missed and struck a window), the doorman at the Dakota rushed out to angrily question the psychotic gunman, who had thrown his weapon down. This employee's name was Jose Perdomo[58] (1935-), a former Miami resident alleged to have known some of his fellow Cuban Exiles who prepped in 1961 for the Bay of Pigs invasion under the supervision of the CIA and Vice President Nixon (before the plan was delayed until the ensuing JFK administration). Tragically, there was nothing Perdomo could do except kick the handgun away. The police came and took the mortally wounded John Lennon to the nearest hospital, where he was worked on by surgeons and pronounced dead.

In the early morning hours, May Pang rushed to David Bowie's New York City loft apartment. The two watched the TV coverage and tearfully mourned together, not far from where she and John had witnessed that saucer-shaped UFO.

Even in death, for John Lennon, it was a small world.

---

1. Wikipedia contributors, "May Pang," *Wikipedia.*
2. May Pang, "Loving John," *Warner Books,* 1983
3. Wikipedia contributors, "Mind Games, Capitol Records, 1973," *Wikipedia.*
4. "John Lennon's UFO Encounter," *Anomalien,* March 30, 2015.
5. Chris Dyer, "Imagine All the Aliens! John Lennon's Sketch of a UFO," *Daily Mail,* March 6, 2019.
6. Wikipedia contributors, "George Harrison," *Wikipedia.*
7. Cynthia Lennon, "A Twist of Lennon," *Avon Books,* 1978.
8. Raechel Shewfelt, "John Lennon Believed In Flying Saucers. Here's How You Can Buy His Drawing of a UFO," *Yahoo Entertainment,* March 27, 2019.
9. "Jackie Gleason: Here, There, and Everywhere Lyrics," *Songlyrics.com.*
10. "Jackie Gleason: Yesterday Lyrics," *Songlyrics.com.*
11. "Rural Communes in Northern California, 1969-1970," *The Bob Fitch Photography Archives.*
12. Matt Sergiou, "About the Occult Beatles," *The Occult Beatles.*
13. Wikipedia contributors, "Magic Alex," *Wikipedia.*
14. Wikipedia contributors, "The Dakota," *Wikipedia.*
15. "People" *Time magazine,* Feb. 19, 1973.
16. "Lennon, Ono, Attend Watergate Hearing 40 Years Ago Today," *retronewser.com,* June 27, 2013.

17. Daniel Bates, "Richard Nixon Tried to Deport John Lennon Because He Considered Him a 'Dangerous Political Enemy,' According to New Documentary," *Daily Mail U.K.*, June 15, 2018.
18. Mucho Mongo, acoustic guitar recording originally created in 1973, not released on an album during Lennon's lifetime, various versions on *YouTube.com*.
19. Wikipedia contributors, "Harry Nilsson," *Wikipedia*.
20. Various versions exist, including one on *YouTube.com*, September 24, 2009.
21. Wikipedia contributor, "The U.S. vs. John Lennon," *Wikipedia*.
22. Ray Coleman, "Lennon: The Definitive Biography," *Harper Perennial*, 1993.
23. "John Lennon Sees a UFO in New York City, 1974," *Dangerous Minds*, April 13, 2015.
24. David Halperin, "John Lennon, May Pang, and the UFO – Their Story," *davidhalperin.net*, February 11, 2016.
25. The Red Kobra, "John Lennon Describes Seeing a UFO Over New York," *Youtube* video, August 1974.
26. One example: August 11th, a startling similar-sounding UFO report from New Jersey: "eight police officers from several jurisdictions observed low-flying saucer-like objects with red, blue, white, and yellow body lights." "1974: August UFO & Alien Sightings," Think About It.
27. Minnie Wright, "John Lennon: Beatles Star's Ex Reveals Truth About His UFO Sighting," *Express*, January 24, 2020.
28. The Randlesham Forest Incident, "John Lennon UFO Encounter 1974," *YouTube* video.
29. Josef Allen Hynek "May Pang Talks About John Lennon's UFO on ABC News," *YouTube* video.
30. Steve Bagnell, "John Lennon UFO Sketch 'a Fake' Claims Former Girlfriend May Pang," *North Wales Bulletin*, June 24, 2015.
31. Wikipedia contributors, "Walls and Bridges," *Wikipedia*.
32. Bryce Zabel, "The Night John Lennon Saw a UFO," *Medium.com*, August 21, 2020.
33. Wikipedia contributors, "David Bowie," *Wikipedia*.
34. "David Bowie Shares His UFO Experiences with Creem Magazine, 44 Years Ago," *Paranormal Pop Culture*, 2021.
35. Wikipedia contributors, "Lester Bangs," *Wikipedia*.
36. Wikipedia contributors, "Ziggy Stardust," *Wikipedia*.
37. Richard Padula, "The Day The UFOs Stopped Play," *BBC World Service Report*, October 24, 2014.
38. P. Seaburn, "David Bowie and the Music of Space Aliens and UFOs," *Mysteriousuniverse*, January 12, 2016.
39. Wikipedia contributors, "Diamond Dogs Tour," *Wikipedia*.
40. *Nixonlibrary.gov*, daily presidential records, June 1974.
41. Article in *bowiewonderworld.com* (site has changed to pay-only since article discovered and quoted herein)
42. Wikipedia contributors, "Ringo Starr," *Wikipedia*.
43. Wikipedia contributors, "Goodnight Vienna," *Wikipedia*.
44. Wikipedia contributors, "The Day The Earth Stood Still," *Wikipedia*.
45. Loomyaire, "Goodnight Vienna -1974 Ringo Starr TV Commercial" *YouTube* video.
    361 Michael Seth Starr. *Ringo: With a Little Help."* 2015.
46. 362 Wikipedia contributors, "Paul McCartney," *Wikipedia*.
47. 363Wikipedia contributors, "Venus and Mars," *Wikipedia*.

48. 364 Wikipedia contributors, "Julian Lennon," *Wikipedia.*
49. 365 Wikipedia contributors, "New York City blackout of 1977," *Wikipedia.*
50. 366 Wikipedia contributor, "Uri Geller," *Wikipedia.*
51. "Classic Hoaxes: Uri Geller-The Greatest Prankster of All Time?" *Pranksters.com.*
52. 367Wikipedia contributors, "The Truth About Uri Geller," *Wikipedia.*
53. "John Lennon Told Me He'd Met UFO Aliens," *Urigeller,* November 2, 1996.
54. "Uri Geller's Legend About John Lennon and the "Alien Egg": Fact or Fiction?" *Aliens UFO Sightings,* April 2015.
55. Wikipedia contributors, "Nobody Told Me," *Wikipedia.*
56. Wikipedia contributors, "Mark David Chapman," *Wikipedia.*
57. Wikipedia contributors, "Murder of John Lennon," *Wikipedia.*
58. Wikispooks contributors, "Jose Sanjenis Perdomo," *Wikispooks.*

EPILOGUE

THE CURSE OF THE NIXON-GLEASON ALIEN ENCOUNTER?

"The principal actor, Richard Nixon himself, never faced criminal prosecution for his role in the Watergate affair and related crimes. However, most of his inner circle saw their careers end in disgrace, and most of them actually did serve some prison time, 'bearing Nixon's sins' while he personally skated."

As we've seen, the Nixon-Gleason extraterrestrial saga is an eerie, strange, and ironic affair that spawned other similar side stories, such as John Lennon's unusual life and death in America. But there are still more dark tragedies that effectively crept into the lives of those mentioned in our sprawling, celebrity-filled legend. Is there a possible "curse" that has resulted from the Nixon-Gleason Homestead visit? Bad news affected nearly everyone and everything involved.

For example, to avoid a sure impeachment and unprecedented

ouster by the United States Congress, Richard M. Nixon became the only American president to ever resign from office in disgrace, leaving the White House on August 9, 1974. He went into self-exile, living nearly alone at his beachfront estate in San Clemente, California, for many years. He walked the beach, past barely clad sun worshipers, decked out in his usual suit, tie, and leather shoes, often a pathetic, out-of-place character who said little to strangers. Aides had to watch him closely because it was feared that he might lose the will to live after his steep and sudden fall from grace and power. A top official in his last White House weeks worried about possible suicide *in office* and limited Nixon's access to pills.[1] In exile, Nixon kept busy by preparing to defend himself in court against the lawsuits leveled against him. He wrote long, ponderous books and generally remained out of the political arena, which had to have frustrated him. He did strike up a mild friendship in the '80s with businessman Donald Trump; Nixon's wife even said after one of Trump's talk-show appearances that he could be president himself someday.

At first, in the late summer of 1974, the public, pundits, and Nixon alike felt that he would have to go on trial for authorizing various Watergate-based crimes and even go to prison if convicted. Some reports have indicated that Mr. Nixon's drinking problem and mental health issues produced a fragile mental state during his final White House days, including talking to some of the presidential portraits on the walls and later speaking incoherently, if at all, while intoxicated. Nixon had always been monitored for depression and paranoia, something that likely became a greater concern after his resignation.[2] He received an uplifting reprieve from this dire fate when, on September 8, 1974, President Gerald R. Ford pardoned him of all crimes committed.[3] This move, in turn, likely cost Ford the 1976 election, which was won by a liberal Democrat—Nixon's worst nightmare.

Meanwhile, several of the president's aides also resigned in scandal; most of them wound up in court and then in penitentiaries, including E. Howard Hunt. He first lost his wife in a dreadful plane crash in late 1972.[4] Twelve persons who died in the tragic accident were in some way connected to the Watergate scandal, the break-in which Hunt helped organize and monitored in a hotel room across the street. Ten thousand dollars in cash was found in his late wife's purse (in one hundred dollar bills), and it was speculated that Hunt's spouse was a paymaster for some of the Watergate burglars. If so, this might be another clue that President Nixon needed *more* cash by early 1973 to finish paying hush money to his arrested minions and their lawyers. Hence, an incentivized Nixon showed Gleason the secrets of ET visitation within a Homestead laboratory to raise more funds.

And what was the fate of E. Howard Hunt, the possible ET-revelation catalyst, after his 33-month prison term? He wrote spy novels and kept a low profile, especially after getting remarried. However, in his last year, he contracted lupus, pneumonia, severe hearing loss, cancers of the jaw and prostate, and gangrene, which forced the amputation of his left leg. All this before he finally passed away in Miami in January 2007,[5] not long after giving deathbed confessions to some of his government knowledge (but apparently nothing on ETs).[6]

As we know, Jackie Gleason's health tanked in the '70s and '80s as he began drinking and smoking more while socializing and sleeping less. His blood pressure issues were complicated by his weight, phlebitis, diabetes, and, eventually, very painful clotted hemorrhoids. In 1978, The Great One suffered a serious heart attack at age sixty-two. He underwent a delicate six-hour, open-heart, triple bypass surgery, with surgeons stripping some of his leg veins to utilize near his heart.[7] He recovered and resumed his career, but he quickly resumed his bad habits too. He continued smoking, eventually leading to emphysema. At one point in 1986, he was informed that his cancer was spreading and would someday take his life. His mobility became limited, and then he became bed-bound by the spring of 1987.

Jackie Gleason had stopped co-sponsoring his annual golf tournament as of 1980, growing bitter toward the corporate support that he and Inverrary had once enjoyed. The pro-am was renamed and continued right outside his door, without his participation. After a few years, it was no longer held at the Lauderhill site. In April 2020, the Inverrary Country Club closed its doors permanently.[8]

Jackie's fabulous, custom-built Glea Manor home, fronting a lake on the golf course, was badly damaged by fire in 1984. He had a large section of it rebuilt at a considerable cost. The cause of the fire remains unknown.

As we know, his marriage went down the drain in the months following the nocturnal Homestead visit. Despite Beverly's desire for reconciliation, he moved aggressively toward a divorce, which was granted in November 1975. The couple had no children, but the end was most unpleasant for both sides.

Speaking of phlebitis, Richard Nixon nearly lost his life in a dramatic scare of the painful disease that hospitalized him shortly after he abruptly left office.[9] His quiet retirement at La Casa Pacifica on the West Coast was necessary due, in part, to the need for rest and recovery. His wife Patricia Nixon (1912-1993)[10] suffered a stroke in 1976 and in 1983 but recovered both times. Retired Richard Nixon rarely spoke to anyone in his former administration and may not have communicated with Jackie Gleason ever again.

As they aged, the Nixons eventually moved to the New York area. He never returned to Key Biscayne again. He sold his two small beachfront properties there in 1976, as did Bebe Rebozo. In 2004, these homes were all bulldozed to the ground to make way for more upscale residences.[11] The old Secret Service checkpoints in the neighborhood were removed. Today, few in the area are likely even aware that the small strip of land was once the center of great activity and power.

Charles "Bebe" Rebozo was apparently in the mood to talk—finally—about his time with the Nixons in the immediate aftermath of the president's resignation. To the surprise of many, he began working on a book that might have revealed some shocking secret which was most unlike him. But he had mounting legal bills to pay. It proved to be a dreadful mistake. According to *Wikipedia*: "Rebozo in 1974 received a letter threatening his life...According to a *New York Times* article dated November 27, 1975, a completed manuscript of a biography on Bebe Rebozo that was scheduled to be published by Farrar, Straus & Giroux was stolen from the home of Thomas Kiernan." In addition to Rebozo's biography, "several tape recordings of interviews and several research files...were taken." Other news coverage at the time pointed out that "thieves ignored jewelry and other items of value"[12] at the Kiernan home, *Wikipedia* added. It seems obvious that someone knowledgeable in the U.S. government wanted juicy secrets kept muzzled. Was Rebozo about to blow the lid off the Nixon-Gleason tour of Homestead AFB? Did Rebozo also go along with them that fateful night? He would have had a blockbuster story to tell, just like Beverly Gleason. It could have been worth a most lucrative book deal...and a blatant breaking-and-entering job for a military intelligence agent, perhaps. The culprit who purloined the book data was never identified, and the materials apparently were never found.

Rebozo took the hint and shut down all further tell-all attempts. He remained mute to the media. Perhaps not coincidentally, he was indicted for money laundering a $100,000 donation from Howard Hughes to the Nixon election campaign but managed to beat the rap. He evidently remained friends with Nixon, and, according to one account, Bebe sat by Richard's bedside as the former leader lay dying. Four years later, after being confined to a wheelchair due to increasingly bad health, Rebozo died in a Miami hospital of complications from a brain aneurysm.

Howard Hughes, meanwhile, went entirely mad in the early '70s and died a bizarrely malnourished, drug-addicted, lonely man with long, unclipped fingernails, hair, and beard. Subsequent X-ray images revealed five broken-off hypodermic needles in his arms, but his official cause of death was listed as "kidney failure."[13]

The apparent curse continued, even hitting Homestead Air Force Base. It was flattened—nearly wiped off the map!—by Hurricane Andrew in 1992.[14] The destroyed site was eventually rebuilt and officially re-designated as "Homestead Air Reserve Station" (HARS) on April 1, 1994. As Andrew approached South Florida, by the way, the prized base evacuated its fighter aircraft to Wright-Patterson AFB in Ohio. Was that *all* that was taken there from the South Florida installation?

Over the decades since 1973, the city of Miami[15] has suffered numerous destructive storms and tense racial protests, angry riots, and public property damage, including arson and looting, most notably and memorably in 1980, 1989, 1991, and 2020. Miami Beach's mayor in 1973, Charles F. "Chuck" Hall—who spoke with Jackie Gleason on a November 1972 TV talk show—suddenly died of a heart attack at age fifty-six on August 10, 1974,[16] the day after President Nixon left the White House.

Jackie's spreading liver and colon cancer caused his Glea Manor death at age seventy-one[17] on June 24, 1987, a day after he changed his will.[18] After a funeral mass, Gleason was entombed at a private Catholic cemetery in Miami. Three days later, Richard Nixon's brother Donald[19] died of pneumonia at age seventy-two. On June 26, 1987, Nixon's economics advisor passed away as well.[20]

Richard Nixon eventually suffered from the same dreaded cerebral hemorrhage that had already taken his wife's life in 1993. Biographers noted that Nixon took her death hard, grieving deeply and crying openly at her televised funeral. He was felled by a major stroke, resulting in a coma lasting four days and finally death, at age eighty-one on April 22, 1994.[21] His body was buried at his presidential library in Yorba Linda, California, alongside his late spouse. In June 2022, new stories reexamining the late Mr. Nixon's scandals popped up like unwanted mushrooms in the media landscape, prodded by the fiftieth anniversary of the Watergate fiasco.[22] Some noted that Nixon conveniently escaped trial and conviction for his crimes, thanks to Ford's pardon. "However, most of his inner circle

PAUL BLAKE SMITH

saw their careers end in disgrace, and most of them actually did serve some prison time, bearing Nixon's sins."[23] The ex-president didn't fare well in the contemporary blitz of media accounts. However, the fact that a deeply political animal like Nixon was barred from almost all future legal practice, government decision-making, and policy influence may have served as nearly the worst punishment of all.

Vice President Spiro Agnew—who, like Beverly McKittrick, grew up in Baltimore—grew increasingly mired in scandal in 1973 and resigned in disgrace before the year was out.[24] As *Wikipedia* put it: "In 1973, Agnew was investigated by the U.S. Attorney for the District of Maryland on suspicion of criminal conspiracy, bribery, extortion and tax fraud. Agnew took kickbacks from contractors during his time as Baltimore County Executive and Governor of Maryland. The payments had continued into his time as vice president; they had nothing to do with the Watergate scandal, in which he was not implicated. After months of maintaining his innocence, Agnew pleaded no contest to a single felony charge of tax evasion and resigned from office." Saying that he felt "totally abandoned" by fellow conservative politicos, a bitter "Agnew declined to take any and all phone calls from President Nixon," *Wikipedia* noted, but he attended the man's April 1994 funeral.[25] Agnew lived a quiet life in the Palm Springs area, golfing, penning his memoirs, *Go Quietly...Or Else*, and becoming a consultant to foreign businesses. He was discovered to be ill from leukemia as the years went by and fell at home in September 1996. Agnew was hospitalized and died of his blood cancer.[26]

National Security Advisor S. Everett Gleason died at age sixty-nine on November 20, 1974, at his home in Washington D.C.[27] He was suffering from lung cancer, and his death was not unlike Jackie's sad demise thirteen years later.

During his retirement years, L. Gordon Cooper repeatedly emphasized in media interviews that he had personally witnessed ET craft. His descriptions were included in a 2002 documentary titled *Out of the Blue*. He died at age seventy-seven of heart failure on October 4, 2004,[28] and portions of his ashes were taken into space in 2007 and 2012. What information he decided to keep to himself on UFOs and ET visitation remains a mystery and likely always will.

Comedian Bob Hope enjoyed a long and successful career after 1973, yet he suffered from vision problems that grew as he aged and became frailer. He converted to Catholicism seven years before his 2003 death, two months after his 100th birthday. Pneumonia was his official cause of death.[29] A year later, Bob's friend, former President Ronald Reagan, died in 2004 of Alzheimer's Disease, having suffered from the disorder since at least 1990. Gerald Ford left the presidency in January 1977 and spent four decades golfing and promoting political and charitable causes; he passed away the day after Christmas in 2006.

As mentioned, John Lennon was brutally murdered on December 8, 1980. His former aide and lover, May Pang, helped produce a June 2022 documentary motion picture, *The Lost Weekend: A Love Story*, which included memories of their August 1974 UFO sighting.[30] Pang was married to David Bowie's producer from 1989 to 2000. She keeps a safety deposit box filled with John Lennon's doodles, more elaborate drawings, and photographs. One wonders if more depictions of Nixon or UFOs are present.

On January 5, 2015, a main-belt asteroid was named *342841-DavidBowie* in honor of the British rock star who so loved the topic of life beyond Earth.[31] On January 10, 2016, Bowie died of liver cancer in his New York City apartment, two days after his sixty-ninth birthday.[32] A group of respected Belgian astronomers soon created a "Bowie asterism" in homage; it is an astrological alignment featuring the seven celestial stars which were aligned near the planet Mars at the time of Bowie's death.[33]

Sadly, there really were no happy Hollywood endings for *anyone* involved here—minus Jackie's second wife, Beverly, who lived quietly in Maryland for five more decades. His first wife, Genevieve, died at age ninety-six in 2012. Like Beverly, she never produced any memoirs or revelations about her illustrious former husband. Little is known about Jackie's two daughters by his first spouse, who always stayed out of the spotlight. Jackie's third wife, Marilyn Taylor Gleason, remained at Glea Manor for a few years after Jackie's death, then sold the estate in 1992 under the stipulation it be maintained just as the TV star created it. Luckily, it was purchased by a wealthy Connecticut businessman who kept the Gleason memorabilia, pool table, and five well-stocked bars—but not the paranormal book collection, which was donated to the University of Miami. Marilyn moved to a beachfront condo for her remaining years and generally avoided the limelight, also declining to pen a tell-all autobiography. She dated no one else, according to her son, and passed away at age ninety-three in April 2019.[34] She was interred with Jackie in their large, white crypt in Miami.[35] The exterior of Jackie Gleason's sealed sarcophagus is inscribed with the words *"And away we go."*

---

1. Jonathan P. Baird, "Trump Is Proving To Be More Dangerous Than Nixon," *Concord Monitor*, December 7, 2020.
2. Gabe Mirkin, "Richard Nixon Battled Paranoia and Depression," *Villages News*, December 25, 2018.
3. Wikipedia contributors, "Pardon of Richard Nixon," *Wikipedia*.
4. "E. Howard Hunt Wife Plane Crash," *diarimeluso.weebly.com*, April 4, 2017.
5. Various press reports compiled: "E. Howard Hunt Dies," *kennedyandkings.com*, February 15, 2007.
6. Erik Hedegaard, "The Last Confession of E. Howard Hunt," *Rolling Stone*, April 5, 2007.
7. Rebelander Basilan, "Jackie Gleason's Challenging Final Years," *Amo Mama*, September 15, 2019.
8. Paul Owers, "Historic Country Club To Close As Sport's Popularity Declines," *CoStar News*, September 26, 2019.
9. "Relative Describes Nixon As In Pain and Depressed," *New York Times*, September 12, 1974.
10. Wikipedia contributors, "Pat Nixon," *Wikipedia*.
11. "Nixon Presidential Retreat in Key Biscayne Torn Down," *Herald Tribune*, July 22, 2004.
12. "AG Studies Theft of Data on Rebozo," *New York Times*, November 27, 1975.
13. Oisin Curran, "The Tragic Life and Curious Death of Howard Hughes," *HowStuffWorks.com*, May 1, 2020.
14. Wikipedia contributors, "Hurricane Andrew," *Wikipedia*.
15. Wikipedia contributors, "Miami," *Wikipedia*.

16. Wikipedia contributors, "Chuck Hall (Florida politician)," *Wikipedia*.

17. Eric Pace, "Jackie Gleason Dies of Cancer, Comedian and Actor was 71," *New York Times*, June 25, 1987.

18. "Jackie Gleason Changed Will On Deathbed," *A.P.*, July 23, 1987.

19. Wikipedia contributors, "Donald Nixon," *Wikipedia*.

20. Wikipedia contributors, "Arthur F. Burns," *Wikipedia*.

21. Wikipedia contributors, "Death and State Funeral of Richard Nixon," *Wikipedia*.

22. Howard Homonoff, "Watergate's 50th Anniversary, A Multi-Media Guide For Today," *Forbes*, June 29, 2022.

23. R.K. Lindgren, "The "Nixonian Fate" 50 Years Later," *When God Plays Dice*, June 3, 2022.

24. Richard Kreitner, "October 10, 1973: Vice President Spiro Agnew Resigns," *The Nation*, October 10, 2015.

25. "Once-Bitter Agnew Attends Funeral, Talks of Reconciliation," *Deseret News*, April 28, 1994.

26. Robert Shogan, "Spiro Agnew Dies; Nixon VP Quit in Disgrace," *Los Angeles Times*, September 18, 1996.

27. "S. Everett Gleason, Historian, Dies," *New York Times*, November 22, 1974.

28. "Space Pioneer Gordon Cooper Dies; Cooper Believed in UFO Cover-up," *CNN*, October 4, 2004.

29. Pat Dowell, "Comedian Bob Hope Dies at 100," *NPR*, July 28, 2003.

30. Kenneth Womack, "May Pang Opens Up About John Lennon's "Lost Weekend" In Her "Love Story" Documentary," *Salon magazine*, June 10, 2022.

31. Chris Spears, "It's No Space Oddity: Mile-Wide David Bowie Asteroid To Forever Float In Outer Space," *CBS News*, January 11, 2016.

32. Wikipedia contributors, "Death of David Bowie," *Wikipedia*.

33. Daniel Brown, "David Bowie Constellation – The Surprising Truth," *phys.org*, January 21.

34. Steve Rothhaus, "Jackie Gleason Widow, Marilyn Taylor Gleason, Dies," *South Florida Sun Sentinel*, April 4, 2019.

35. Find A Grave obituary, https://www.findagrave.com/memorial/198069095/marilyn-ann-gleason – It mentions how Marilyn said in 2014 of Jackie: "He always had great ideas. Onward and upward. That was his motif."

ABOUT THE AUTHOR

I'm the author of 5 books from one publishing company, and I now have a new nonfiction book coming out from another publisher. I still live in still live in southern Missouri, long after my four years at SE Missouri State University. I enjoy biographies, sports, and history.

https://www.facebook.com/PaulBlakeSmithauthor

BIBLIOGRAPHY

Chris Matyszczyk, "Canada's Ex-Defense Minister: U.S. Knows How Aliens Can Make Us Greener," *CNET*. February 27, 2011. https://www.cnet.com/culture/canadas-ex-defense-minister-u-s-knows-how-aliens-can-make-us-greener/.

"Frank Gannon (White House Central Files: Staff Member and Office Files)." *Richard Nixon Presidential Library and Museum*. Yorba Linda, CA. http://www.nixonlibrary.gov/finding-aids/frank-gannon-white-house-central-files-staff-member-and-office-files

Wikipedia contributors, "Richard Nixon," *Wikipedia*, https://en.wikipedia.org/wiki/Richard_Nixon

Wikipedia contributors. "San Clemente, California," *Wikipedia*, https://en.wikipedia.org/wiki/San_Clemente_California

David Emery, "Did President Nixon Hide Proof of Alien Life in a Time Capsule?" *Snopes.com*, March 24, 2018. https://www.snopes.com/fact-check/nixon-alien-life-time-capsule/.

Wikipedia contributors, "Jackie Gleason," *Wikipedia*, https://en.wikipedia.org/wiki/Jackie_Gleason

Ultra-top-secret-MTD, allegedly from Defense Intelligence Agency, January 1989

Wikipedia contributors, "John Lennon," *Wikipedia*, https://en.wikipedia.org/wiki/John_Lennon

"Beverly Gleason," *IMDB*, https://www.imdb.com/name/nm11740952/

Wikipedia contributors, "Paul Hellyer," *Wikipedia*, https://en.wikipedia.org/wiki/Paul_Hellyer

Vicky Verma, "At least Four Alien Species Have Been Visiting Earth For Thousands Of Years From Andromeda," *howandwhys*.com, August 2021, https://www.howsandwhys.com/four-alien-species/

Aired May 16, 2021, reported by correspondent Bill Whitaker, CBS television network

Wikipedia contributors, "Douglas Caddy," *Wikipedia*, https://en.wikipedia.org/wiki/Douglas_Caddy

Russell Baker, "A Very Wretched Relationship," *New York Books*, April 4, 2013, https://www.nybooks.com/articles/2013/04/04/eisenhower-nixon-wretched-relationship/

Salla, Michael, ed., "SOM1-01 - Special Operations Manual / Extraterrestrial Entities and Technology, Recovery and Disposal," *bibliotecapleyades.net*, December, 1996.

Zack White, "Astrobiologist: 'Surely we will meet humans from other worlds,' mysterioussociety.com, November 24, 2021. https://mysterioussociety.com/astrobiologist-surely-we-will-meet-humans-from-other-worlds?fbclid=IwAR3o3Zp-sA6o7xGxr-WKR0SvlqlUJLPxzHvxvOcV3o4zuJQ7HOZYuuGYrE8

"It's Official: Scientists Discovered A 'Second Earth' *Ideas for Tips* www.ideasfortips.life/its-official-researchers-have-discovered-a-second-earth

Wikipedia contributors, "Linda Moulton Howe," *Wikipedia*, https://en.wikipedia.org/wiki/Linda_Moulton_Howe

Linda Moulton Howe, "Maze of Deception," *earthfiles.com,* 2020, https.//earthfiles.com

Wikipedia contributors, "Central Intelligence Agency," *Wikipedia*, https://ttps://en.wikipedia.org/wiki/Central_Intelligence_Agency

Wikipedia contributors, "Roswell incident," *Wikipedia*, https://en.wikipedia.org/wiki/Roswell_incident

Wikipedia contributors, "Project Blue Book," *Wikipedia*, https://en.wikipedia.org/wiki/Project_Blue_Book

Wikipedia contributors. "Area 51," *Wikipedia*, https://en.wikipedia.org/wiki/Area_51

Wikipedia contributors, "J. Edgar Hoover," *Wikipedia*, https://en.wikipedia.org/wiki/J._Edgar_Hoover

Wikipedia contributors, "NASA," *Wikipedia*, https://en.wikipedia.org/wiki/NASA

Wikipedia contributors, "Apollo program," *Wikipedia*, https://en.wikipedia.org/wiki/Apollo_program

Heathcliff Peters, "UFOs and US Presidents: US Presidents Talks About UFOs," *Astral Citizens*, February 2022. https://astralcitizens.com/us-presidents-talk-about-UFOs/

Richard Nixon, "NASA statement/speech," *nasa.gov.*, January 5, 1972, https://history.nasa.gov/stnixon.htm

Wikipedia contributor, "Ronald Reagan," *Wikipedia*, https://en.wikipedia.org/wiki/Ronald_Reagan

Wikipedia contributors, "Camp David," *Wikipedia*, https://en.wikipedia.org/wiki/Camp_David

Steve Hammons, "Alleged Briefing to President Reagan on UFOS," *AmericanChronicle*, November 27, 2007, https://bibliotecapleyades.net/exopolitica/exopolitics_reagan01.htm

"Aztec, New Mexico UFO Crash Recovery 1948," *Noufors*, noufors.com/Aztec_New_Mexico_ufo_crash_recovery_of_1948.html.

"Presidential Daily Diary, May 1970" Richard *Nixon Museum and Library,*https://nixonlibrary.gov/sites/default/files/virtuallibrary/documents/PDD/1970/027%20May%201-15%201970.pdf

Wikipedia contributors, Mamie Eisenhower, *Wikipedia*, https://en.wikipedia.org/wiki/Mamie_Eisenhower

"Jackie Gleason Claims Presidents Told Him UFOs are Real," *Alien UFO Sightings*, https://alien-ufo-sightings.com/2014/04/jackie-gleason-claims-presidents-told-him-ufos-are-real/

Wikipedia contributors, "Key Biscayne,' *Wikipedia*, https://en.wikipedia.org/wiki/Key_Biscayne

Wikipedia contributors, "Miami-Dade County, Florida," *Wikipedia*, https://en.wikipedia.org/wiki/Miami-Dade_County,_Florida

Wikipedia contributors, "Homestead Air Reserve Base," *Wikipedia*, last updated July 2022, https://en.wikipedia.org/wiki/Homestead_Air_Reserve_Base

Sean McCaughan, "Nixon Winter White House, Private Beach, Helipad Adjacent,"

Curbed Miami," May 22, 2012, https://miami.curbed.com/2012/5/22/10374802/
nixon-winter-white-house-compound-with-private-beach-helipad-adjacent

Wikipedia contributors, "Homestead Air Reserve Base," *Wikipedia*, https://en.wiki
pedia.org/wiki/Homestead_Air_Reserve_Base

"'Mr. Peacemaker' Nixon Is Welcomed in Florida," *New York Times*, January 27, 1973,
https://www.nytimes.com/1973/01/27/archives/mr-peacemaker-nixon-is-
welcomed-in-florida.html

Wikipedia contributors, "Homestead, Florida," *Wikipedia* July 28,
2022,https://en.wikipedia.org/wiki/Homestead,_Florida

"UFO Sighting in Homestead, Florida (United States) on Friday 15 October 2010"
UFO Hunters, https://Florida (United States) on Friday 15 October 2010 - UFO
Hunters (ufo-hunters.com)

Wikipedia contributors, "Bebe Rebozo," *Wikipedia*, https://en.wikipedia.org/wiki/
Bebe_Rebozo

William Saffire, "Before The Fall," *Belmont Tower Books*, 1975

Don Fulsom, "Gangster in the White House," *Crime Magazine*, September 11, 2009,
https://crimemagazine.com/gangster-white-house

Dave Rolland, "Richard Nixon and Key Biscayne," *Jitney Books*, April 9, 2020, https://
jitneybooks.com/richard-nixon-key-biscayne/

Phillip Shabecoff, "Secret Service Director Says That Most of $1.9-Million Spent on
Nixon's Homes Was for Security," *The New York Times*, June 28, 1973, https://www.
nytimes.com/1973/06/28/archives/secret-service-director-says-that-most-of-19mil
lion-spent-on-nixons.html

Wikipedia contributors, "John F. Kennedy," *Wikipedia*, https://en.wikipedia.org/
wiki/John_F_Kennedy

Timothy Good, "Need To know," *Pegasus Books*, paperback edition, November 2007

Henry Applebaum, "Vernon Walters - Renaissance Man," *Studies in Intelligence*,
Volume 46, 2002, https://cia.gov/static/20dc4319f6e8d3a9d63b7076a30b3e1d/
Vernon-Walters-Renaissance-Man.pdf

Howard Jones, "A Beach-Head Too Far?" *Lessons Not Learned at the Bay of Pigs*, August
28, 2008, https://combatreform.org/airbornebayofpigs.htm

Jeff Shain, "Flashback: Jackie Gleason's Inverrary Classic," *Pro Golf Weekly*, February
22, 2018.
https://progolfweekly.com/flashback-jackie-gleasons-inverrary-classic/

Elaine Raffel, "A Slice of Beatle History Hits the Palm Beach Market," *Second Shelters*,
May 13, 2020,https://secondshelters.com/2020/05/13/a-slice-of-beatle-history-hits-
the-palm-beach-market/

Antonio Fins, "Richard Nixon toured Mar-a-Lago a month before he resigned presidency," *The Palm Beach Post*, February 18, 2019, https://www.palmbeachpost.com/
story/news/politics/government/2019/02/18/presidents-day-day-nixon-toured-
mar-a-lago-then-resigned-month-later/5916381007/

Christina Stoehr, "Biography reveals Jackie Gleason's many flaws" *Baltimore Sun*,
July 18, 1992, https://www.baltimoresun.com/news/bs-xpm-1992-07-19-
1992201248-story.html

Stephanie Nolasco, "Jackie Gleason 'embraced' lasting success on 'The Honeymooners,' never regretted playing Ralph Kramden," *Fox News*, January 1, 2019, https://www.foxnews.com/entertainment/jackie-gleason-embraced-lasting-success-on-the-honeymooners-never-regretted-playing-ralph-kramden

Audrey Meadows, Joe Daily, "Love, Alice: My Life as a Honeymooner," *Crown Publishers*, September 1994

"The Jackie Gleason Collection," *University of Miami Libraries, Special Collections,*, Florida, https:scholar.library.miami.edu/gleason/

Lobosco, David, "A Trip Down Memory Lane: Jackie Gleason and UFO," *greatentertainersarchives* , August 1, 2011, https://greatentertainersarchives.blogspot.com/2011/08/jackie-gleason-and-ufos.html

Foundation Interviews, "Leonard Stern on Jackie Gleason on 'The Honeymooners,'" *YouTube* video, 4:29, August 2016, https:// www.youtube.com/watch?v=4XCHhlTgCFU

Luke Stangel, "Jackie Gleason's Spaceship-Like House Is Listed for $12M," *Realtor.com,* August 6, 2018, https://www.realtor.com/news/celebrity-real-estate/jackie-gleason-spaceship-party-house/

Brent Swancer, "The Strange Story of Nikola Tesla and the Aliens," *mysteriousuniverse.org,*, January 19, 2021, https://mysteriousuniverse.org/2021/01/the-strange-story-of-nikola-tesla-and-the-aliens/

Donald Bain, "Long John Nebel: Radio Talk King, Master Salesman, and Magnificent Charlatan," *MacMillan Books*, January 1974

Wikipedia contributors, "Long John Nebel," *Wikipedia* August 2017, https://en.wikipedia.org/wiki/Long_John_Nebel

Winnie Muriuki, "Jackie Gleason Net Worth 2022: Age, Height, Weight, Wife, Kids, Bio-Wiki," *Wealthy Persons* www.wealthypersons.com/jackie-gleason-net-worth-2020-2021/.

Bob Woodward and Carl Bernstein, "Nixon Debated Paying Blackmail, Clemency: 'Keep Cap on Bottle,'" *The Washington Post*, May 1, 1974, https://www.washingtonpost.com/92abb252-ae9e-11e1-a163-d43a3ca733b4_story.html

Samuel Rushay, "Listening to Nixon: An Archivist's Recollections on His Work with the White House Tapes," *National Archives*, 2007, https://www.archives.gov/publications/prologue/2007/fall/tapes.html

Larry Holzwarth, "10 Crimes of the Nixon Administration," *historycollection.com*, March 27, 2018, https://historycollection.com/10-crimes-of-the-nixon-administration/

Jonathan Poletti, "Was Richard Nixon Gay? Let's Look at the Facts," *medium.com*, April 30, 2020, https://medium.com/queertheory/was-nixon-gay-93c92d075b89

Douglas Brinkley and Luke Nichter, "The Nixon Tapes: 1973," *Houghton Mifflin Harcourt*, September 2015

"You could get a million dollars," *Miller Center*, March 21, 1973, https://millercenter.org/the-presidency/educational-resources/you-could-get-a-million-dollars

Wikipedia contributors, "Herbert W. Kalmbach," *Wikipedia*, https://en.wikipedia.org/wiki/Herbert_W._Kalmbach

PAUL BLAKE SMITH

Anthony Ripley, "Kalmbach Pleads Guilty to 2 Campaign Charges: May Be Jaworski Witness," *The New York Times*, February 26, 1974, https://www.nytimes.com/1974/02/26/archives/kalmbach-pleads-guilty-to-2-campaign-chargs-may-be-jaworski-witness.html

UPI, "Nixon Aide Guilty on Political Fund," *The New York Times*, 1974 November 16, , https://www.nytimes.com/1974/11/16/archives/nixon-aide-guilty-on-political-fund-.html

Don Fulsom, "The Mob's President: Richard Nixon's Secret Ties to the Mafia," *Crime Magazine*, February 5, 2006, https://www.crimemagazine.com/mobs-president-richard-nixons-secret-ties-mafia

Eric Meisfjord, "The Truth About Larry King And Jackie Gleason's Relationship," *Grunge*, January 23, 2021, https://www.grunge.com/318553/the-truth-about-larry-king-and-jackie-gleasons-relationship/#:~:text=Jackie%20Gleason%20really%20was%20%27The%20Great%20On

The Honeymooners 1955, Season 1, Episode 14, "The Man from Space" – IMDb, https://www.imdb.com/title/tt0604654/

"1965 Press Photo Jackie Gleason and Richard Nixon golfing in Miami, FL." *eBay*, https://pages.ebay.com/vault/

"The Hills of Inverrary, COA in Lauderhill, Florida," https://www.thehillsofinverrary.org

Peter Burke, "Jackie Gleason's former Lauderhill home for sale" *Local10*, February 25, 2016, https://www.w.local10.com/entertainment/2016/02/25/jackie-gleasons-former-lauderhill-home-for-sale/

Stephanie Nolasco, "Jackie Gleason 'embraced' lasting success," *Fox News*, January 1, 2019.

George H. Williamson, "A Message From Our Space Brothers," *bibliotecapleyades*, June 21, 1954, https://www.bibliotecapleyades.net/bb/williamson.htm

Brett Swancer, "The Strange Story of Nikola Tesla and the Aliens," *mysteriousuniverse*https://mysteriousuniverse.org/2021/01/the-strange-story-of-nikola-tesla-and-the-aliens/

Brett Swancer, "David Bowie and the Music of Space, Aliens and UFOs," *mysteriousuniverse*, https://mysteriousuniverse.org/2016/01/david-bowie-and-the-music-of-space-aliens-and-ufos/

"The Prestige (2006) - David Bowie as Tesla," – *IMDb*, https://www.imdb.com/title/tt0482571/characters/nm0000309

Jame Bacon, "How Sweet It Is: The Jackie Gleason Story," *St. Martin's Press*, June 1, 1986, Foreword by Jackie Gleason

Frank Kelly, "The Great Drunk: Lushing Large with Jackie Gleason," *Modern Drunk Magazine*.August 2002, https://drunkard.com/08_02_gleason2/

Timothy G. Beckley, "And Away We Go... The Night Jackie Gleason Saw the Corpses of the Little Men from Mars,"*UFO Digest*," June 19, 2015, https://www.ufodigest.com/article/and-away-we-go-the-night-jackie-gleason-saw-the-corpses-of-the-little-men-from-mars/

According to the eventually-released report, Gleason kept in touch at times with Miami FBI Special Agent Kenneth W. Whittaker

Jack Doyle, "Richard Nixon and television," *The Pop History Dig*, March 2018, https://pophistorydig.com/topics/tag/richard-nixon-and-television/

Wikipedia contributors, "Nixon White House tapes," *Wikipedia*, https://en.wikipedia.org/wiki/Nixon_White_House_tapes

Katherine G, "Things You Might Not Know About 'All In The Family'," *Fame10*, April 11, 2017, https://www.fame10.com/entertainment/10-things-you-didnt-know-about-family-matters/

David Coleman, "Nixon's Presidential Approval Ratings" History in Pieces historyin-pieces.com/research/Nixon-approval-ratings.

Richard D. Lyons, "Science Adviser to Nixon Leaving for Industry Job" *The New York Times* January 3. 1973www.nytimes.com/1973/01/03/archives/science-advisor-to-nixon-leaving-for-industry-job-science-advisor.html

HelmerReenberg, "May 2, 1972 - President Richard Nixon's Remarks on the Death of FBI Director J. Edgar Hoover," *Bing* video www.bing.com/videos/search?q=May+2%2c+1972+-+President+Richard+Nixon%27s+Remarks+on+the+Death+of+FBI+Direc tor+J.+Edgar+Hoover+-+Bing+video&view=detail&mid= B495ED235D693F2E3893B495ED235D693F2E3893&form=VDQVAP&rvsmid =06DB1184F80003AC2F6306DB1184F80003AC2F63&ajaxhist=0

Aine Caine and Abby Jackson, "20 US presidents who belonged to shadowy secret societies," *Insider*, February 19, 2018, https://www.insider.com/us-presidents-who-were-in-secret-societies-2017-4

Thomas Powers, "The Rise and Fall of Richard Helms," *Rolling Stone magazine*, December 16, 1976, https://www.rollingstone.com/culture/culture-news/the-rise-and-fall-of-richard-helms-191224/

Chet Dembeck, "Former CIA Analyst Claims Intelligence Agencies Have Proof ET Exists - But Hide," *Unknown Boundaries*, June 3, 2022, https://unknownboundaries.com/former-cia-analyst-claims-intelligence-agencies-have-proof-et-exists-but-hide/

"Inside the Department of Dirty Tricks," *The Atlantic*, August 1, 1979, https://ww.the-atlantic.com/magazine/archive/1979/08/inside-the-department-of-dirty-tricks/305460/

The released letter is on stationary headed: "Office of Dwight D. Eisenhower" in "Gettysburg, Pennsylvania"

Timothy Good, "Need to Know," January, 2006

Wikipedia contributors, "Robert Seamans," *Wikipedia*, https://en.wikipedia.org/wiki/Robert_Seamans

Wikipedia contributors, "Nicolaus Copernicus," *Wikipedia*, https:///en.wikipedia.org/wiki/Nicolaus_Copernicus

Wikipedia contributors, "Charles Messier," *Wikipedia*, https:en.wikipedia.org/wiki/Charles_Messier

"Houston Space Center Is Named For Johnson," *The New York Times*, February 19, 1973, https://www.nytimes.com/1973/02/20/archives/houston-space-center-is-named-for-johnson.html

Gerhard Peters and John Woolley, ""Informal Remarks at the Jackie Gleason Inver-rary Classic, Lauderhill, Florida," *The American Presidency Project*, https://www.presidency.ucsb.edu/documents/informal-remarks-the-jackie-gleason-inverrary-classic-lauderhill-florida

Wikipedia contributors, "Gordon Cooper," *Wikipedia*, https://en.wikipedia.org/wiki/Gordon_Cooper

"What did Richard Nixon say about Bohemian Grove?" *NSN Search response*, https://nsnsearch.com/how-to/what-did-richard-nixon-say-about-bohemian-grove/

Wikipedia contributors, "Freemasonry," *Wikipedia*, https://en.wikipedia.org/wiki/Freemasonry

"Major Gordon Cooper, USA Astronaut, and UFOs," *UFO Evidence*, October 4, 2004, https://ww.ufoevidence.org/news/article157.htm#:~:text=During%20the%20final%20orbit%2C%20Major%20Gordon%20Cooper%20told,it%20was%20picked%20up%20by%20Muchea%27s%20tracking%20radar

Marcus Lowth, "The UFO Conspiracy Revelations of NASA Astronaut Gordon Cooper," *UFO Insight*, March 27, 2017, https://www.ufoinsight.com/ufos/cover-ups/ufo-nasa-gordon-cooper

"Astronauts and UFOs: Reports and Statements by USA Astronauts," *UFOlogie*, undated, https:///ufologie.patrickgross.org/htm/astronauts.htm#cooper

Alex Stuckey, "Listen: Apollo 11 Crew Now Isolated From Everyone Except Nixon," *Houston Chronicle,*July 4, 2019 , https://www.chron.com/local/mission-moon/cigarettes-and-rocket-fuel-podcast/article/Listen-Apollo-11-crew-now-isolated-from-rest-of-14037419.php

El Toro, "Gordon Cooper & UFOs: An Astronaut Speaks Out About Aliens," *Newcarz*, March 14, 2022, https://newcarsz.com/gordon-cooper-ufos-an-astronaut-speaks-out-about-aliens/

Timothy G. Beckley, "And Away We Go: The Night Jackie Gleason Saw The Corpses of Little Green Men From Mars," *UFO Digest,* June 19, 2015, https://www.ufodigest.com/article/and-away-we-go-the-night-jackie-gleason-saw-the-corpses-of-the-little-men-from-mars/

Wikipedia contributors, "National Enquirer," *Wikipedia*, https://en.wikipedia.org/wiki/National_Enquirer

Wikipedia contributors, "Lauderhill, Florida," *Wikipedia*, https://en.wikipedia.org/wiki/Lauderhill,_Florida

Charles Feiglstok, "Away He Goes, or Does He? The Strange Jackie Gleason Caper," *People magazine*, March 24, 1975, printed online https://online.pakasak.com/archive/away-he-goes-or-does-he-the-strange-jackie-gleason-caper-vol-3-no-11/

John Franch, "The Secret Life of J. Allen Hynek," *The Skeptical Inquirer*, Jan/Feb 2013, https://skepticalinquirer.org/2013/01/the-secret-life-of-j-allen-hynek/

John Greenewald, "Jackie Gleason and the Pickled Aliens," *The Black Vault*, May 25, 2015, https://www.theblackvault.com/casefiles/jackie-gleason-and-the-pickled-alien-by-kenny-young/

"How Sweet It Ain't: The Jackie Gleasons Split," *People*, March 24, 1975.

Beverly Gleason, "Jackie Gleason Saw the Bodies of Space Aliens at Air Force Base," *The National Enquirer*, Number 556, August 16, 1983, https:///www.priory-of-sion.com/biblios/links/gleason.html

"Arthur Godfrey," *Washington Post*, May 13, 2002, https://www.washingtonpost.com/archive/local/2002/05/16/arthur-godfrey/e31208e9-fa70-4d10-8fbb-da113d723a1a/

"Arthur Lincoln 'Rawhide' Godfrey," May 2003, https://www.findagrave.com/memorial/27127412/arthur-lincoln-godfrey

Stephen Bull, "Bebe Rebozo's Driving," *Nixon library*, February 13, 1973, https://nsarchive.gwu.edu/document/21237-730213-bebe-rebozo-driving

Wikipedia contributors, "Walter Tkach," *Wikipedia*, https://en.wikipedia.org/wiki/Walter_R._Tkach

Wikipedia contributors, "Ron Ziegler," *Wikipedia* , https://en.wikipedia.org/wiki/Ron_Ziegler

"MAJ William Henry 'Bill' Shaw," https://www.findagrave.com/memorial/169024218/william-henry-shaw

Craig Basse, "David Rippetoe, former deputy at MacDill command," October 18, 2005, https://www.tampabay.com/archive/1990/11/20/david-rippetoe-former-deputy-of-macdill-command/

"Brig. Gen Alonzo J. Walter Jr.," *Military Hall of Honor*, https://militaryhallofhonor.com/honoree-record.php?id=229636

Nick Redfern, "Are There Really Dead Aliens Stored Away in Military Facilities?" November 2021, https://mysteriousuniverse.org/2021/11/are-there-really-dead-aliens-stored-away-in-military-facilities/

Paul Seaburn, "Connections between Wright-Patterson AFB, Ray Szymanski and hidden aliens," *Mysterious Universe*, September 2017, https://www.sott.net/article/362309-Connection-of-Wright-Patterson-AFB-Ray-Szymanski-and-hidden-aliens

Vicky Verma, "Are There Crashed UFOs & Dead Alien Bodies In So-Called Hangar 18 of Ohio Military Base?" *Hows and Whys*, December 2021, https://www.howandwhys.com/crashed-ufos-dead-alien-bodies-in-hangar-18/

Wikipedia contributors, "Terry Lee Gabreski (nee Walter)," *Wikpedia*, https://en.wikipedia.org/wiki/Terry_Gabreski

Wikipedia contributors, "Papua New Guinea," *Wikipedia* https:://en.wikipedia.org/wiki/Papua_New_Guinea

"1955: The Hopkinsville Alien Invasion," *Think About It*, updated March 18, 2021, https://www.thinkaboutitdocs.com/the-hopkinsville-alien-invasion-of-1955/

Marcus Lowth, "The Bizarre and Forgotten Broad Haven School UFO Incident of 1977," *UFO Insight*, February 21, 2017, https://www.ufoinsight.com/ufos/close-encounters/broad-haven-school-ufo-incident

"1954 French UFO Humanoid Encounters," https:////www.ufosnw.com/sighting_reports/older/1954french/1954french.htm

Wikipedia contributors, "Night Skies," *Wikipedia*, https://en.wikipedia.org/wiki/Night_Skies

Wikipedia contributors, "E.T., The Extra Terrestrial," *Wikipedia*, https://en.wikipedia.org/wiki/E.T._the_Extra-Terrestrial

Mitch Marcus director,"Presidential Encounters," *Hangar 1: The UFO Files*, 2014, https://www.imdb.com/title/tt3558504/

The Mike Douglas Show, November 1972, https://www.imdb.com/title/tt2552834/

"Major Gordon Cooper, USA Astronaut, and UFOs," *Unexplainable.net*, October 4, 2004, https://ww.ufoevidence.org/news/article157.htm

Wikipedia contributors,"List of The Honeymooners Sketches," *Wikipedia*, https://en.wikipedia.org/wiki/List_of_The_Honeymooners_sketches

Wikipedia contributors, "Smokey and the Bandit," *Wikipedia*, https://en.wikipedia.org/wiki/Smokey_and_the_Bandit

Wikipedia contributors, "Mr. Billion," *Wikipedia*, https://en.wikipedia.org/wiki/Mr._Billio

Kenny Young Archives, https://kenny.anomalyresponse.com

Wikipedia contributors, "Easton, MD," *Wikpedia*, https://en.wikipedia.org/wiki/Easton,_Maryland

Mary Williams, "Sydell Spear, Devoted Employee of Jackie Gleason," *South Florida Sun Sentinel*, December 27, 1993, https://www.sun-sentinel.com/news/fl-xpm-1993-12-28-9312280067-story.html

Wikipedia contributors, "Hugo Black, Jr.," *Wikipedia*, https://en.wikipedia.org/wiki/Hugo_Black_Jr

Anthony Braglia, "Opening the Door to 'The Blue Room' - Where UFO Debris is Hidden," *UFO Chronicles*, June 13, 2012, https://www.theufochronicles.com/2012/06/opening-door-to-blue-room-where-ufo.html?m=1

Christopher Maag, "Bergen County Became Richard Nixon's Adopted Home," *The Daily Record*, August 10, 2014, https://www.dailyrecord.com/story/news/local/new-jersey/2014/08/10/bergen-county-became-richard-nixons-adopted-home/13862573/

Various articles by Tim Beckley and Kenny Young on Jackie Gleason & Richard Nixon, https://greyfalcon.us/Jackie%20Gleason.htm

Jay Francis, "Dr. Kissinger's Key UFO Role Revealed," *UFO Digest*, July 27, 2011, https://www.ufodigest.com/article/dr-henry-kissingers-key-ufo-role-revealed/

History.com Editors, "Nixon Resigns," *History.com*,, last updated August 5, 2022, https://www.history.com/this-day-in-history/nixon-resigns

Presidential daily records, Nixon Library. February 1974, https://www.nixonlibrary.gov/sites/default/files/virtuallibrary/documents/PDD/1974/118%20February%2016-28%201974.pdf

Wikipedia contributors, "Redstone Arsenal," *Wikipedia*, https://en.wikipedia.org/wiki/Redstone_Arsenal

The Redstone Rocket. "Published in the Interest of Personnel at Redstone Arsenal, Al." The Redstone Rocket, September 14, 2022. https://www.theredstonerocket.com/.

Wikipedia contributors, "Lyndon B. Johnson," *Wikpedia*, https://en.wikipedia.org/wiki/Lyndon_B._Johnson

Wikipedia contributors, "Cape Canaveral," *Wikipedia*, https://en.wikipedia.org/wiki/Cape_Canaveral

Wikipedia contributors, "Ed Gurney," *Wikipedia*, https://en.wikipedia.org/wiki/Edward_Gurney

Curtis Sutherly, "UFO Mysteries: A Reporter Seeks the Truth," *Llewellyn Publications*, December 2001

"Freemasons Honor Former President, Brother Gerald R. Ford Masonic Historic Event," *baumbach.com*, 2006, Baumbach.com/BrotherGeraldFord/.

Marcus Lowth, "Michigan, 1966 – The Swamp Gas Incidents," *UFO Insight*, September 2018, https://www.ufoinsight.com/ufos/close-encounters/michigan-1966-swamp-gas-incidents#:~:text=In%20March%201966%20a%20wave%20of%20U-FO%20sightings,most%20detailed%20of%20all%20the%20sightings%20on%20record.

Wikipedia contributors, "Jimmy Carter," *Wikipedia*, htttps://en.wikipedia.org/wiki/Jimmy_Carter

History.com Editors, "Jimmy Carter Files Report On UFO Sighting," September 2021, https://www.history.com/this-day-in-history/carter-files-report-on-ufo-sighting

Bryce Zabel, "UFOs Hovered Over 1976 Election," September 8, 2020, https://medium.com/on-the-trail-of-the-saucers/the-ufo-factor-in-the-1976-election-d1ac7cdc1b31

Wikipedia contributors, "Norman Miller," *Wikipedia*, https://en.wikipedia.org/wiki/Norman_Charles_Miller

Grant Cameron, "Ronald Reagan's UFO Sightings," *Free Republic, freerepublic.com*, January 1, 2011, https://freerepublic.com/focus/f-chat/2650247/posts

Bill Paynter "Ancient Aliens," Season 15, Episode 12, aired April 18, 2020, https://www.imdb.com/name/nm11741027/

Steve Hammons, "Reagan's 1987 U.N. Speech on 'Alien Threat' Resonates Now," *Culture Ready*, July 29, 2015, https://www.cultureready.org/blog/reagans-1987-un-speech-alien-threat-resonates-now

Francis Ridge, "USS Curtis Carrying Nuclear Weapons Buzzed By UFO, April 7, 1954," *Water UFO*, https://waterufo.net/item.php?id=1080

Lucy Wang, "Jackie Gleason's Spaceship-Like House Hits Market For #12M," *Dwell*, August 15, 2018

Wesley Brown, "Gleason Showed Real Hustler Skills in Augusta," *The Augusta Chronicle*, July 12, 2014, https://www.augustachronicle.com/story/lifestyle/2014/07/12/stub-820/14405224007/

Wikipedia contributors, "Frank Edwards," *Wikipedia*, https://en.wikipedia.org/wiki/Frank_Edwards_(writer_and_broadcaster)

Charles Lear, "UFOs on the Radio," *PodcastUFO.com*, March 15, 2020, https://podcastufo.com/ufos-on-the-radio/

Richard Geldreich prefers to relay his UFO/ET information on his Twitter page: https://twitter.com/richgel999

Wikipedia contributors, "S. Everett Gleason," *Wikipedia*, https://en.wikipedia.org/wiki/S._Everett_Gleason

Wikipedia contributors, "Nathan F. Twining," *Wikipedia*, https://en.wikipedia.org/wiki/Nathan_F._Twining

"President Eisenhower's daily appointment logs," *Eisenhowerlibrary*, February 1954, https://www.eisenhowerlibrary.gov/sites/default/files/research/online-documents/presidential-appointment-books/1954/february-1954.pdf

John Austin, "JFK Saw Evidence of Aliens and UFOs While He Was President, Former Pilot Says," *Express.com*, May 31, 2017, https://www.express.co.uk/news/weird/811560/President-JFK-pilot-aliens-UFOs-Unacknowledged-Dr-Steven-Greer

Richard Nixon, "Statement on the Death of General Eisenhower," *Presidency.ucsb*, March 28, 1969, https://www.presidency.ucsb.edu/documents/statement-the-death-general-eisenhower

Dary Matera, "Bio" https://darymatera.com/bio.html

"Eisenhower Met Space Aliens-The Story They Tried to Hide for 28 Years," *National Enquirer*, October 19, 1982.

Donna Hawthorn, "Starseed Origins," https://starseedorigins.webs.com/starseed-origins

Dante Santori and Gil Carlson, "The Book of Alien Races," *Primedia E-Launch LLC*, 2014

Michael Salla, "Russian PM Not Joking – Extraterrestrials Live Among Us, According to MIB Documentary," *Exopolitics.org*,, January 2, 2013, https://exopolitics.org/tag/dmitry-medvedev/

Full_Strength_Beer, "Skinny Bob- Alien," *Youtube*, 2011, https://www.youtube.com/watch?v=r6Ql5HPaEz8

Paul B. Smith, "MO41, The Bombshell Before Roswell: 2020 Revised and Updated," *Argus Books*, https://-argusbooks.com/authorssmithpaul.htm

"Club of Presidents,"*Thunderbird Country Club*, https://www.thunderbirdcc.org/presidents#:~:text=President%20Eisenhower%20on%20two%20occasions%20brought%20his%20Vice,the%20Club%20and%20become%20"one%20of%20the%20guys."

Heather Wade hosted that show after original host Art Bell retired, and at times the podcast "The Kingdom of Nye," www.https://www.thekingdomofnye.com

Gaia staffers, "Project SERPO and and the Zeta Reticuli Exchange Program," *Gaia.com*, November 26, 2019, https://www.gaia.com/article/project-serpo-zeta-reticuli-exchange-program

Project Serpo data, compiled at https://serpo.org

Wikipedia contributors, "Zeta Reticuli," *Wikipedia*, https://en.wikipedia.org/wiki/Zeta_Reticuli

Len Kasten, "Secret Journey to Planet Serpo: A True Story of Interplanetary Travel," *Bear & Company*, May 2013

"Charles Hall and the Tall White ETs," https://www.bibliotecapleyades.net/vida_alien/esp_hall02.htm

"10 Shocking Secrets of the Tall White Aliens, Revealed by Charles Hall," *alienufos-*

ightnings.com, https://alien-ufo-sightings.com/2019/11/10-shocking-secrets-about-the-tall-white-aliens-revealed-by-charles-hall/

Corey Goode, *The Cosmic Insider*, https://coreygoode.com

Wikipedia contributors, "Gary McKinnon," *Wikipedia*, https://en.wikipedia.org/wiki/Gary_McKinnon

Mark, "MUFON goes to Florida city / Homestead, FL, 1-15-2014" January 15, 2014, https://jfkkilledmarilynmonroe.blogspot.com

Earthfiles.com data summarizing the work of UFO investigators Leonard Stringfield and Ron Madeley, subscriber content, 2005 and 2010

Wikipedia contributors, "Bermuda Triangle," *Wikipedia*, https://en.wikipedia.org/wiki/Bermuda_Triangle

Wikipedia contributors, "Bob Hope," *Wikipedia*, https://en.wikipedia.org/wiki/Bob_Hope

Wikipedia contributors, "Spiro Agnew," *Wikipedia*, https://en.wikipedia.org/wiki/Spiro Agnew

Wikipedia contributors, "Gerald Ford," *Wikipedia*, https://en.wikipedia.org/wiki/GeraldFord

"Bob Hope House, John Lautner's Modernist Masterpiece," *Modern Palm Springs*, https://moderntourspalmsprings.com/bob-hope-house/

Nicolette Wenzell, "Explore Palm Springs: Bob Hope House," *Palm Springs Life*, July 22, 2013, https://www.palmspringslife.com/explore-palm-springs-bob-hope-house/

"Bob Hope's UFO House in Palm Springs, CA (Listed for $25 Million)," *Home Stratosphere*, July 6, 2020, https://www.homestratosphere.com/bob-hopes-ufo-house-in-palm-springs-ca-listed-for-25-million/

Joi-Marie McKenzie, "Bob Hope's UFO House Has Sold For $13 Million," *ABC News*, December 1, 2016, https://abcnews.go.com/Lifestyle/bob-hopes-ufo-house-sold-13-million/story?id=43899883

"Bob Hope Says Nixon Seems In Need of Rest," *New York Times*, February 24, 1975, https://www.nytimes.com/1975/02/24/archives/bob-hope-says-nixon-seems-in-need-of-rest.html

Ann Brenoff, "Bob Hope's House In Toluca Lake, Calif, Had Enough Room For Nixon to Land a Helicopter," *Huffington Post*, September 24, 2013, https://www.huffpost.com/entry/bob-hope-house_n_3982079

Jeff Shain, "Flashback: Jackie Gleason's Inverrary Classic," *Pro Golf Weekly*, February 22, 2016, https://progolfweekly.com/flashback-jackie-gleasons-inverrary-classic/

Harry S Truman Presidential Library record of the documentary, https://www.trumanlibrary.gov/movingimage-records/mp76-83

"Homestead UFO House," *Abandoned Florida*, July 3, 2013, https://www.abandoned-fl.com/the-ufo-house/

"Condon, Gretchen," *Altmeyer Funeral Home*, October 2020, https://altmeyerfuneralandcremation.com/obituaries/larry-william-bryant/

"Citizens Against UFO Secrecy," at 3518 Martha Custis Drive, Alexandria, VA 22302.

PAUL BLAKE SMITH

Editors of Publications International, "Jackie Gleason Sees a UFO," *How Stuff Works*, https://science.howstuffworks.com/space/aliens-ufos/jackie-gleason-ufo.htm

"Beckley, Tim, Grey Falcon," *greyfalcon.us*, https://greyfalcon.us/Jackie%20Gleason.htm

K. T. Frankovich , *Educate Yourself*, 2005, https://educate-yourself.org/cn/hurricanandrewaccountsexcisedsections15aug04.shtml

K. T. Frankovich , *Where Heavens Meet* (Oakville: Language of Souls Publications, 1999).

K.T. Frankovich , "The Lime Grove Encounters," *Soul Guidance*, https://www.soulguidance.com/houseofthesun/ET/greys/limegrove.html

Miamiteacher, *Amazon.com*, Review, September 11, 2004, https://www.amazon.com/Where-Heavens-Meet-K-Frankovich/dp/1894368177

"UFOs and American Presidents," *UFO Casebook*, June 17, 2011, https://www.ufocasebook.com/2011/ufopresidents.html

Wikipedia contributors, "Oklahoma City Air Force Station," *Wikipedia*, https://en.wikipedia.org/wiki/Oklahoma_City_Air_Force_Station#:~:text=Oklahoma%20City%20Air%20Force%20Station%20%28ADC%20ID%3A%20P-52%2C,to%20the%20s

Nixon.gov, presidential daily schedule for January 1974, https:www//.nixonlibrary.gov/sites/default/files/virtuallibrary/documents/PDD/1974/116%20January%2016-31%201974.pdf

"Arab Oil Embargo," *Brittanica.com*, https:///www.britannica.com/event/Arab-oil-embargo

"1974: January UFO & Alien Sightings," *Think About It*, https://www.thinkaboutitdocs.com/1974-january-ufo-alien-sightings/

"The 1974 UFO Chronology," *NICAP*, https://www.nicap.org/chronos/1974fullrep.htm

Jeff Parrott, "Ronald Reagan Spoke at the First CPAC Gathering in 1974. Here's What He Said," *Deseret.com*, https://www.deseret.com/indepth/2021/2/26/22303493/ronald-reagan-spoke-at-the-inaugural-cpac-in-1974-here-is-what-he-said-washington-dc

Wikipedia contributors, "Ray Price," *Wikipedia*, https://en.wikipedia.org/wiki/Ray_Price_

Wikipedia contributors, "Ben Rich," *Wikipedia*, https://en.wikipedia.org/wiki/Ben_Rich

Gaia staff, "Ben Rich, Lockheed-Martin, and UFOs," *Gaia.com*, December 3, 2019, https://www.gaia.com/article/ben-rich-lockheed-martin-and-ufos

Wikipedia contributors, "Henry Kissinger," *Wikipedia*, htttps://en.wikipedia.org/wiki/Henry_Kissinger

Richard Markosian, "Aliens at Dugway Proving Ground: Spaceships Taking Off From "The New Area 51"?" *Utah Stories*, April 18, 2018, https://utahstories.com/2018/04/aliens-at-dugway-proving-ground-spaceships-taking-off-from-the-new-area-51/

Wikipedia contributors, "Harry Reid," *Wikipedia*, https://en.wikipedia.org/wiki/Harry_Reid

Brett Bachman, "Former Senator Harry Reid: I Was Told Lockheed-Martin Had UFO Crash Fragments," *Salon.com*, May 1, 2021, https://www.salon.com/2021/05/01/former-sen-harry-reid-i-was-told-lockheed-martin-had-ufo-crash-fragments/

Arium Walla, "Second Director of Lockheed Skunk Works Shocking Comments About UFO Technology," *bibliotecaleyades.net*, June 23, 2015, https://www.bibliotecapleyades.net/ciencia/ciencia_flyingobjects163.htm

"Extraterrestrials UFOs Are Real," *UFOresearchnetwork.com*, September 2, 2010, https://uforesearchnetwork.proboards.com/thread/923/rich-ufos-real-deathbed-confession

"Ben Rich, Area 51, & Taking ET Home," October 14, 2014, https://www.blueblurrylines.com/2014/10/ben-rich-area-51-taking-et-home.html

Wikipedia contributors, "Whittier, California," *Wikipedia*, https://en.wikipedia.org/wiki/Whittier,_California

Wikipedia contributors, "H.R.Haldeman," *Wikipedia*, https://en.wikipedia.org/wiki/H._R._Haldeman

U.S. Department of Defense in Washington D.C., https://www.defense.gov

Drew Costigan, "The Holloman AFB Film – Fact or Fiction?" *Youtube* video, 2018, https://www.youtube.com/watch?v=BTMmtPGEdMw

R. Graham, "When the Government Gave Hollywood Footage of a "Real" Alien Landing," *Mysteriousuniverse.org*, January 2019, https://mysteriousuniverse.org/2019/01/when-the-government-gave-hollywood-footage-of-a-real-alien-landing/

Chris Matthews, "How Kennedy Brought Down Nixon," *The Daily Beast*, July 14, 2017, https://www.thedailybeast.com/how-kennedy-brought-down-nixon

Compilation of articles, including excerpt from writer Frank Thomas, who quotes plotting Nixon as saying "If he (Kennedy) runs (in 1976) I'll kick his ass," "Four More Years–The Presidency of Richard Nixon," https://www.alternatehistory.com/forum/threads/four-more-years-the-presidency-of-richard-m-nixon.194381/

Wikipedia contributors, "Franklin D. Roosevelt," *Wikipedia*, https://en.wikipedia.org/wiki/Franklin_D_Roosevelt

"1971 Emenegger/Sandler UFO Landing Film," *Think About It*, last updated March 14, 2021, https://ww.thinkaboutitdocs.com/1971-emeneggersandlerufo-landing-film/

Natalia Megas, "45 Years After Watergate, H.R. Haldeman's Wife Finally Speaks," *The Daily Beast*, May 2017, https://www.thedailybeast.com/a-watergate-widow-finally-speaks

Nixon.gov, May 1971 daily schedule, https://www.nixonlibrary.gov/sites/default/files/virtuallibrary/documents/PDD/1971/051%20May%201-15%201971.pdf

Chris Whipple, "How H.R. Haldeman Became the Model for Ruthless White House Chiefs of Staff," *History.net*, July 19, 2017, https://www.historynet.com/nixons-s-o-b/

Wikipedia contributors, "Charles Colson," *Wikipedia*, https://en.wikipedia.org/wiki/Charles_Colson

LBJ Library, Johnson Daily Diary Collection, https://lbjlibrary.net/collections/daily-diary.html

Grant Cameron, "Disney, UFOs, and Disclosure," *presidentialufo.com*, July 11, 2002, https:///rense.com/general27/dis.htm

Robbie Graham, "When the Government Gave Hollywood Footage of a 'Real' Alien Landing," *mysteriousuniverse.org*, January 2019, https://mysteriousuniverse.org/2019/01/when-the-government-gave-hollywood-footage-of-a-real-alien-landing/

Wikipedia contributors, "John L. McLucas," *Wikipedia*, https://en.wikipedia.org/wiki/John_L._McLucas

"Evidence! Holloman AFB Story True?" *Pegasus Research Consortium*, https://www.thelivingmoon.com/49ufo_files/03files2/Hollowman_AFB_UFOs.html

Art Campbell, "Eisenhower's Incredible Journey," *UFOcrashbook.com*, https://ww.ufocrashbook.com/eisenhower.html

Wikipedia contributors, "La Casa Pacifica," *Wikipedia*, https://www.en.wikipedia.org/wiki/La_Casa_Pacifica

Tom Owens, "1988-10-14: UFO Coverup? Live! With Mike Farrell," *Youtube* video, July 28, 2019, https://www.youtube.com/watch?v=enQ4sGsiEf4

"Jamie Shandera," *NOUFORS*, https://noufors.com/Jaime_Shandera.htm

Wikipedia contributors, "United States Air Force," *Wikipedia*, https://en.wikipedia.org/wiki/United_States_Air_Force

"Paul R. Shartle obituary," *Ancient Faces*, https://www.ancientfaces.com/person/paul-r-shartle-birth-1922-death-2001/25692283

Paul Shartle's wife Geraldine also died in 2001, gravesite at https://www.findagrave.com/memorial/58084092/paul-robert-shartle

"Paul Shartle obituary," *Tributes*, https://www.tributes.com/obituary/show/Paul-Robert-Shartle-93049105

Jaded Truth, "UFO's (It Has Begun) Past, Present, and Future Documentary," *Youtube* video, September 30, 2017 https://www.youtube.com/watch?v=6CJdUA8LQg0

Drew Costigan, "The Holloman AFB UFO: Fact or Fiction?" *Youtube* video, April 2018, https://www.youtube.com/watch?v=BTMmtPGEdMw

Wikipedia contributors, "Steven Spielberg," *Wikipedia*, https://en.wikipedia.org/wiki/Steven_Spielberg

Wikipedia contributors, "Close Encounters of the Third Kind," *Wikipedia*, https://en.wikipedia.org/wiki/Close_Encounters_of_the_Third_Kind

"Today's Blind Items: Government Cooperation," *Crazy Days and Nights*, November 26, 2018, https://www.crazydaysandnights.net/2018/11/todays-blind-items-government.html

Christopher Welch, "What Did President Reagan Know About UFOs?" *Vigeeks*, March 20, 2020, https://vigeeks.com/reagan-ufo/

Huyen Dang, "Spielberg, Close Encounters, and Conspiracy Theories," *todaypressworld.com*, September 8, 2022, https://todaypressworld24.com/?p=5976&fbclid=IwAR004MGaCFkJfuypqeyWMYXoRf1sHw6BvBAWmuELkoVXJnx-cHzDcZLgBAmM

Linda Moulton Howe, "An Alien Harvest, Special Limited Edition," January 1, 1989

Ancient Aliens, "Aliens and the Presidents," 2020, described in Internet Media Database, https://www.imdb.com/title/tt12127180/fullcredits

Wikipedia contributors, "May Pang," *Wikipedia*, https://en.wikipedia.org/wiki/May_Pang

May Pang, "Loving John," *Warner Books*, 1983

Wikipedia contributors, "Mind Games, Capitol Records, 1973," *Wikipedia*, https://en.wikipedia.org/wiki/Mind_Games_(John_Lennon_album)

"John Lennon's UFO Encounter," *Anomalien*, March 30, 2015, https://anomalien.com/john-lennons-ufo-encounter/

Chris Dyer, "Imagine All the Aliens! John Lennon's Sketch of a UFO," *Daily Mail*, March 6, 2019, https//www.dailymail.co.uk/news/article-6777043/John-Lennons-never-seen-sketch-UFO-drawn-thought-saw-one-New-York.html

Wikipedia contributors, "George Harrison," *Wikipedia*, https://en.wikipedia.org/wiki/George_Harrison

Cynthia Lennon, "A Twist of Lennon," *Avon Books*, 1978

Raechel Shewfelt, "John Lennon Believed In Flying Saucers. Here's How You Can Buy His Drawing of a UFO," *Yahoo Entertainment*, March 27, 2019, https://www.yahoo.com/entertainment/john-lennon-believed-flying-saucers-heres-can-buy-drawing-ufo-204755604.html

"Jackie Gleason: Here, There, and Everywhere Lyrics," *Songlyrics.com*, https://www.songlyrics.com/jackie-gleason/here-there-and-everywhere-lyrics/

"Jackie Gleason: Yesterday Lyrics," *Songlyrics.com*, https://genius.com/Jackie-gleason-yesterday-lyrics

"Rural Communes in Northern California, 1969-1970," *The Bob Fitch Photography Archives*, https://exhibits.stanford.edu/fitch/browse/rural-communes-in-northern-california-1969-1970?f%5Btopic_facet%5D%5B%5D=Hamrick%2C+Donald+James%2C+1935-&f%5Btopic_facet%5D%5B%5D=Harbinger+Commune&per_page=20&sort=score+desc%2C+pub_year_isi+desc%2C+title_sort+asc

Matt Sergiou, "About the Occult Beatles," *The Occult Beatles*, https://theoccultbeatles.wordpress.com/category/articles/

Wikipedia contributors, "Magic Alex," *Wikipedia*, https://en.wikipedia.org/wiki/Magic_Alex

Wikipedia contributors, "The Dakota," *Wikipedia*, https://en.wikipedia.org/wiki/The_Dakota

"People" *Time magazine*, Feb. 19, 1973, https://ttps://content.time.com/time/subscriber/article/0,33009,906881,00.html

"Lennon, Ono, Attend Watergate Hearing 40 Years Ago Today," *retronewser.com*, June 27, 2013, https://retronewser.com/2013/06/27/lennon-ono-attend-watergate-hearing-in-washington-40-years-ago-today-1973/

Daniel Bates, "Richard Nixon Tried to Deport John Lennon Because He Considered Him a 'Dangerous Political Enemy,' According to New Documentary," *Daily Mail U.K.*, June 15, 2018, https::/www.dailymail.co.uk/news/article-5849009/Richard-Nixon-considered-John-Lennon-dangerous-political-leader-tried-deport-hm.html

Mucho Mongo, acoustic guitar recording originally created in 1973, not released on an album during Lennon's lifetime, various versions on YouTube.com, via https://www.youtube.com/watch?v=BpYwM9OSPYo

Wikipedia contributors, "Harry Nilsson," *Wikipedia*, https://en.wikipedia.org/wiki/Harry_Nilsson

Wikipedia contributor, "The U.S. vs. John Lennon," *Wikipedia*, https://en.wikipedia.org/wiki/The_U.S._vs._John_Lennon

Ray Coleman, "Lennon: The Definitive Biography," *Harper Perennial*, 1993

"John Lennon Sees a UFO in New York City, 1974," *Dangerous Minds*, April 13, 2015, https://dangerousminds.net/comments/john_lennon_sees_a_ufo_in_new_york_city_1974

David Halperin, "John Lennon, May Pang, and the UFO – Their Story," *davidhalperin.net*, February 11, 2016, https:///www.davidhalperin.net/john-lennon-may-pang-and-the-ufo-1-their-story/

The Red Kobra, "John Lennon Describes Seeing a UFO Over New York," *Youtube* video, August 1974 https://www.youtube.com/watch?v=Xm1xhgB1-9E

Minnie Wright, "John Lennon: Beatles Star's Ex Reveals Truth About His UFO Sighting," *Express*, January 24, 2020, https://www.express.co.uk/entertainment/music/1232867/John-Lennon-Beatles-May-Pang-UFO-sighting

The Randlesham Forest Incident, "John Lennon UFO Encounter 1974," *YouTube* video, https://www.youtube.com/watch?v=Jdw4cibPh-U&t=54s

Josef Allen Hynek "May Pang Talks About John Lennon's UFO on ABC News," *YouTube* video, https://www.youtube.com/watch?v=BNl_jwuQgtE

Steve Bagnell, "John Lennon UFO Sketch 'a Fake' Claims Former Girlfriend May Pang," *North Wales Bulletin*, June 24, 2015, https://www.dailypost.co.uk/news/north-wales-news/john-lennon-ufo-sketch-a-9517521

Wikipedia contributors, "Walls and Bridges," *Wikipedia*, https://en.wikipedia.org/wiki/Walls_and_Bridges

Bryce Zabel, "The Night John Lennon Saw a UFO," *Medium.com*, August 21, 2020, https://medium.com/on-the-trail-of-the-saucers/did-john-lennon-really-see-a-ufo-ba938fe154c5

Wikipedia contributors, "David Bowie," *Wikipedia*, https://en.wikipedia.org/wiki/David_Bowie

"David Bowie Shares His UFO Experiences with Creem Magazine, 44 Years Ago," *Paranormal Pop Culture*, 2021, https://www.paranormalpopculture.com/2019/02/david-bowie-shares-his-ufo-experiences.html

Wikipedia contributors, "Lester Bangs," *Wikipedia*, https://en.wikipedia.org/wiki/Lester_Bangs

Wikipedia contributors, "Ziggy Stardust," *Wikipedia*, https://en.wikipedia.org/wiki/Ziggy_Stardust_(character)

Richard Padula, "The Day The UFOs Stopped Play," *BBC World Service Report*, October 24, 2014, https://www.bbc.com/news/magazine-29342407

P. Seaburn, "David Bowie and the Music of Space Aliens and UFOs," *Mysteriousuniverse*, January 12, 2016 https://mysteriousuniverse.org/2016/01/david-bowie-and-the-music-of-space-aliens-and-ufos/

Wikipedia contributors, "Diamond Dogs Tour," *Wikipedia* , https://en.wikipedia.org/wiki/Diamond_Dogs_Tour

Nixonlibrary.gov, daily presidential records, June 1974, https://www.nixonlibrary.gov/sites/default/files/virtuallibrary/documents/PDD/1974/126%20June%2016-30%201974.pdf

Wikipedia contributors, "Ringo Starr," *Wikipedia*, https://en.wikipedia.org/wiki/Ringo_Starr

Wikipedia contributors, "Goodnight Vienna," *Wikipedia*, https://en.wikipedia.org/wiki/Goodnight_Vienna

Wikipedia contributors, "The Day The Earth Stood Still," *Wikipedia*, https://en.wikipedia.org/wiki/The_Day_the_Earth_Stood_Still

Loomyaire, "Goodnight Vienna -1974 Ringo Starr TV Commercial" *YouTube* video,, https://www.youtube.com/watch?v=zqBH-9yyQMU

Michael Seth Starr. *Ringo: With a Little Help."* 2015

Wikipedia contributors, "Paul McCartney," *Wikipedia*, https://en.wikipedia.org/wiki/Paul_McCartney

Wikipedia contributors, "Venus and Mars," *Wikipedia*, https://en.wikipedia.org/wiki/Venus_and_Mars_(Wings_album)

Wikipedia contributors, "Julian Lennon," *Wikipedia*, https://en.wikipedia.org/wiki/Julian_Lennon

Wikipedia contributors, "New York City blackout of 1977," *Wikipedia*, https://en.wikipedia.org/wiki/New_York_City_blackout_of_1977

Wikipedia contributor, "Uri Geller," *Wikipedia*, https://en.wikipedia.org/wiki/Uri_Geller

"Classic Hoaxes: Uri Geller-The Greatest Prankster of All Time?" *Pranksters.com*, https://pranksters.com/uri-geller/

Wikipedia contributors, "The Truth About Uri Geller," *Wikipedia*, https://en.wikipedia.org/wiki/The_Truth_About_Uri_Geller

"John Lennon Told Me He'd Met UFO Aliens," *Urigeller,* November 2, 1996, https://www.urigeller.com/uri-reveals-secrets-about-john-lennon/

"Uri Geller's Legend About John Lennon and the "Alien Egg": Fact or Fiction?" Aliens UFO SightingsApril 2015, https://alien-ufo-sightings.com/2015/04/uri-gellers-legend-about-john-lennon-and-the-alien-egg-fact-or-fiction/

Wikipedia contributors, "Nobody Told Me," *Wikipedia*, https://en.wikipedia.org/wiki/Nobody_Told_Me

Wikipedia contributors, "Mark David Chapman," *Wikipedia*, https://en.wikipedia.org/wiki/Mark_David_Chapman

Wikipedia contributors, "Murder of John Lennon," *Wikipedia*, https://en.wikipedia.org/wiki/Murder_of_John_Lennon

Wikispooks contributors, "Jose Sanjenis Perdomo," *Wikispooks* , https://wikispooks.com/wiki/José_Sanjenís_Perdomo

Jonathan P. Baird, "Trump Is Proving To Be More Dangerous Than Nixon," *Concord Monitor*, December 7, 2020, https://www.concordmonitor.com/Forum-Baird-37540163

Gabe Mirkin, "Richard Nixon Battled Paranoia and Depression," *Villages News*, December 25, 2018, https://www.villages-news.com/2018/12/25/richard-nixon-battled-paranoia-and-depression/

Wikipedia contributors, "Pardon of Richard Nixon," *Wikipedia*, https://en.wikipedia.org/wiki/Pardon_of_Richard_Nixon

"E. Howard Hunt Wife Plane Crash," April 4, 2017, diarimeluso.weebly.com/blog/e-howard-hunt-wife-plane-crash#:~:text=When%20Hunt%27s%20wife%20-Dorothy%20was%20killed%20in%20a,hus-band%2C%20E.%20Howard%20Hunt%27s%20Wife%20Watergate%27s%20Darkest%20Secret.

Various press reports compiled: "E. Howard Hunt Dies," *kennedyandkings.com*, February 15, 2007, https://www.kennedysandking.com/obituaries/e-howard-hunt-dies

Erik Hedegaard, "The Last Confession of E. Howard Hunt," *Rolling Stone*, April 5, 2007, https://www.rollingstone.com/feature/the-last-confession-of-e-howard-hunt-76611/

Rebelander Basilan, "Jackie Gleason's Challenging Final Years," *Amo Mama*, September 15, 2019, https://news.amomama.com/170668-jackie-gleasons-challenging-final-years.html

Paul Owers, "Historic Country Club To Close As Sport's Popularity Declines," *CoStar News*, September 26, 2019, https://product.costar.com/home/news/shared/1467674839?market=37

"Relative Describes Nixon As In Pain and Depressed," *New York Times*, September 12, 1974, https://www.nytimes.com/1974/09/12/archives

Wikipedia contributors, "Pat Nixon," *Wikipedia*, https://en.wikipedia.org/wiki/Pat_Nixon

"Nixon Presidential Retreat in Key Biscayne Torn Down," *Herald Tribune*, July 22, 2004, https://www.heraldtribune.com/story/news/2004/07/22/nixon-presidential-retreat-in-key-biscayne-torn-down/28816821007/

"AG Studies Theft of Data on Rebozo," *New York Times*, November 27, 1975, https://www.nytimes.com/1975/11/27/archives/da-studies-theft-of-data-on-rebozo-papers-on-friend-of-nixon-stolen.html

Oisin Curran, "The Tragic Life and Curious Death of Howard Hughes," *HowStuffWorks.com*, May 1, 2020, https://history.howstuffworks.com/historical-figures/howard-hughes.htm

Wikipedia contributors, "Hurricane Andrew," *Wikipedia*, https://en.wikipedia.org/wiki/Hurricane_Andrew

Wikipedia contributors, "Miami," *Wikipedia* , https://en.wikipedia.org/wiki/Miami

Wikipedia contributors, "Chuck Hall (Florida politician)," *Wikipedia*, https://en.wikipedia.org/wiki/Chuck_Hall_(Florida_politician)#:~:text=Charles%20F.%20Hall%20%281918%20–%20August%2010%2C%201974%29,Beach%20from%201971%20until%20his%20death%20in%201974.

Eric Pace, "Jackie Gleason Dies of Cancer, Comedian and Actor was 71," *New York*

Times, June 25, 1987, https://www.nytimes.com/1987/06/25/obituaries/jackie-glea-son-dies-of-cancer-comedian-and-actor-was-71.html

"Jackie Gleason Changed Will On Deathbed," A.P., July 23, 1987, https://apnews.-com/article/63e6224c1c6c5780f9ab914bfc0b6853

Wikipedia contributors, "Donald Nixon," Wikipedia, https;//en.wikipedia.org/wiki/Donald_Nixon

Wikipedia contributors, "Arthur F. Burns," Wikipedia, https://en.wikipedi-a.org/wiki/Arthur_F._Burns

Wikipedia contributors, "Death and State Funeral of Richard Nixon," Wikipedia, https://en.wikipedia.org/wiki/Death_and_state_funeral_of_Richard_Nixon

Howard Homonoff, "Watergate's 50th Anniversary, A Multi-Media Guide For Today," Forbes, June 29, 2022, https://www.forbes.com/sites/howard-homonoff/2022/06/29/watergates-50th-anniversary-a-multi-media-guide-for-today/?sh=686d973a2e0c

R.K. Lindgren, "The "Nixonian Fate" 50 Years Later," When God Plays Dice, June 3, 2022, https://godplaysdice.com/2022/06/03/the-nixonian-fate-50-years-on/

Richard Kreitner, "October 10, 1973: Vice President Spiro Agnew Resigns," The Nation, October 10, 2015, s://www.thenation.com/article/archive/october-10-1973-vice-president-spiro-agnew-resigns/

"Once-Bitter Agnew Attends Funeral, Talks of Reconciliation," Deseret News, April 28, 1994, https://www.deseret.com/1994/4/28/19105916/once-bitter-agnew-attends-funeral-talks-of-reconciliation

Robert Shogan, "Spiro Agnew Dies; Nixon VP Quit in Disgrace," Los Angeles Times, September 18, 1996, https:////www.latimes.com/archives/la-xpm-1996-09-18-mn-45094-story.html

"S. Everett Gleason, Historian, Dies," New York Times, November 22, 1974, https://www.nytimes.com/1974/11/22/archives/s-everett-gleason-historian-69-dies.html

"Space Pioneer Gordon Cooper Dies; Cooper Believed in UFO Cover-up," CNN, October 4, 2004, https://www.cnn.com/2004/TECH/space/10/04/gordon.cooper/index.html

Pat Dowell, "Comedian Bob Hope Dies at 100," NPR, July 28, 2003, https://www.n-pr.org/2003/07/28/1359556/comedian-bob-hope-dies-at-100

Kenneth Womack, "May Pang Opens Up About John Lennon's "Lost Weekend" In Her "Love Story" Documentary," Salon magazine, June 10, 2022, https://www.salon.-com/2022/06/10/may-pang-opens-up-about-john-lennons-lost-weekend-in-her-love-story-documentary/

Chris Spears, "It's No Space Oddity: Mile-Wide David Bowie Asteroid To Forever Float In Outer Space," CBS News, January 11, 2016, https://www.cbsnews.com/col-orado/news/its-no-space-oddity-mile-wide-david-bowie-asteroid-to-forever-float-in-outer-space/

Wikipedia contributors, "Death of David Bowie," Wikipedia, https://en.wikipedi-a.org/wiki/Death_of_David_Bowie

Daniel Brown, "David Bowie Constellation – The Surprising Truth," phys.org,

PAUL BLAKE SMITH

January 21, 2016, https://phys.org/news/2016-01-david-bowie-constellation-truth.html#:~:text=The%20"David%20Bowie%20constellation"%20was%20defined%20by%20the,the%20sky%20–%20or%20constellation%20–%20at%20all.Steve Rothhaus, "Jackie Gleason Widow, Marilyn Taylor Gleason, Dies," *South Florida Sun Sentinel*, April 4, 2019, https://www.sun-sentinel.com/news/obituaries/fl-ne-jackie-gleason-widow-dead-20190403-story.htmlFind A Grave obituary, https://www.findagrave.com/memorial/198069095/marilyn-ann-gleason – It mentions how Marilyn said in 2014 of Jackie: "He always had great ideas. Onward and upward. That was his motif."

APPENDIX

My previous book, *President Eisenhower's Close Encounters*, aired a
shocking, electrifying government report dated January 8, 1989. It
was a Defense Intelligence Agency briefing about the history of UFOs
and ETs in America, labeled "Ultra Top Secret." It included data on
actual face-to-face meetings with friendly off-world visitors. The
explosive material was mysteriously leaked to a paranormal podcast
host in mid-2017. Evidently, the report was once an important explanation of the alien situation for the incoming administration of new
President George H. W. Bush. My publishers at that time printed
almost all of the document but accidentally left off the final pages,
entitled "Assessment of the Situation." It's a key summation that
deserves attention. As we can see here, it mentions a secret airbase in
the Nevada desert that houses aliens and government agents interacting with them (see "Kewper Stein" in the Introduction and the
"Project Serpo" notion). This might have been the main site for the
"diplomatic exchanges" mentioned in this book, but it is the author's
opinion that some of them may have been conducted at Homestead
AFB during Nixon's reign.

Here are the missing pages, 38-44, to wrap up this book,

containing information that quite possibly describes the actions of President Richard Milhous Nixon when he was in charge of the federal response to this top-secret communication and travel program, data so white-hot that likely even Jackie Gleason was not allowed to learn of it.

Ultra-Top-Secret document title page 38 here— "Assessment of the Situation, Statement of Position"

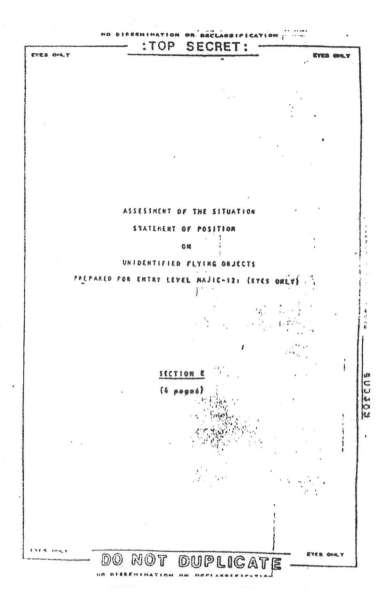

:TOP SECRET:

EYES ONLY   EYES ONLY

ASSESSMENT OF THE SITUATION

STATEMENT OF POSITION

ON

UNIDENTIFIED FLYING OBJECTS

PREPARED FOR ENTRY LEVEL MAJIC-12: (EYES ONLY)

SECTION E

(6 pages)

EYES ONLY   EYES ONLY

DO NOT DUPLICATE

NO DISSEMINATION OR DECLASSIFICATION

Ultra-Top-Secret document page 39 here—titled "Assessment of the Situation" followed by pages 40, 41, 42, 43, and 44.

:TOP SECRET:

ASSESSMENT OF THE SITUATION

In any attempt to properly assess the present situation as it relates to the issue of national security or the risk of cultural upheaval, it is important to take full advantage of hindsight and historical retrospective. It is both an interesting footnote of history and a key point of reference that the human race itself is directly responsible for its being contacted in this century by beings from other worlds.

Through dialogs with representatives of these alien pilots of the flying disc-crafts, we have learned that our own scientific curiousity led to the visitations which have been ongoing throughout this century.

In 1895, the Yugoslavic electrical scientist, Nikola Tesla, most noted for his introduction of alternating current to electrical power transmission and for a laboratory device named after him (the Tesla coil) embarked on a series of researches that have made this the saucer century. Tesla had long proposed that it was possible to directly broadcast pure electrical energies at a distance without loss of power and without wires. By 1899, and with the aid of government and private scientific backing, Tesla had chosen a site near Colorado Springs, Colorado to conduct a massive and never repeated experiment. Nikola Tesla's purpose was to gather the Earth's own magnetic field and to use the Earth as a huge transmitter to send signals to outer space in an attempt to contact whoever might be living there. Tesla had no idea that the specific type of power he had generated was coursing through space and caused great havoc many light years away. Modern science has all but forgotten Tesla's work. The sorts of energies and magnetic waves he was working with were never fully defined or explained and almost all of his original designs are lost or were destroyed by their creator in his later years. But it is now obvious that this single action by a scientific outlaw generated serious concerns among the other intelligences in the near reaches of our galaxy. Although others have attempted to use radio waves to broadcast messages into outer space, none used the energies that Tesla did.

We have now determined by discussion with the extraterrestrials who have contacted this government since 1947 that the type of power Tesla used is a very important form of energy. It has apparently been largely overlooked by modern electrical engineers and physicists although certain information gathered by the Central Intelligence Agency (CIA) indicates a strong program of research of this type inside the Soviet Union. According to the alien sources we have debriefed, Tesla's work was a technical fluke at least one hundred years ahead of it's time. Development of these energy fields will only logically occur after we have fully understood laser beam devices.

The extraterrestrials have reportedly been visiting and regularly monitoring the progress of life on Earth for thousands of our years and they were very concerned about this odd signal we sent coursing through space. Among other things, it seems that these energy waves can disturb the process of ecology, alter weather patterns and damage ozone levels in whatever planetary atmosphere they might encounter.

Evidently, Tesla was sending huge amounts of an unknown form of energy into space along with his intended signals but was unable to detect these due to the fact that instruments for their measurement did not and do not now exist.

The extraterrestrial intelligences (EI's) attempted to respond to his transmissions in a form of binary code that they routinely use for long range communications (evidently these energies act instantly at a distance and are not limited to the speed of light) and ask that he cease sending. Of course, Tesla had no way of understanding the message he received back from space. Fortunately, the anger of local residents at the side effects of his research forced him to shut down the Colorado Springs experiments in the same year he began them.

This, then, was the actual start of the so-called "flying saucer age" in our times. As it became clear that our people were on the verge of an explosion of technical progress, the EI's decided on a long term program of carefully calculated and seemingly random contact with the eventual goal of raising our awareness of our place in the galactic community. With the advent of the Atomic Age, this program was escalated to include eventual diplomatic contact with many of Earth's governments. The same approach of staging apparent "accidental" contact was chosen for it's low psychological impact on the human race. This was the situation in the case of the United States of America (re: Roswell and Aztec, New Mexico files, this briefing).

The problem with direct contact was stated early in our relationship by one of the extraterrestrial biological entities (EBE's). " Right now there are people on this planet who do not know that your moon circles your world or how long it takes your world to orbit your star (sun). I am not speaking of a small number, but perhaps as many as half of the global population. We have been mistaken for being gods or devils in your past and this sort of slow education is best. As a cultural myth, we stand the best chance of acceptance by the masses of your citizens."

There are now hundreds of compiled studies of the EBEs, their worlds and their objectives. In several cases, volunteers from our armed forces have participated in diplomatic and cultural exchanges during the 1970's and early 1980's and have visited some of the EBE's worlds. The following is a short assessment of the situation as we now understand it.

    * There are four basic types of EBEs so-far confirmed;
      And they are listed here in descending order of their
      influence on our studies.

        A. Earth-like humanoids. There are several
          variations more-or-less like ourselves. The
          majority of these are friendly and are the
          bulk of our EBE contacts. Most have a high
          degree of psychic ability and all use science,
          and engineering of an advanced nature.

THE NIXON-GLEASON ALIEN ENCOUNTER   271

B. Small humanoids or "Greys". The Greys, so-called
for the hue of skin possessed by most of this
type, are a sort of drone. The are not unlike
the worker ants or bees. They are a type of
genetic clone incapable of sexual reproduction.
With little or no independent will, they are
mostly under the psychic control of the Earth-
like humanoids who raise them like pets (or a
kind of slave). A detailed explaination of this
cultural oddity and it's role in the form of
space travel these EBEs employ is addressed
elsewere in this briefing. Assuming the Greys
are under benign control, they are harmless.

C. Non-humanoid EBEs. These are in several classes
and come from worlds where dominant morphology
took a different evolutionary course. Many of
these are dangerous not for organized hostile
intentions, but because such creatures do not
hold human life as sacred. To them, we are
animals despite our intelligence. A few are
friendly because their cultures forbid all acts
against living creatures. Thus far, contact has
been minimal with only a handful of unfortunate
encounters.

D. Transmorphic Entities. Of all the forms of EBE
studied so-far by Operation Majestic, these are
the most difficult to understand or even to give
a description of. Essentially, such entities are
not "beings", or "creatures"! TEs exist in some
other dimension or plane which is to say not in
our space or time. They do not use devices to
travel in space. Only once has a member of an
MJ-12 contact team been privileged to be present
when introduced by an Earth-like EBE to a TE. In
essence these entities are composed of pure mind
energy. They are not unlike "ghostly spirits"
and seem to be only curious about our universe.
They are said (by other EBEs) to be capable of
taking on any physical form that they "channel"
their energy into as matter.

* The principle means of travel used by the humanoid EBE is
of a mechanical nature and involves very large craft that
cannot land on a planet. These employ the forms of energy
discovered accidently by Nikola Tesla to cause themselves
to be thrust from or pulled towards the stars they wish
to visit. Some alteration or control of the passage of
time onboard the intransit craft is used as well.

A055389

- Since the huge interstellar (between stars) craft cannot approach the powerful gravity and magnetic fields of the stars from which they draw their power, they are placed into a "parking orbit" far outside the planetary family (solar system) of any star they approach. This may be millions of miles from the world the EBE's wish to visit. Smaller craft, often but not always disc-shaped, are used to travel the distances remaining. These draw their power and propel themselves by use of "electrogravity". This is a means of balancing a gravity wave against an electromagnetic wave in a manner that generates a third kind of wave similar to that which powers their larger vessel. This journey between worlds takes time in the small craft, and the humanoid EBE's suspend the effects of aging by freezing themselves in small chambers. The psychic powers of the humanoid EBE's are not lessened during this state of "suspended animation", so they are still able to control their craft. Towards that end and to provide for some external control over unforeseeable circumstances while frozen, the humanoid EBE's developed a host/parasite culture thousands of years ago with the small "Grey" EBE's. Since then, these Greys have become an extension of their controller's senses to such a degree that most humanoid EBE's rely heavily on their use at all times. "They are not unlike the sybiotic empathy between a pack of hunting dogs or a team of horses, and their Earthly masters - simply like tools or partners in work," explained one EBE.

- During the current wave of interest in our planet by the EBE's, there have been three interstellar craft, or "mother ships" stationed outside our solar system. These have been rotated at twenty-two (22) year intervals since the early 1930's. During a contact debriefing in 1964, an EBE explained that this was no hardship for them. "Our genetic science is about where yours will be in another millenia or two. Although the basic grasp of engineering the DNA will come within another eighty (80) years or so, if you survive as a species. Our friends will still be living when we return home. And most of us bring our families with us so we can watch our children mature." Their family structure is very different from ours and often includes several "models" of each set of parents, specifically engineered to produce offspring of certain mental character adapted to different physical forms needed in their culture. All of these live together as a family unit often as many as would be in a small village or neighborhood in our civilization.

THE NIXON-GLEASON ALIEN ENCOUNTER   273

• Onboard the "mother ship" almost every race and culture
is represented. There is no recognizable form of
government behind the actions of these representatives
from many worlds. It has been explained that as any
species evolves physically, it evolves psychically or
spiritually. The outcome of this process is that any
form of political organizing, including the politics
of religious structure, becomes a "personal moral
transgression" of higher shame to any who practice such
pursuits, than any good that could come from them.
Although this attitude makes any discussion of their
faith or beliefs nearly impossible, it has become very
clear that most races capable of interstellar travel
support the principles of self-determination. In short
that there is no empire of conquerors threatening our
planet. "A little cross-cultural nudge, like urging
a small child to walk towards you, is o.k. But these
guys wouldn't let Darth Vader sweep their streets," as
a member of a Majestic diplomatic task group put it
after several years of analysis of contacts.

Many volumes could be written and have been on the details of this ongoing contact process. Much of the contact of individual citizens by these
EBE's seems absurd on the surface and we remain largely incapable of controlling such contact. The pattern developing, however, seems to indicate that
a course of action is not directly needed. Little threat to national
security has occured. In fact, the EBE's have informed us that we are a sort
of "protectorate" not unlike a wildlife preserve in their eyes. They will
not protect us from ourselves, but are not interested in making us become
like them either. There do appear to be forces in outer space that are
hostile in the sense that they would exploit us although not conquer us.
And we have been informed that a large part of the alien presence on Earth
is to insulate us from doing any damage to the alien's own culture until we
are more morally evolved as a species. With these things in mind we arrive
at a statement of official position.

STATEMENT OF POSITION

"In so far as no threat, either implied nor expressed and either of a
military, civil or societal nature has been forwarded by the visitation of
the association of visiting extraterrestrials against the governments and
the peoples of these United States of America; and in so far as great and
many cultural and technical advances have been derived by such exchange,
we hereby grant full, complete diplomatic status and recognition to these
individuals from beyond our world. Furthermore, let it be known that we
seek to provide shelter, comfort and aid in all their peaceful endeavors
in so far as these are respective of the laws of our land and the right to
self-determination and free will expressed in our national constitution.
And until such time as the objectives or methods of either parties in this
agreement shall deem otherwise, this bond between our peoples shall remain
in effect."

The preceding diplomatic treaty was drafted by the directorate of the MAJESTIC-12 operation and a joint committee of extra-terrestrial visitors and representatives of the U.S. Diplomatic Corps, as a statement of intent. It was ratified and signed at Kirtland Air Force Base, Texas on July the eighteenth, 1954 by President Dwight D. Eisenhower and an individual on the behalf of the EBE's.

Each subsequent holder of the executive office has continued to uphold the intent of this policy towards these aliens.

Beyond the statement of intent, basic agreement has been reached on the following negotiated issues:

- The extraterrestrials will refrain where and when possible from open display of their presence to the public at large.

- The extraterrestrials will submit substantiating proof and listings of all persons contacted from among the public at large or that have been removed from the Earth for purpose of contact or cultural exchange. In no case shall anyone abducted by the EBE's be subjected to knowing harm or kept against their will for longer then forty-eight (48) hours.

- The extraterrestrials will avoid any willful contact with representatives of the public news media or any private investigators of the UFO phenomenon, groups or writers dedicated to the same intentions.

- The U.S. government will provide through the Defense Logistics Agency's Reutilization and Marketing Service such items as needed for the personal comfort of those visiting EBE's who may be sequestered in it's care.

- The U.S. government will provide a section of the MAJESTIC headquarters base in Nevada as an embassy compound for the EBE visitors and equip it to their needs.

- Any exchange of technical, scientific or social information will be conducted item-for-item and in such manner as to assure that both parties have equal gain from the process.

Except for many facinating details which are available under separate cover through either Operation Majestic (MAJOPSHQ) or the Defense Intelligence Agency's Office of Counterintelligence, this concludes the assessment of the situation and statement of position section of this preliminary briefing paper.

THE NIXON-GLEASON ALIEN ENCOUNTER   275

CHAPTER EIGHT

MORE FROM FOUNDATIONS

True Investigative Stories of Corrupt Doctors

HEALERS OR DEALERS?

RICHARD P. ALLISON

Healers or Dealers by Richard Allison

A #1 Best-selling New Release in Pharmacology Pain Medicine and Medical Law and Legislation!

Do no harm?

There is an innate trust built into us since childhood that our doctor spent years learning and studying how to help people. But what if that trust is broken? Are they all brought to justice for the confidences they've betrayed and the countless lives they've helped ruin?

In *Healers or Dealers?*, readers get a front-row seat to the jaw-dropping true accounts written by the retired investigator who experienced them and attempted to hold these doctors accountable.His stories show a direct correlation between doctors' questionable conduct with illegal administrating, dispensing, and prescribing of opioids and the craze that plagues our nation today. Couple this with the addictions that unwaveringly rival those we see in the worst of America's inner cities...

and a pharmaceutical opioid epidemic is born.

Made in the USA
Las Vegas, NV
25 July 2023

75244227R00166